BIRDING

in Seattle and King County

Site Guide and Annotated List
by Eugene S. Hunn

Second Edition

Trailside Series
August 2012

Seattle Audubon Society
for birds and nature

Birding in Seattle and King County
by Eugene S. Hunn

Second Edition

Note: All photographs are used with permission from the photographers, who retain their copyrights. Topographic maps are printed courtesy of Washington State.

Front cover: Savannah Sparrow © Kathrine Lloyd
Back cover (clockwise, left to right): Spotted Towhee © Kathrine Lloyd; Horned Grebe © Tim Kuhn; Rufous Hummingbird © Doug Parrott; Eugene S. Hunn © Eugene S. Hunn

Published and distributed by: Seattle Audubon Society
Copyediting and production by: Constancy Press, LLC
Cover design by: Lorie Ransom
Design help from: Gwynn Harris
Black-and-white maps by: Amber L. Pearson, Krystle Jumawan, and Kelly Cassidy

Printed in Nansha, Panyu District, China, by Everbest Printing Co.
through Four Colour Print Group
August 2012

To obtain more copies of this book, write or call:
Seattle Audubon Society   (206)523-4483
8050 35th Avenue NE
Seattle WA 98115
www.seattleaudubon.org

ISBN 0-914516-06-X   US $21.95

DEDICATION

This edition of *Birding in Seattle and King County* is dedicated to three stalwart King County birders who have inspired many of us in years past: Merilyn Hatheway, who welcomed a crowd of birders to view the male Black-throated Blue Warbler that frequented her Mercer Island feeder throughout the winter of 1994-1995 (1926-1995); Kevin Li, dedicated to restoring Purple Martins to King County (1956-2006); and Thais Bock, founder of the Kent-Auburn Christmas Bird Count (1917-2010).

Juvenile Franklin's Gull at Juanita Bay Park, August 20, 2009 (© Gregg Thompson).

TABLE OF CONTENTS

Photography Credits

American Tree Sparrow, Marymoor Park, October 30, 2009 (© Gregg Thompson).

List of Maps

ACKNOWLEDGMENTS

This revised edition of *Birding in Seattle and King County* has benefitted mightily from the editorial expertise and enthusiasm of Constance Sidles, president of Constancy Press, LLC, and chair of Seattle Audubon's Publications Committee. She dedicated hundreds of hours to copyediting the manuscript and verifying every detail. Her husband, John Sidles, contributed his technical expertise to make the design and production of this book possible. Krystle Jumawan and Amber Pearson worked long hours to make the maps readable and accurate. Lorie Ransom designed the cover, and Gwynn Harris helped design the book. Amy Davis, Rachel Lawson, and Melissa Willoughby proofread the text. Evan Houston reviewed the bird list. Dennis Paulson edited the dragonfly list, and Idie Ulsh the list of butterflies. I also wish to acknowledge my gratitude to the many photographers who contributed their work generously to help make this book both beautiful and informative. I am in debt to the avid King County birders, too numerous to mention, who have contributed their observations and analyses over the years. Many have been credited in the text with respect to one or another extraordinary sighting. Any errors that may come to light too late to correct should be laid at my feet.—*Eugene Hunn*

Barrow's Goldeneye, Montlake Fill (© Doug Parrott).

PREFACE TO THE REVISED EDITION

Birding in Seattle and King County: Site Guide and Annotated List was first published by the Seattle Audubon Society as part of their Trailside Series in 1982. I proposed the project then as a counterweight to the trend for bird guides of increasing geographic scope but with minimal detail about local patterns with respect to habitat and season. It was to have been a modest effort in my spare time but in the end required several years of data-dredging and field-truthing before we saw the finished product.

The data was collated and the text prepared without the benefit of a computer. I used graph paper to organize all published and many unpublished sightings for the county by species and date, which could then be translated into the bar graphs of seasonal abundance printed in that first edition. I soon realized that while we knew quite a bit about bird distributions in the western third of the county, very little was on record with regard to the less readily accessible, mountainous, eastern two-thirds of the region. So, accompanied on several occasions by Alan Richards and my wife Nancy, I hiked and climbed along the Cascade Crest, noting both common and unusual birds.

My final tally for King County in 1982 was 307 species of verified occurrence. Twenty-two maps drawn by Brian Vanderburg and a handful of black-and-white photographs provided graphic context, with a cover adapted from an evocative pen-and-ink illustration by Elizabeth Mills showing Barrow's Goldeneyes on Lake Union (a bit of a stretch, as they are not often seen there, though they are common nearby at the Hiram M. Chittenden Locks). We printed 10,000 copies, thinking the second 5,000 came at a real bargain rate but not considering the limits of the market. Twenty-five years later the last copy was sold (or given away)!

The current Seattle Audubon Society board, on the advice of its Publications Committee, proposed that I prepare a revised edition for publication in 2010, amending the original edition as needed but with the added attraction of color illustrations. The board did so because the first edition of *Birding in Seattle and King County* had proved its worth. It helped inspire an explosion of interest in local birding and perhaps inspired comparable efforts to document the birdlife of San Juan (Lewis and Sharpe 1987), Whatcom (Wahl 1995), and Yakima (Stepniewski 1999) Counties, for starters.Dave Beaudette, a dedicated and mostly solitary observer, took it upon himself to test the limits of King County birding as defined by the first edition. He explored every nook and cranny of the county, with particular attention to the waters of our Puget Sound fringe and the mountain crests. His meticulous notes helped add many new species to the King County list. He long held records for personal all-time King County (313) and King County year (237) lists, before moving to more hospitable climes.

Beaudette's listing records have only recently been challenged by the obsessive efforts of a coterie of King County listers, notably Matt Bartels (249 for the year in 2007) and myself (325 all-time). The explosion of King County bird reports since 1982 is due as well to many more keen observers, some having adopted particular King County places as their personal turf. To name just a few of these key places and their stewards: the Union Bay Natural Area, better known as the Montlake Fill, subject of detailed multi-year censuses by Fayette Krause, Dennis Paulson, Kevin Aanerud, Ellen Ratoosh, Chris McInerny, and now Constance Sidles (see her recent personal accounts, *In My Nature* 2009 and *Second Nature* 2011) and Brett Wolfe; Green Lake by Eugene Hunn and Martin Muller; Woodland Park by Tom Aversa; Discovery Park by David Hutchinson and Penny Rose, as well as Neil

Buff-breasted Sandpiper feeding at Marymoor Park, August 31, 2005 (© Steve Caldwell).

Zimmerman's Christmas Bird Count crews; Magnuson Park by Jan Bragg; Juanita Bay Park by MaryFrances Mathis and Ryan Merrill; Wallace Swamp Creek Park by Linda Phillips; Marymoor Park by Michael Hobbs and his merry band of Thursday-morning birders (who are responsible for a number of outstanding rarities, such as BUFF-BREASTED SANDPIPER, SMITH'S LONGSPUR, and BURROWING OWL, to name just a few); Lake Sammamish State Park by Hugh Jennings; the Preston-Snoqualmie Trail by Rob Conway; the Snoqualmie Valley from Duvall to Carnation (including Stillwater, one of my favorite haunts) by Mike Wile; Vashon Island by Ed Swan (see his *The Birds of Vashon Island* 2005); and the Naches Pass region by Dave Beaudette and many of us since. As a result, the "official" county list now stands at 377 species, 70 more than in 1982.

King County birding has benefitted immensely from the evolution of nearly instantaneous electronic communication and the development of well-organized efforts to share observations in the field and encourage careful documentation of unusual sightings. For many years we relied on a bird-sightings telephone hotline staffed by a series of dedicated volunteers. I hosted the hotline through the late 1980s and early 1990s until it was made obsolete by the BirdBox, brainchild of Bob Morse, sponsored by the Washington Ornithological Society (WOS), and funded by a gift from Ruby Egbert. This automated telephone system relied on an antique computer that finally died in early 2009. However, the BirdBox in turn has been made largely obsolete by the development of Tweeters, our current email life-line maintained at the University of Washington behind the scenes by Dan Victor and Hal Opperman.

The flood of raw data posted to Tweeters would be overwhelming if not for the consistent hard work of the *WOSNews* quarterly sightings column authors, Russell Rogers from 1993 until 2000, Tom Aversa through 2009, and now Ryan Merrill, and the regional editors for the series of regional reports published first by the National Audubon Society as *Audubon Field Notes* (1949-1970), then as *American Birds* (1971-1994), *Field Notes* (1994-1998), and now by the American Birding Association as *North American Birds* (1999-2009). (The volume numbers run consecutively throughout this series.) Their efforts cover the entire state and more but often include significant King County records as well as excellent color photography. Meanwhile, the next generation of birders may make eBird—a continental bird reporting network hosted by the Cornell Lab of Ornithology—the place to go for data.

This revised edition expands the 160-page first edition to well over 250 pages, including galleries of full-color bird images from King County. I have added several inset maps for key birding sites, such as Marymoor Park, Juanita Bay Park, the scattered Kent and Auburn wetlands, and the Naches Pass region, with the assistance of Amber Pearson and Krystle Jumawan, our cartographers. The bar graphs have been redone, and all species recorded ten or fewer times to date in the county are detailed, giving dates, locations, and observers.

The Christmas Bird Count (CBC) summaries have been thoroughly revised to incorporate count data recorded since 1982. I draw data from four CBC circles. We have 100 years of data for the Seattle CBC, three decades of data from the East Lake Washington and Kent-Auburn CBCs, and now ten years of winter bird censuses for our newest count, Vashon. Each of these four counts is sponsored by a local Audubon chapter. In *Birding in Seattle and King County* 1982, I proposed a breeding bird atlas project modeled on that of Great Britain and Ireland (Sharrock 1976). That effort began statewide in 1987 but began for King County in earnest in 1994 and was essentially complete by 2000. The King County Atlas effort was expanded to include a four-county transect published with a link on the Seattle Audubon website as Sound to Sage Breeding Bird Atlas (the direct website address is: http://www.soundtosage.org). These birding surveys provide systematic data countywide for both winter and summer.

Juvenile Red-necked Phalarope feeding on Main Pond at Montlake Fill, August 20, 2009 (© Kathrine Lloyd).

Checklist of King County Birds

This list may be used to record the species you have seen in King County. Recognizable subspecific forms are indented. Species considered "casual" or "accidental" in King County are italicized. Families are separated by an extra space. Species followed by (I) are non-native species, introduced since Euroamerican settlement. Those followed by (X) have been extirpated from King County.

___ Greater White-fronted Goose
   ___ *"Tule" White-fronted Goose*
___ *Emperor Goose*
___ Snow Goose
___ *Ross's Goose*
___ Brant
___ Cackling Goose
   ___ *"Aleutian" Cackling Goose*
   ___ *"Minima" Cackling Goose*
   ___ *"Taverner's" Cackling Goose*
___ Canada Goose
   ___ *"Great Basin" Canada Goose*
   ___ *"Lesser" Canada Goose*
   ___ *"Dusky" Canada Goose*
___ *Mute Swan (I)*
___ Trumpeter Swan
___ Tundra Swan
___ Wood Duck
___ Gadwall
___ Eurasian Wigeon
___ American Wigeon
___ *American Black Duck (IX)*
___ Mallard
___ Blue-winged Teal
___ Cinnamon Teal
___ Northern Shoveler
___ Northern Pintail
___ *Baikal Teal*
___ Green-winged Teal
   ___ *"Eurasian" Teal*
___ Canvasback
___ Redhead
___ Ring-necked Duck
___ *Tufted Duck*

___ Greater Scaup
___ Lesser Scaup
___ *King Eider*
___ Harlequin Duck
___ White-winged Scoter
___ Surf Scoter
___ Black Scoter
___ Long-tailed Duck
___ Bufflehead
___ Common Goldeneye
___ Barrow's Goldeneye
___ Hooded Merganser
___ Common Merganser
___ Red-breasted Merganser
___ Ruddy Duck

___ Ring-necked Pheasant (I)
___ Ruffed Grouse
___ *Spruce Grouse*
___ White-tailed Ptarmigan
___ Sooty Grouse
___ *Wild Turkey (I)*

___ *Mountain Quail (IX)*
___ California Quail (I)
___ *Northern Bobwhite (IX)*

___ Red-throated Loon
___ Pacific Loon
___ Common Loon
___ *Yellow-billed Loon*

___ Pied-billed Grebe
___ Horned Grebe
___ Red-necked Grebe
___ Eared Grebe

_____ *Stilt Sandpiper*
_____ *Buff-breasted Sandpiper*
_____ *Ruff*
_____ Short-billed Dowitcher
_____ Long-billed Dowitcher
_____ Wilson's Snipe
_____ Wilson's Phalarope
_____ Red-necked Phalarope
_____ *Red Phalarope*

_____ *Black-legged Kittiwake*
_____ *Sabine's Gull*
_____ Bonaparte's Gull
_____ *Black-headed Gull*
_____ *Little Gull*
_____ Franklin's Gull
_____ Heermann's Gull
_____ Mew Gull
_____ Ring-billed Gull
_____ Western Gull
_____ California Gull
_____ Herring Gull
_____ Thayer's Gull
_____ *Iceland Gull*
_____ *Slaty-backed Gull*
_____ Glaucous-winged Gull
_____ Glaucous Gull
_____ *Great Black-backed Gull*
_____ Caspian Tern
_____ *Black Tern*
_____ Common Tern
_____ *Arctic Tern*
_____ *Forster's Tern*
_____ *Elegant Tern*

_____ *Pomarine Jaeger*
_____ Parasitic Jaeger
_____ *Long-tailed Jaeger*

_____ Common Murre
_____ Pigeon Guillemot
_____ Marbled Murrelet
_____ Ancient Murrelet
_____ *Cassin's Auklet*
_____ Rhinoceros Auklet

_____ *Horned Puffin*
_____ *Tufted Puffin*

_____ Rock Pigeon (I)
_____ Band-tailed Pigeon
_____ *Eurasian Collared-Dove (I)*
_____ *White-winged Dove*
_____ Mourning Dove

_____ *Yellow-billed Cuckoo*

_____ Barn Owl

_____ *Flammulated Owl*
_____ Western Screech-Owl
_____ Great Horned Owl
_____ Snowy Owl
_____ Northern Pygmy-Owl
_____ *Burrowing Owl*
_____ Spotted Owl
_____ Barred Owl
_____ *Great Gray Owl*
_____ Long-eared Owl
_____ Short-eared Owl
_____ Northern Saw-whet Owl

_____ Common Nighthawk
_____ *Common Poorwill*

_____ Black Swift
_____ Vaux's Swift

_____ *Black-chinned Hummingbird*
_____ Anna's Hummingbird
_____ *Costa's Hummingbird*
_____ Calliope Hummingbird
_____ Rufous Hummingbird
_____ *Allen's Hummingbird*

_____ Belted Kingfisher

_____ Lewis's Woodpecker
_____ *Acorn Woodpecker*
_____ *Williamson's Sapsucker*
_____ *Yellow-bellied Sapsucker*
_____ Red-naped Sapsucker
_____ Red-breasted Sapsucker
_____ Downy Woodpecker

___ Hairy Woodpecker
___ American Three-toed Woodpecker
___ Black-backed Woodpecker
___ Northern Flicker
   ___ "Red-shafted" Flicker
   ___ "Yellow-shafted" Flicker
___ Pileated Woodpecker

___ Olive-sided Flycatcher
___ Western Wood-Pewee
___ Willow Flycatcher
___ *Least Flycatcher*
___ Hammond's Flycatcher
___ *Gray Flycatcher*
___ Dusky Flycatcher
___ Pacific-slope Flycatcher
___ *Black Phoebe*
___ *Eastern Phoebe*
___ Say's Phoebe
___ *Vermilion Flycatcher*
___ *Ash-throated Flycatcher*
___ *Tropical Kingbird*
___ Western Kingbird
___ Eastern Kingbird
___ *Scissor-tailed Flycatcher*

___ *Loggerhead Shrike*
___ Northern Shrike

___ *White-eyed Vireo*
___ Cassin's Vireo
___ *Blue-headed Vireo*
___ Hutton's Vireo
___ Warbling Vireo
___ Red-eyed Vireo

___ Gray Jay
___ Steller's Jay
___ *Blue Jay*
___ Western Scrub-Jay
___ Clark's Nutcracker
___ *Black-billed Magpie*
___ American Crow
___ Common Raven

___ Horned Lark

___ Purple Martin
___ Tree Swallow
___ Violet-green Swallow
___ Northern Rough-winged Swallow
___ Bank Swallow
___ Cliff Swallow
___ Barn Swallow

___ Black-capped Chickadee
___ Mountain Chickadee
___ Chestnut-backed Chickadee

___ Bushtit

___ Red-breasted Nuthatch
___ *White-breasted Nuthatch*

___ Brown Creeper

___ Rock Wren
___ *Canyon Wren*
___ Bewick's Wren
___ House Wren
___ Pacific Wren
___ Marsh Wren

___ American Dipper

___ Golden-crowned Kinglet
___ Ruby-crowned Kinglet

___ *Blue-gray Gnatcatcher*

___ Western Bluebird
___ Mountain Bluebird
___ Townsend's Solitaire
___ *Veery*
___ Swainson's Thrush
___ Hermit Thrush
___ American Robin
___ Varied Thrush

___ *Gray Catbird*
___ Northern Mockingbird
___ *Sage Thrasher*
___ *Brown Thrasher*

___ European Starling (I)

___ *White Wagtail*

____ American Pipit

Bohemian Waxwing

____ Cedar Waxwing

Phainopepla

Tennessee Warbler

____ Orange-crowned Warbler

____ Nashville Warbler

Northern Parula

____ Yellow Warbler

Chestnut-sided Warbler

Black-throated Blue Warbler

____ Yellow-rumped Warbler

   ____ "Audubon's" Warbler

   ____ "Myrtle" Warbler

____ Black-throated Gray Warbler

____ Townsend's Warbler

____ Hermit Warbler

Blackburnian Warbler

____ Palm Warbler

Black-and-white Warbler

American Redstart

Ovenbird

Northern Waterthrush

____ MacGillivray's Warbler

____ Common Yellowthroat

Hooded Warbler

____ Wilson's Warbler

____ Yellow-breasted Chat

Green-tailed Towhee

____ Spotted Towhee

____ American Tree Sparrow

____ Chipping Sparrow

Clay-colored Sparrow

Brewer's Sparrow

   ____ _"Timberline" Sparrow_

____ Vesper Sparrow

Lark Sparrow

Black-throated Sparrow

Sage Sparrow

____ Savannah Sparrow

____ Fox Sparrow

   ____ _"Red" Fox Sparrow_

____ "Slate-colored" Fox Sparrow

____ "Sooty" Fox Sparrow

____ Song Sparrow

____ Lincoln's Sparrow

____ Swamp Sparrow

____ White-throated Sparrow

Harris's Sparrow

____ White-crowned Sparrow

   ____ "Puget Sound" White-crowned Sparrow

   ____ "Gambel's" White-crowned Sparrow

____ Golden-crowned Sparrow

____ Dark-eyed Junco

   ____ "Oregon" Junco

   ____ "Slate-colored" Junco

   ____ _"Gray-headed" Junco_

____ Lapland Longspur

Smith's Longspur

Chestnut-collared Longspur

Rustic Bunting

____ Snow Bunting

____ Western Tanager

Rose-breasted Grosbeak

____ Black-headed Grosbeak

____ Lazuli Bunting

Indigo Bunting

Painted Bunting

Bobolink

____ Red-winged Blackbird

____ Western Meadowlark

____ Yellow-headed Blackbird

Rusty Blackbird

____ Brewer's Blackbird

Common Grackle

____ Brown-headed Cowbird

Hooded Oriole

____ Bullock's Oriole

Baltimore Oriole

Brambling

____ Gray-crowned Rosy-Finch

____ Pine Grosbeak

___ Purple Finch	___ *Hoary Redpoll*
___ Cassin's Finch	___ Pine Siskin
___ House Finch	___ *Lesser Goldfinch*
___ Red Crossbill	___ American Goldfinch
___ White-winged Crossbill	___ Evening Grosbeak
___ Common Redpoll	___ House Sparrow (I)

Bohemian Waxwing, Magnuson Park, November 27, 2010 (© John Puschock).

1. INTRODUCTION

Why write a book about King County birds? My main motive is to advance our knowledge of the natural environment in which we live and upon which our welfare ultimately depends. Birds—a most conspicuous element of the environment—can provide careful observers with a sensitive barometer of the quality of life around them. The more detailed the knowledge, the more finely tuned the barometer. I have sought here to summarize as accurately as possible the current status of the county's birdlife in a form that may serve equally well the needs of the curious novice, the avid birder, or the professional wildlife biologist or resource manager.

My second goal in writing this guide is to supply motive and means to the reader to explore the birding potential of King County. I did not select King County because of its extraordinary potential in that regard, for many Washington counties have richer and more diverse habitats. Rather, King County's most obvious asset is the fact that it surrounds Seattle. It is "backyard" for King County's nearly two million people, of which a sizable fraction piles into their cars, boats, and planes every weekend, intent on going somewhere else. If this book could encourage a thousand people to drive a thousand miles less each year in search of recreation, that would be more than a gallon of gasoline saved for every word I write!

This book may also aid the cause of conserving King County's prize habitats for those who find sense and satisfaction in the appreciation of natural history. Some of the birding localities recommended in the site guides are in imminent danger of "improvement." I indicate the current status of conservation efforts in such cases. Effective habitat conservation depends on the public's heightened sensitivity to the unique character of familiar places. I hope to cultivate that sensitivity here by stimulating the reader's awareness of King County's multifaceted landscape and diverse birdlife.

Finding the birds depends on understanding their habits in relation to the characteristics of the environment. Accordingly, I first describe (in Chapter 2) the

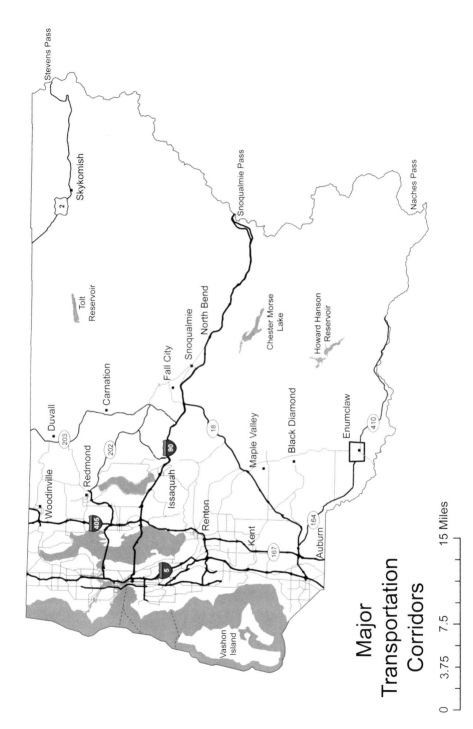

Major Transportation Corridors

0	3.75	7.5	15 Miles

types of habitats found within King County and the corresponding sorts of birds likely to be seen there. Next, Chapter 3 is a guide to the myriad locations in King County which are especially productive or promising for birding. In Chapter 4 I present distribution charts which include all bird species ever reported from King County, if such sightings have been confirmed. Graphs of bird distributions allow the reader to discover at a glance which birds are likely to be found at a given season. The novice should use these graphs in conjunction with an illustrated guide to the birds of North America. For the expert, the graphs and accompanying annotations provide a concise summary of the phenology (that is, distribution patterns in time and space) of every bird species reliably reported for the county through 2010, abstracted from thousands of individual sightings. Finally, bibliographic references direct the critical reader to more detailed accounts of scientific and historical interest.

Thanks to advances in digital color printing, we are able to offer brilliant photographs of a substantial sample of King County's birds, generously donated by a number of skilled local photographers. All bird photos were taken in King County.

HISTORICAL PERSPECTIVE

A guide to the birds of King County is not unprecedented. Earl J. Larrison's *Field Guide to the Birds of King County, Washington* was published in 1947 in this same Seattle Audubon Society Trailside Series. The present guide is not a revision of that earlier work, as a different approach seems appropriate, one which makes use of the changes that have occurred not only in local bird populations but also in available knowledge about them.

Although many of Larrison's species summaries remain accurate today, dramatic changes are evident. Figure 1 summarizes the more striking cases of status changes during the previous century as of 1980. To prepare this chart, I consulted Larrison's King County book and three detailed summaries of Seattle's birdlife from still earlier periods: Samuel F. Rathbun's accounts based on his residence here during the 1890s, Thomas D. Burleigh's report of a year's residence in Seattle during 1920, and Robert C. Miller and Elizabeth L. Curtis's review of the status of birds on the University of Washington campus as of 1940 (see Bibliography).

In Figure 1, 27 species are charted, of which 23 are native. Casual species are omitted from consideration. As of 1982 (when the original edition of this book was published), 11 native species had increased in abundance, while 12 had decreased or showed indications of decline. Four species had declined over a large area of the western United States. These species include the YELLOW-BILLED CUCKOO, hard hit by destruction of its pristine riparian forest habitat in California; and the LEWIS'S WOODPECKER, PURPLE MARTIN, and WESTERN BLUE-BIRD, all hole nesters showing marked population reductions since the meteoric rise of the EUROPEAN STARLING. Other declines seem to have been more local,

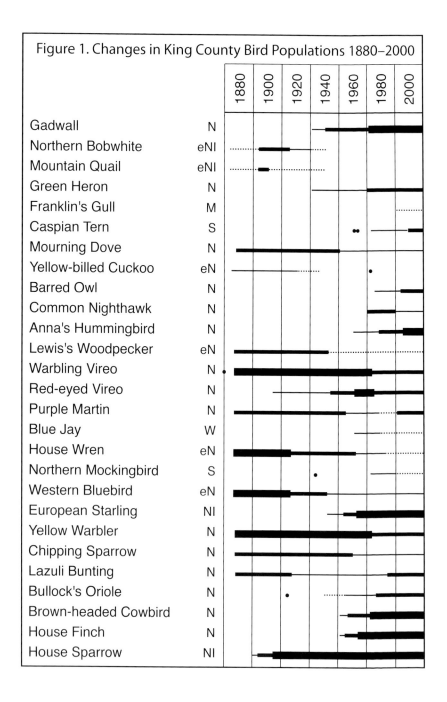

Figure 1. Changes in King County Bird Populations 1880–2000

perhaps reflecting habitat transition from the original forest (before about 1890) to rough-cleared land (through World War II), to spreading suburbia (post-war). The disappearance of NORTHERN BOBWHITE and MOUNTAIN QUAIL (both introduced) and declines in populations of MOURNING DOVE, HOUSE WREN, LAZULI BUNTING, and CHIPPING SPARROW may reflect this pattern. WARBLING and RED-EYED VIREOS and the YELLOW WARBLER are common species which seem to have been in decline since 1970. The VIREOS continue to be squeezed between the ever-expanding city and the mountain foothills, while the gleaming Yellow Warbler retreats with every swamp reclamation project. Even more important has been the impact of nest parasitism on these three species by the burgeoning BROWN-HEADED COWBIRD population. It is painful to watch a harried Yellow Warbler trying to satisfy the demands of a baby cowbird five times its size. The decline of the COMMON NIGHTHAWK has been more difficult to fathom, as it once nested commonly on downtown Seattle rooftops. It is no stranger to the city, and yet in the past several decades it has nearly disappeared.

Birds on the increase up to 1982 were mostly those that benefit from human disturbance; they are, in a word, weeds of the bird world. Most notorious among these is the EUROPEAN STARLING and its sidekick, the HOUSE (or "English") SPARROW. Properly included here also are ANNA'S HUMMINGBIRD (which would not last a month without exotic winter-blooming shrubs and red-colored sugar water), BROWN-HEADED COWBIRD, and the HOUSE FINCH. NORTHERN MOCKINGBIRDS and BLUE JAYS might fit here as well, though they seem less citified and remain rare. BARRED OWLS in 1980 had their toe just in the door. The explosion in their local populations is more recent. The BULLOCK'S ORIOLE is truly a boon to local birding, but the reasons for its success, like that of the GREEN HERON and GADWALL, are not apparent.

Recent Changes (since 1982)

Our local avifauna is dynamic, responding to local habitat changes as well as to broader shifts in climate and landscape. Some of these changes are readily understood, while others remain puzzling. I discuss below the more prominent changes in King County birdlife since the first edition of this guide was published in 1982 (see Figure 2).

GREATER WHITE-FRONTED GOOSE: a rare winter visitor as of 1982, this goose is now regular each winter in small numbers, with sizable flocks regularly noted during migration.

CACKLING GOOSE: The "Canada Goose" was split by the North American Classification Committee of the American Ornithologists' Union (AOU) in 2000 into two species. The larger goose is still called the Canada Goose *(Branta canadensis)* and includes the large, pale-breasted resident "Great Basin" Canadas *(B. c. moffitti)* and migrant "Lesser" Canadas *(B. c. parvipes)*, with a few "Dusky" Canadas *(B. c. occidentalis)* straggling through. Since the late 1960s, numbers of "Great Basin" Canada Geese—transplanted from flooded nest sites along the Columbia River east of the Cascades—have exploded, the trend continuing despite efforts to capture and export supernumerary geese, which are considered pests by some for fouling lawns and footpaths. The new species is the smaller tundra-nesting Cackling Goose *(Branta hutchinsii)*, which includes the Mallard-sized *B. h. minima (*which nests on the shores of the Bering Sea in western Alaska), as well as significant numbers of the larger, paler-breasted "Taverner's" Cackling Goose *(B. h. taverneri)*, and possibly an occasional endangered "Aleutian" Cackling Goose *(B. h. leucopareia)*. The "Minima" race was considered a rare late-fall migrant in the first edition of this guide, referred to then as "Cackling Canada Goose." At that time, most wintered in northern California. In recent years their numbers in winter have exploded, with one winter flock in Kent in January 2008 estimated at 3,000. "Taverner's" Cackling Geese may also be quite numerous, though differentiating "Taverner's" Cackling Geese from "Lesser" Canadas is next to impossible. Just how often "Aleutian" Cackling Geese visit King County is very difficult to judge, as many "Minimas" show white collars, a key distinctive feature of the "Aleutian geese." Sorting through the large winter goose flocks has become something of a growth industry.

TRUMPETER SWAN: Trumpeters were rare early-winter visitors as of 1982. Since 2006 they have expanded their winter range south from near Snohomish into the Snoqualmie Valley, where flocks of several hundred swans, the great majority Trumpeters, are now regular, with smaller groups wintering at Kent and Auburn. This increase reflects steady growth in Trumpeter Swan wintering populations in the Skagit Valley, their traditional stronghold, and likely results from their protected status on their Alaskan breeding grounds.

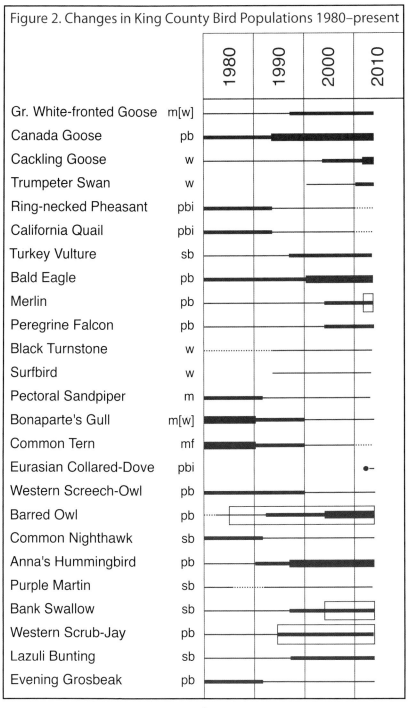

Figure 2. Changes in King County Bird Populations 1980–present

SCOTERS: All three scoters are still quite common in winter off our saltwater shores, but wildlife censuses document a nearly 90 percent decline in their Puget Sound populations (cf. Nysewander et al. 2005). The reasons for these declines are not clear but may involve loss of habitat supportive of scoter winter food supplies.

RING-NECKED PHEASANT and CALIFORNIA QUAIL: Both of these introduced galliform species were common residents in 1982 but are now very scarce. Pheasants may survive due to continuing Washington Department of Fish & Wildlife releases for hunters, but few of the birds released survive more than a few days.

COMMON LOON: There were no recent nesting records of Common Loons in King County as of 1982. Several pairs were recorded nesting on the large Cascade water supply reservoirs during the Washington Breeding Bird Atlas project. Perhaps 10 pairs regularly nest today on our large, inaccessible mountain lakes.

GREBES: WESTERN GREBE winter flocks consisting of several hundred birds are still the norm off West Point in Discovery Park and in Lake Washington at the Cedar River mouth in Renton. This should not deceive us into imagining that Western Grebe populations are healthy. Careful surveys of winter Western Grebe flocks in Puget Sound indicate a decline of 95 percent since the 1970s (cf. Puget Sound

This page: Trumpeter Swan in foreground and Tundra Swan in background in a field south of Carnation, February 3, 2008. Note the differences in bill shape and color that help distinguish these two species from each other (© Eugene Hunn). *Opposite page: Lazuli Bunting on territory at Montlake Fill, summer 2008* (© Doug Parrott).

Action Team 2007). HORNED and RED-NECKED GREBES also seem to have suffered declines, as have scoters, as noted above. The health of the Puget Sound marine ecosystem may be a major factor, but the alteration of wetland nesting habitat in eastern Washington and the northern Great Plains may play an equal role. On the other hand, since the split of CLARK'S from Western Grebes, we have gained a new species for the county list. Clark's Grebes are rare but regular in large Western Grebe flocks, mixed with a very few apparent hybrids. Finally, we should note the quite unexpected nesting of several pairs of Western Grebes in Juanita Bay in 2007. There were few if any prior Western Grebe nesting records west of the Cascades.

BROWN PELICAN: Our first record of a Brown Pelican in King County came in the winter of 1983, the second not until 1995. Since then we have come to expect a few stragglers each year from the now abundant late summer and fall coastal flocks. This is no doubt due to the prohibition of DDT, which had decimated nesting populations in southern California and northern Mexico through the 1970s. The striking success of OSPREYS, BALD EAGLES, and PEREGRINE FALCONS may be attributed to the same policy shift. Thank you, Rachel Carson!

TURKEY VULTURE: Turkey Vultures have apparently increased substantially during the nesting season. They are now fairly common March through October from the Snoqualmie Valley through the Cascade foothills to the Cascade Crest.

BALD EAGLE: In 1982 I knew of just three Bald Eagle nests in King County. As of 2007, 77 active nests were located in King County (Stinson et al. 2007). Bald Eagles are now routinely encountered throughout the year just about everywhere in the county and have recently been implicated in raids on GREAT BLUE HERON rookeries, to the dismay of some observers.

MERLIN: Merlins nested in a north Seattle neighborhood in 2008 and 2009 and are now regularly observed all year round. Meanwhile, AMERICAN KESTRELS appear to be somewhat less common than formerly.

PEREGRINE FALCON: No active nests were known in King County in 1982. Today at least 10 pairs breed regularly, including a pair on a downtown skyscraper (a nest you can monitor by closed-circuit TV in the lobby of the 1201 Third Avenue Building). There are also pairs beneath several Seattle bridges, as well as pairs at Snoqualmie Falls and on Rattlesnake Ledge.

SHOREBIRDS: The old Boeing Ponds have been cleaned up and remodeled as the Green River Natural Resources Area (GRNRA). Unfortunately, observing shorebirds at the new Boeing Ponds is difficult, with productive and accessible shorebird habitat now reduced to a few scattered, seasonally wet fields, mostly in Kent and Auburn. We still may record nearly two dozen shorebird species over the course of the year, but most are quite sporadic.

BLACK TURNSTONE and SURFBIRD: As of 1982 I could find just two Black Turnstone records and one of a Surfbird for King County. Beginning in the early 1990s, a substantial winter flock of these two rock-loving species has taken up residence on the breakwater at Duwamish Head in West Seattle.

PECTORAL SANDPIPER: Once fairly common as a fall migrant on the coast and in the Seattle area, Pectoral Sandpipers are now increasingly hard to find.

BONAPARTE'S GULL: At times abundant through 1982, Bonaparte's are now rarely encountered in such large flocks. Meanwhile, FRANKLIN'S and LITTLE GULLS, rarities associated with these Bonaparte's flocks, have all but disappeared from western Washington.

COMMON TERN: In 1982 I said that "Shilshole Bay is alive with Common Terns in August and September…." No longer. In the past few years Common Terns have all but disappeared. I don't know why.

EURASIAN COLLARED-DOVE: First recorded in 2007, Eurasian Collared-Doves are showing up in increasing numbers every year, with several reports in the spring of 2008. Groups of a dozen and more were located in 2009 along the southern margin of the county. It seems likely that this species will soon become established, if it is not already, in King County. Apparently, there is no stopping the colonization of North America by this species, which arrived on its own in Florida in 1982.

OWLS: BARRED OWLS colonized Washington in 1965 and first nested in King County in Discovery Park in 1981. Now Barred Owls are by far the most conspicuous owl throughout the county. A pair has nested in my backyard for the past several years. Perhaps not coincidentally, WESTERN SCREECH-OWLS and GREAT HORNED OWLS—and of course SPOTTED OWLS—have declined precipitously. Western Screech-Owls used to be common in Seward Park year-round but can no longer be found there. While Barred Owls likely prey on Western Screech-Owls and are known to drive out and/or hybridize with their close relative, the Spotted Owl, it is difficult to imagine how they might displace the much larger and more powerful Great Horned. Another mystery.

COMMON NIGHTHAWK: This species continues to decline. It has abandoned the city and the suburbs and hangs on in cut-over foothill terrain east of the Snoqualmie Valley.

ANNA'S HUMMINGBIRD: First noted in our area in 1965, having spread north from California, Anna's Hummingbirds are now common urban residents, nesting as early as February. Anna's Hummingbirds remain scarce away from hummingbird feeders and ornamental plantings.

PURPLE MARTIN: Purple Martin nesting pairs were reduced to just a handful in the county in the 1980s. A concerted effort during the past decade to mount starling-proof gourds on lake and shoreline pilings for nesting has been extraordinarily successful. The late Kevin Li spearheaded the effort in and around Seattle. Once again the Purple Martin's rich, gurgling calls brighten our summer outings. By 2007 there were some 125 nesting pairs in the county at 18 sites, nine on Vashon Island and nine scattered along the shore of Puget Sound, the Duwamish River, and Lake Washington. However, for some reason numbers declined sharply in 2008 and 2009 to some 30 pairs (S. Kostka and R. Siegrist, unpublished data).

BANK SWALLOW: Rated a rare summer vagrant in 1982, Bank Swallows have become regular breeders. We now know of three substantial Bank Swallow colonies in King County, in cutbanks along the Green, White, and Snoqualmie Rivers.

WESTERN SCRUB-JAY: Since the first county record in 1977, reports have gradually increased, with nesting first documented in Enumclaw in 1994. The birds are now regular at several Seattle locations and the Green River Valley, mostly in urban and suburban habitats.

MOUNTAIN CHICKADEE: Prior to 1982 this species was reported only as a rare winter straggler, mostly during invasion years. It is now known to nest in small numbers at the Cascade Crest between Naches and Green Passes.

MOUNTAIN BLUEBIRD: Considered a rare straggler in 1982, Mountain Bluebirds have now been recorded nesting each summer at the Cascade Crest at Naches Pass and in the silver-snag burn north of Windy Gap.

LAZULI BUNTING: Lazuli Buntings have increased dramatically in the last few years in the Snoqualmie Valley and at Kent and Auburn. A pair nested at Montlake Fill in Seattle in 2008 and 2009.

EVENING GROSBEAK: In the late 1970s large flocks of Evening Grosbeaks gathered in early May on the University of Washington campus, feeding on maple seeds. A few years later such visitations were history. Evening Grosbeaks may still be widespread at any season, but total numbers seem significantly reduced since the 1970s.

Burrowing Owl, the Renton post office, March 19, 2010 (© Gregg Thompson).

GETTING STARTED IN BIRDING

For the fledgling birder, this book needs a companion field guide. There are a number of excellent guides available that illustrate in full color nearly every species listed here. None is perfect; each has its peculiar strengths and weaknesses. My first field guide was Chandler S. Robbins, Bertel Bruun, Herbert S. Zim, and Arthur Singer's *A Guide to Field Identification: Birds of North America* (1966), known as "Robbins" or "The Golden Guide" for short. It sold new for $2.95 in 1967. A key advantage of Robbins was the placement of range maps, verbal accounts, and illustrations for each species together on facing pages. All regularly occurring North American species were treated, not only those of the west.

Robbins's major competition came from Roger Tory Peterson's *A Field Guide to Western Birds* (1961; revised edition 1990). Both were soon superceded by the

Western Scrub-Jay, Montlake Fill, fall 2010 (© Gregg Thompson).

National Geographic's *Field Guide to the Birds of North America*, now in a sixth edition, which adopts the Robbins guide format and remains unique in including virtually every rarity recorded in North America. The current "bible" for the serious birder is *The Sibley Guide to Birds* by David Allen Sibley, published in 2007. Sibley's artwork is superior, and the guide is a gold mine of useful identification tips. The recent explosion of new guides of all sorts defies a brief summary. I will note only several regional guides useful for beginning birders: *Birds of Washington State* by Brian H. Bell and Gregory Kennedy (2006) narrows the options to our home state, while *Birds of the Puget Sound Region* by Bob Morse, Tom Aversa, and Hal Opperman (2003) sharpens the focus further to the 12 counties circling Puget Sound. Crisp photographs serve to illustrate this truly pocket-sized guide.

Birding is an inexpensive sport. The single essential investment of any consequence is a pair of binoculars, for which you could spend anywhere from $100 to $2,000. You should shop around to find the brightest, most durable, and most convenient pair within your price range. For a detailed discussion of binoculars and other birding equipment, I suggest you consult a book that introduces the sport, such as George Laycock's *The Bird Watcher's Bible* (1994).

With new binoculars, the illustrated field guide of your choice, and *Birding in Seattle and King County* at hand, you're ready to embark on a birding adventure. Just so you won't get lost, I'd like to suggest the following maps and trip-and-trail guides to assist in route finding.

Get a good city map of Seattle with adequate details. Seattle maps vary as to scope and detail of the larger regional insets. You may also want to purchase maps of the eastside suburbs, inclusive of Bellevue, Redmond, Kirkland, and Issaquah; and of south King County suburbs, inclusive of Renton, Kent, Auburn, and Federal Way. These cover the urban and suburban sectors of the county. The King County GIS (KCGIS) Virtual Map Counter website (search on "King County maps") offers a range of maps, some of which you can download and print if you have access to a computer and printer. For example, you might find useful Metro Transit Maps, the King County Bicycling Guidemap, a series of walking maps, a King County Regional Trails map, and the Cougar Mountain Regional Wildland Park map. These and other maps are also available at the Map Counter at the King County Map and Records Center on the first floor of the King Street Center Building on the east side of 2nd Ave. S between S Jackson and S King Sts. (open 8 a.m. until 4:30 p.m. weekdays).

The Mt. Baker-Snoqualmie National Forest map, published by the U.S. Forest Service, is available at ranger stations in Skykomish, North Bend, and Enumclaw for a nominal fee. This map shows the logging roads and hiking trails of the mountainous eastern portion of the county better than the county road map. The Forest Service has recently published a more detailed map of the Snoqualmie Ranger District (2007) which covers most of the eastern half of King County. The

Alpine Lakes Protection Society has published an Alpine Lakes Wilderness Area map (2002) that employs sophisticated topographical shading to highlight the precipitous terrain. This map covers montane King and adjacent Kittitas Counties. If you plan to do any backcountry hiking, you should purchase the appropriate U.S. Geological Survey topographical maps, usually available at mountaineering supply stores.

For those with an interest in exploring the mountain areas of eastern King County by trail, The Mountaineers have published *100 Hikes in Washington's Alpine Lakes* by Vicky and Ira Spring and Harvey Manning (3rd ed., 2000). Twenty-odd trail routes in the county are included in this collection. If you wish to reach the alpine summits in hope of finding ROSY-FINCHES or WHITE-TAILED PTARMIGANS, Fred Beckey's *Cascade Alpine Guide: Climbing & High Routes, 1: Columbia River to Stevens Pass* (2000) provides descriptions of off-trail approaches and climbing routes.

Closer to home you may wish to explore the innumerable trails and back roads of the so-called Issaquah Alps, that is, Cougar, Squak, and Tiger Mountains. Consult Manning's *Guide to Trails of Cougar Mountain and Squak Mountain: including prospectus for a Cougar Mountain Regional Park,* published by the Issaquah Alps Trails Club (IATC) in 1981. Additional dimensions of the natural history of the Issaquah Alps are explored in Marvin A. Pistrang's *Bedrock and Bootsoles: An Introduction to the Geology of the Issaquah Alps* and Manning's *The Flowering of the Issaquah Alps,* both published by the IATC in 1981. William K. Longwell, Jr.'s *Guide to Trails of Tiger Mountain* (IATC, revised 1981) provides a detailed introduction for the Tiger Mountain area.

The Mountaineers' *Footsore* series by Harvey Manning, describing "walks and hikes around Puget Sound," is a gold mine of information about promising back roads and unexpected pockets of near-wilderness just outside of town. Volume 1 covers Seattle and the region south and east to Dash Point, North Bend, and Greenwater; Volume 2 adds the foothill regions between the US-2 and I-90 corridors; and Volume 4 treats Vashon Island. I enjoy Manning's wry wit and acerbic commentary, and you probably will, too. Unfortunately, these guides are now out of print and rather out of date, likely available only in library archives.

The Hancock Timber Resource Group publishes a Snoqualmie Forest Recreation Area Access map that covers the maze of unpaved logging roads in the lower foothills of the Cascades north of I-90. Contact them at 1-360-879-4200.

If your birding should take you farther afield, you will find *A Birder's Guide to Washington* (American Birding Association, 2003) by Hal Opperman and members of the Washington Ornithological Society, essential. This popular guide summarizes the status of all of Washington's birds and describes hundreds of birding sites throughout the state.

Keeping Notes and Sharing Your Discoveries

A systematic diary of your bird sightings is a mine of memories. More important, careful records maintained over the years provide a solid factual basis for assessing long-term environmental changes around your home base. These are compelling personal and scholarly reasons to keep careful records. Start now or sooner.

Now and then, waxing nostalgic, I turn back to the notes I made of my first year's birding, in California in 1967. I can recall my first encounter with the SOOTY SHEARWATER—that "wave-master"—as thousands of birds streamed past just outside the view windows of San Francisco's Cliff House lounge one threatening October afternoon. I see them now as clearly as I did then.

Commercial bird diaries, organized by species or date, are adequate for starters. Those organized by species are particularly useful, in that your sightings are automatically collated. At the end of the year you may readily review the dates and locations of all your sightings of, for example, Pileated Woodpeckers. (This system

This page: Say's Phoebe, Marymoor Park, March 22, 2010 (© Gregg Thompson). *Opposite page: Lapland Longspur, Montlake Fill, October 8, 2007* (© Marv Breece).

never has adequate space reserved for robins and starlings.) On the other hand, the day-by-day record books are easier to use when it comes to entering a day's observations or summarizing the birds found at a given locality. The disadvantage is that extracting an annual summary by species requires much leafing back and forth. A modest investment in one of the currently available birding software packages such as AviSys will overcome these limitations, or you can learn to use eBird.

Initially you may be satisfied simply to note the more unusual occurrences of a given species. However, I have gradually come to the point of recording religiously every species seen on every field trip and estimating the numbers of individuals of each. I use a new loose-leaf binder each year with a page for each day in the field. I also briefly note weather conditions, route followed, duration, unusual behavior, nesting activity, and the names of my companions. All of this is grist for the memory mill. Without such records (my own and many others') this book could not have been written.

Keep a "life list" of all the species of birds you have identified over the years. Watch it grow. You will soon come to appreciate the special joy of seeing the rare individual of a species resident elsewhere, far off course in its travels. The Washington Ornithological Society's "Checklist of Washington Birds," updated periodically and published by WOS, may be useful for this purpose. Some avid "listers" (yours truly among them) have dozens of lists: life lists, state lists, county lists, year lists, county year lists, yard lists, and so on. Each is a condensation of your experiences as a birder. Listing is strong motivation to get out from in front of the TV and into the woods. However, no list will substitute for detailed daily records.

Information is a valuable commodity. The information you record in your bird notes may be of value to others, and theirs of value to you. Birding is most enjoyable when you can share the excitement of a new bird find or the satisfaction of new knowledge of familiar birds with someone else who understands. There are dozens of active and expert birders in King County.

If you find an unusual bird, by all means pass the word along. "Unusual" may be defined as: 1) a bird not on the local list, 2) a bird which is not supposed to be here at this time, or 3) a bird which is rarely or irregularly noted at a given time and place. The distribution charts in this guide will help you evaluate the newsworthiness of your King County sightings.

Rare birds create a stir. The birding community turns out en masse to see them, if they are securely "staked out." Birders' phones are ringing off their hooks all over the region. Who saw "the bird" first? Is it really an X? When was it last seen? Where, exactly? Information in action.

A case in point: the BRAMBLING which appeared in mid-January 1982 at a feeder north of Issaquah. By mid-March some 200 people had seen it, some coming from as far away as Oregon, British Columbia, even California and the East Coast. This little finch is something like a cross between an Evening Grosbeak and a Lazuli Bunting. It is a Eurasian native that may not be pictured in your field guides. We may never see another this side of the Pacific.

Yet rarities are more than simply an exciting addition to everyone's "life list." They may give advance notice of expansion of a species's range. The county's first EUROPEAN STARLING in December 1945 heralded the invasions of the 1950s. Will the first EURASIAN COLLARED-DOVE (July 2007) do likewise? Migrants that are off course, such as the BLACK-THROATED SPARROW that came calling at the same feeder visited by the Brambling, are pieces of a larger puzzle. When fitted together they may show the impact of extremes of weather on a bird population, for example in the case of the Black-throated Sparrow, of drought on a desert bird of the Southwest (Hunn 1978).

It is thus very important that such rare birds be accurately identified. If you suspect you have found a most unusual bird, study it well, then write a detailed description of its plumage, shape, size, and behavior. Describe the circumstances of the sighting, such as the weather, the lighting, the length of your observations, your distance from the bird, the optical equipment you used, and the references you consulted. Carefully consider all possible look-alikes. Take a photograph if possible. Report your find to Tweeters at tweeters@u.washington.edu or leave a message with the Seattle Audubon Society office (206-523-4483). The Washington Bird Records Committee (WBRC) is linked to the WOS website. The WBRC provides special reporting forms for this purpose. Seek confirmation of your identification by more experienced observers. Don't be afraid to make a mistake or admit an error. The observations you report are scientific data and should be able to stand the test of time.

2. KING COUNTY HABITATS

King County, Washington, stretches from the saltwater shore of Puget Sound at sea level to the crest of the Cascade Mountains, reaching 7986 feet elevation (2434 meters) on Mt. Daniel. Seattle is its human core, a leading city of the Northwest, as large or larger than Denver, Calgary, Vancouver, B.C., or Portland, Oregon. The county, containing more than 2100 square miles, is larger than two states—Rhode Island and Delaware—and its population of 1,916, 440 (April 2009 estimate) exceeds that of 13 states. The county represents only 3 percent of Washington's land surface but is home to 29 percent of the state's population.

King County is really two worlds, a montane wilderness and a densely settled lowland. A line drawn from Duvall south through North Bend and Maple Valley to Enumclaw roughly marks the division. The eastern 60 percent of the county is mountainous and rather inaccessible. A huge tract extending south from the Interstate 90 (I-90) corridor to State Route 410 (SR-410) is set aside for municipal watersheds closed to the public. The upper Cedar and Green River Basins are gated just east of Rattlesnake Lake on the Cedar and at Kanaskat on the Green. The front line of the mountains north of North Bend and east of the Snoqualmie Valley has limited access (see the North Fork Snoqualmie River routes described below). A recent deal (2004) transferred Weyerhaeuser timber lands to the Hancock Timber Resource Group under an agreement with King County. King County purchased the development rights to the 90,000-acre Snoqualmie Forest for $22 million. The agreement requires that these lands be managed for sustainable timber production in perpetuity. This should prevent suburban creep from radically domesticating these lands. Vehicle access to the Snoqualmie Forest—at the Spur 10 Gate off the North Fork Road SE—requires a $200 annual permit purchased from the forest management company. Access on horseback, by bicycle, or on foot, however, is unrestricted, with the exception of certain areas in the upper Tolt River Basin closed to public entry by Seattle Public Utilities.

Windy Gap near Naches Pass, an example of wet coniferous forest (© Eugene Hunn).

Public roads penetrate this foothill area from the west along Stossel Creek through the Marckworth State Forest, to Lake Joy and Moss Lake off Kelly Rd. NE southeast of Duvall, and up the Tolt River for a few miles east from Carnation. Forest Service Road 57 (FSR-57) out of North Bend follows the North Fork Snoqualmie River north and east to the western edge of the Mt. Baker-Snoqualmie National Forest.

Deep in the Cascades, the Alpine Lakes Wilderness Area straddles the crest between Snoqualmie and Stevens Passes. It is restricted to horse and boot travel. Yet diligent exploration in this ornithologically little-known backcountry pays dividends. WHITE-TAILED PTARMIGAN have been reported from Granite Mountain, Snoqualmie Peak, and Big Snow Mountain, and rumors, as yet unconfirmed, of the elusive SPRUCE GROUSE come from the Tolt River headwaters. A few endangered SPOTTED OWLS may still nest in isolated patches of old-growth forest, though their nest sites are closely guarded secrets. BLACK-BACKED and AMERICAN THREE-TOED WOODPECKERS are reported every summer from the vicinity of Government Meadow just below Naches Pass. GRAY-CROWNED ROSY-FINCHES breed on some of the higher summits, while BLACK SWIFTS nest somewhere on Mt. Si's sheer face. GOLDEN EAGLES likely nest near the sources of the Skykomish, North Fork Snoqualmie, and Green Rivers.

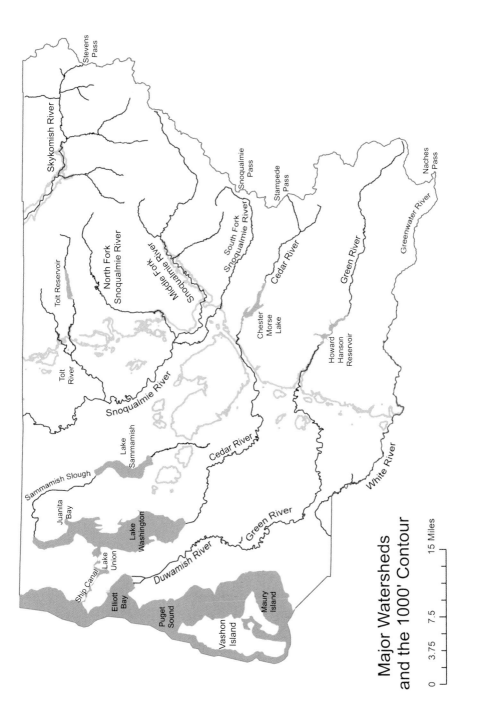

Major Watersheds
and the 1000' Contour

| 0 | 3.75 | 7.5 | 15 Miles |

The county is drained by five major rivers, from north to south: the South Fork Skykomish, the Snoqualmie, the Cedar, the Green, and the White. The Skykomish joins the Snoqualmie north of the county line to form the Snohomish, which reaches the Sound at Everett. The Snoqualmie's three forks join near North Bend. The common stream then drops 272 feet over Snoqualmie Falls—sacred to the indigenous Snoqualmie Indians—before meandering northward through the broad Snoqualmie Valley, the western boundary of the montane zone. It is joined by the Tolt at Carnation. South of the Issaquah Alps (mountain outliers reaching nearly to Lake Washington) the Cedar and Green cut through a gradually moderating hill country. There the boundary of lowland civilization is less clearly drawn. The valley of the White River, sculpted by Mt. Rainier's glacial runoff, opens at Enumclaw and merges with the broad alluvial plain of the lower Green River at Auburn. The White is a river of indecision, as its final destination has shifted between the Puyallup River and Commencement Bay (as now) and the Duwamish River and Elliott Bay. The most recent shift south was engineered by man, intended to further the interests of Tacoma against Seattle as the key port city of the Sound.

The force of the great Puget Lobe of the last continental ice sheet is apparent in the lowlands of King County. Valleys and ridges trend north to south, requiring the westward-flowing rivers to detour to reach the sea. Terminal moraines more than 1000 feet above sea level on the Skykomish and Snoqualmie Rivers indicate the farthest advance of the ice into the foothills. The resulting topography is complex, and one can rarely travel far in a straight line.

The lower courses of the main rivers are now largely given over to farming. The intervening hills are mostly in second-growth woods. Everywhere in the lowlands, however, woods and marsh are in retreat on their urban margins before the relentless march of suburban tract housing and expansive industrial parks. Favorite Kent Valley birding haunts are lost each year to progress.

Still, Seattle itself has a rich array of birdlife. I have personally recorded 265 species within the city limits. Green Lake and the marshes of Union Bay regularly host more than a dozen species of DUCKS in winter, and Lake Washington has as many GULL species. SNOWY OWLS can occasionally be found right in town, while the recent immigrant BARRED OWLS seem to have colonized every available woodlot in the city. The woods of Discovery Park may at this moment hold a brilliant HOODED WARBLER or another equally baffling waif thousands of miles off course. Welcome to the adventure of King County birding.

I recognize 13 basic habitats in King County. Eleven are found in the statewide habitat classification devised by Terry Wahl and Dennis Paulson (1981); I have added urban and aerial distinctions. Habitat associations are essential aids to proper species identification. If you glimpse a small gray bird skimming rapidly up a mountain stream course, you may safely conclude that it was an AMERICAN DIPPER. A largish, earless owl in deep forest may be a BARRED or SPOTTED

OWL, certainly not a SHORT-EARED, while the same perched on a fence post in an open field might be a BARN or SHORT-EARED OWL, certainly not a SPOTTED. A broad-brush habitat classification such as the one used here is a rough guide indicating where each species is most likely to be found; however, it may be more useful for identifying species during the breeding season than during times of migration. During migration, individuals may turn up in a greater variety of settings, in many cases quite different from their breeding season habitat preference. For example, the AMERICAN PIPIT nests in alpine meadows (classed here as wet meadows), but during migration and in winter, it typically occurs along freshwater margins or on farmland and in parks.

Some species of birds are very picky in their choice of habitat. HARLEQUIN DUCKS nest only along rapid mountain rivers and winter on saltwater about rocky prominences. SPOTTED OWLS must have a certain acreage of old-growth timber—preferably on a steep slope—and a snaggle-topped tree to provide a nest platform beneath the forest canopy, where their preferred prey—flying squirrels and red-backed voles—abound. SANDERLINGS, which are regular in migration and winter at West Point in Discovery Park, feed on sand or gravel beaches along saltwater but are almost never seen with the other sandpipers on the muddy freshwater shores of the ponds at Montlake Fill on the University of Washington campus. Other species seem at home almost anywhere. The AMERICAN ROBIN will raise a family as readily in an urban park as on a rural farm, and as well at the seashore as in desert scrub or mountain forest. One type of bird is not better than another; there are places both for specialists and generalists in the economy of nature.

Open Saltwater

This category includes Puget Sound waters from just south of Edmonds to Dalco Passage off Point Defiance at Tacoma, plus the more sheltered waters of Elliott Bay and Quartermaster Harbor, and the Lake Washington Ship Canal as far as the Hiram M. Chittenden Locks. This stretch of Puget Sound is about 90 miles long, with no point over two miles from land. Depths range to 175 fathoms (1050 feet). Much of this area is accessible only by private boat or ferry.

Four ferries cross our section of the Sound: Seattle/Bainbridge Island, Seattle/Bremerton, Fauntleroy/Vashon/Southworth, and Point Defiance/Tahlequah. In my experience, there is little to be seen from the ferries that is not more readily observed from shore, especially if a spotting scope is handy. Prime shoreline vantage points—from north to south—include: Richmond Beach Park; the mouth of Piper's Creek at Carkeek Park; Meadow Point at Golden Gardens Park; West Point in Discovery Park; the West Seattle shoreline from Duwamish Head around Alki Point to Fauntleroy; KVI Beach, Point Robinson, and Tahlequah on Vashon Island; and Redondo Beach and Dash Point State Park along King County's southern shore. Birds most characteristic of this habitat are LOONS, GREBES, COR-

MORANTS, SCOTERS, JAEGERS, GULLS, TERNS, and ALCIDS. Patience is well rewarded, for the offshore scene is in constant flux, although birdlife on the Sound is quite sparse in June and July. Peak numbers and the greatest variety of birds most likely occur in September to November. Find a comfortable lookout and keep your eyes open. With luck you may also see an occasional seal, sea lion, or cetacean.

Rocky Shoreline

Rocky shoreline is scarce in King County. There are small patches of rocks exposed at low tide just north of West Point and some sedimentary outcroppings similarly exposed at Alki Point. The Alki Point shoreline reminds me of Restoration Point on Bainbridge Island, three miles west, a favored location for wintering rock shorebirds. Species favoring this habitat, such as BLACK OYSTERCATCHERS, RUDDY TURNSTONES, WANDERING TATTLERS, and ROCK SANDPIPERS, are not likely to be found, however, as they are rare stragglers to our corner of the Sound, but in recent years a good-sized flock of BLACK TURNSTONES and SURFBIRDS has taken up winter residence along the breakwater at Duwamish Head. BRANTS and HARLEQUIN DUCKS feed by preference in the shallows off these beaches.

Sandy Shoreline, Mudflat, & Salt Marsh

Much of the Puget Sound shoreline in King County is of cobbles, pebbles, or sand. The rich mudflats of the primordial Duwamish River delta have been dredged for port facilities. Small patches of salt marsh remain on Kellogg Island in the Duwamish waterway just above the West Seattle Bridge, at the Mileta Creek estuary on Maury Island, and at KVI Beach (Point Heyer) north of Ellisport on Vashon Island. The last-named site attracts a modest migration of SHOREBIRDS. Special habitat favored by the BARROW'S GOLDENEYE is formed by the barnacle-encrusted pilings on the Seattle waterfront, at Harbor Island, and below the Hiram M. Chittenden Locks. Early each spring, northward-bound BRANTS disperse along hundreds of miles of Puget Sound shallow shoreline, refueling for their long flight to the Bering Sea. PIGEON GUILLEMOTS and BELTED KINGFISHERS nest in burrows in the sand bluffs south of West Point and about Quartermaster Harbor. The guillemots also nest under downtown piers.

FRESHWATER, MARSH, & SHORE

Lake Washington (18 miles long) and Lake Sammamish (7 miles long) are deep lakes with mostly cobbled shores. Where streams enter and exit these lakes, cattail-bordered marshes form, as at Kenmore, Juanita Bay, Yarrow Bay, Mercer Slough, and Union Bay on Lake Washington, and at both ends of Lake Sammamish. These wetlands are especially attractive to DUCKS in migration and winter, and provide important feeding areas for BALD EAGLES. CANADA GEESE—introduced populations of the "Great Basin" race *moffitti*—breed on both lakes. Union Bay attracts the greatest variety of water birds of any spot in the city of Seattle, while the ponds at the Green River Natural Resources Area (GRNRA) in Kent support the greatest variety of nesting waterfowl in the county, with MALLARDS, GADWALLS, NORTHERN SHOVELERS, CINNAMON TEALS, and RUDDY DUCKS breeding regularly. Kenmore's Tracy Owen Station at Log Boom Park and Renton's Gene Coulon Memorial Beach Park, at opposite ends of Lake Washington, each support thousands of waterfowl during winter. The Cedar River mouth hosts a congregation of GULLS that may include extraordinary rarities such as GLAUCOUS, ICE-LAND, SLATY-BACKED, and even a GREAT BLACK-BACKED GULL. The Snoqualmie Valley's oxbow lakes and beaver ponds support nesting WOOD DUCKS,

Opposite page: Richmond Beach, an example of open saltwater habitat (© Eugene Hunn). *This page: Great Black-backed Gull, photographed at the Cedar River mouth in Renton, January 17, 2004* (© Denny Granstrand).

HOODED and COMMON MERGANSERS, and several species of DABBLING DUCKS. Nesting OSPREYS hunt for fish over these lakes and rivers between March and October, and BALD EAGLES are especially numerous when salmon are spawning. Three large water supply reservoirs on the Tolt, Cedar, and Green Rivers have not suffered the distraction of motorized boating and thus support nesting BARROW'S GOLDENEYES and COMMON LOONS. Hundreds of smaller lakes and ponds are scattered from suburbia to the Alpine Lakes Wilderness.

Wet Meadows

Open meadow and marsh habitats in King County are either the result of human clearing or of temperature and moisture extremes. The clearing of fields and pastures by settlers and the regular burning of "prairies" by Indians opened or maintained river bottom grasslands along the Green, Sammamish, and Snoqualmie Rivers. Other periodically flooded bottomlands were too wet to allow forest growth. The few remnants of these extensive open wetlands—patches between Renton and Auburn and scattered sloughs along the Snoqualmie River below Fall City—must be saved to remind us of the former abundance of the DUCKS, GREBES, OSPREYS, RAILS, and BITTERNS now virtually exiled from this area. At higher elevations, wet meadows are natural consequences of the environmental extremes near timberline. Such alpine meadows host breeding AMERICAN PIPITS and WHITE-TAILED PTARMIGANS during the brief summer and provide good hunting for migrating RAPTORS in the fall.

Wet meadow and freshwater marsh habitats, our King County wetlands, are a resource of special value. Wetlands define the boundary between water and land and form a transitional zone where biological diversity is maximal. Regrettably, wetlands are also highly attractive to developers. South of Renton, cattail marsh has nearly succumbed to sprawling industrial parks and warehouse complexes. Industrial, commercial, and residential development crowd the ponds in Kent and Tukwila, hem in the Black River slough, and cordon off the Yarrow Bay marsh on Lake Washington's east shore.

Farmland

Farmlands are artificial meadows with an added attraction for birds provided by farming activities. Soil-dwelling organisms exposed by plowing attract flocks of MEW and RING-BILLED GULLS. Crop residues, lost seed, and stubble, not to mention manure, attract hordes of GULLS, CROWS, ROBINS, AMERICAN PIPITS, and BLACKBIRDS, with their inevitable STARLING escort. Many RAPTOR species hunt the smaller birds and mice supported by the farmer, and they find convenient perches and nesting sites in scattered groves of trees and quiet barns. This habitat is represented best in the Snoqualmie Valley, where hundreds of TRUMPETER SWANS and a variety of GEESE now winter. However, this habitat is in rapid retreat in the Kent-Auburn and Redmond areas on Greater Seattle's urban margin, though patches have been preserved by special farmlands conservation programs and in mitigated wetlands.

RIPARIAN WOODLAND

This streamside variant of the broadleaf forest (see below) reaches its finest development in the towering Black Cottonwood groves bordering the Snoqualmie River, such as are found at Tolt-MacDonald Park in Carnation. The BULLOCK'S ORIOLE is a characteristic breeding bird of this habitat. A flash of bright orange, a raucous cackle, and a finely woven bag nest indicate its presence. A hike along the Snoqualmie Valley Trail between Duvall and Carnation in May or June is an eye-opener. Besides the orioles, look and listen for RED-BREASTED SAPSUCKERS, BLACK-HEADED GROSBEAKS, LAZULI BUNTINGS, RED-EYED VIREOS, YELLOW WARBLERS, and perhaps a stray YELLOW-BREASTED CHAT, a species which has been noted several years running at Stillwater. Along smaller creeks and sloughs, Pacific, Scouler's, and Sitka Willows are the dominant trees. Such riparian woods follow the major river courses deep into the montane zone and fringe the inlets of the larger mountain lakes.

BROADLEAF FOREST

This habitat is patchily distributed in lowland King County, most commonly found at coniferous forest edges, on damp bottomlands, or mixed with coniferous trees such as Douglas Fir in hillside stands. Red Alder, Bigleaf Maple, and Black Cottonwood are dominant species. Pacific Madrone lends a colorful Mediterranean look to the sunny bluffs overlooking the Sound. This habitat is favored by DOWNY WOODPECKERS, BLACK-CAPPED CHICKADEES, and HUTTON'S VIREOS year-round. In the winter, they are joined by both species of KINGLET. In early spring, nests of HAWKS and OWLS are conspicuous in the bare branches.

WET CONIFEROUS FOREST

Before Euroamerican settlement, this habitat type was more extensive than it is today. Urban and suburban development has pushed the forest back, leaving a few remnant enclaves of old growth with trees of impressive magnitude, such as at Schmitz and Seward Parks in Seattle and the Asahel Curtis Picnic Ground just west of Snoqualmie Pass. Old-growth timber, in stands 200 years of age and more, is an endangered forest community in King County; each remaining stand is precious. SPOTTED OWLS, NORTHERN GOSHAWKS, and MARBLED MURRELETS are well-known denizens of extensive old-growth timber. They use this habitat for feeding, roosting, and nesting. In the foothills and mountains, clear-cutting creates a complex geometry of shrubby thickets. In time, these raw squares are clothed in a second-growth forest dominated by Douglas or Noble Fir, depending on elevation. The Green River headwaters along the Cascade Crest north of Naches Pass are an excellent place to study these transitions. At bog edge and swamp, look for Western Red Cedar mixed with Sitka Spruce. Montane forests at middle elevations are dominated by Pacific Silver Fir, as at Snoqualmie Pass. Above 4000 feet, Subalpine Fir, Mountain Hemlock, and Yellow Cedar take over.

SHRUBBY THICKET

This habitat is not localized but rather is scattered within or borders wet coniferous, broadleaf, and riparian forest habitats. Before Euroamerican settlement, such thickets were confined to the zones of transition between stream and forest, or to naturally disturbed sites such as avalanche tracks on steep mountain slopes, burned areas, or floodplains. Now, clear-cutting and farming, road cuts and powerline rights-of-way, ski slopes and vacant lots all provide space for thicket-loving species. Avalanche gullies overgrown with Sitka ("Slide") Alder and mountain willows usually harbor a singing MACGILLIVRAY'S and several WILSON'S WARBLERS.

A Bald Eagle leaving its urban habitat at Montlake Fill to enter its aerial world (© Thomas Sanders).

Blueberry tangles high on Granite Mountain among the silver snags of an ancient burn provide cover for breeding FOX SPARROWS and MOUNTAIN BLUEBIRDS. Mountain bog-margins host LINCOLN'S SPARROWS. In the lowlands, SPOTTED TOWHEES mew and BEWICK'S WRENS hiss and warble from every irrepressible Himalayan Blackberry tangle.

Parks & Gardens

This is scarcely a habitat per se except by virtue of its urban context. City parks and gardens are a complex mosaic of remnant wet coniferous forest, second growth mixed with broadleaf trees, shrubby margins and open meadow, marsh, and seashore. Yet the rich variegation of these islands of shelter in a sea of cement and asphalt, coupled with their proximity to so much humanity, makes them among the most valuable of all wildlife habitats. ANNA'S HUMMINGBIRDS are found almost exclusively in these areas, subsisting on ornamental plantings and bird-feeding stations. Large parks provide a quality of wilderness within the city, as exemplified by nesting BALD EAGLES in Discovery Park and Woodland Park adjacent to Green Lake, as well as at the Talaris Conference Center near the Montlake Fill.

Urban

A few species of birds are adapted to truly urban conditions. Such species prefer the company of downtown crowds. They forage in garbage cans in back alleys and nest in drainpipes and on window sills. The formidable trio of immigrants, the ROCK PIGEON, EUROPEAN STARLING, and HOUSE SPARROW, thrive among cement and fumes. A few native species have likewise adapted to urban life—for example, the HOUSE FINCH, which has greatly expanded its range as a consequence of this preference. CROWS and GLAUCOUS-WINGED GULLS thrive on garbage, and CANADA GEESE make pests of themselves at shoreline parks and playgrounds, wherever there is grass for them to graze. Less obtrusive are the PURPLE MARTINS, recovered from near oblivion thanks to nesting gourds hung up on shoreline pilings. OSPREYS and PEREGRINE FALCONS, quite scarce until recently, have adapted to nesting on cell-phone towers, downtown skyscrapers, and bridges.

Aerial

SWIFTS and SWALLOWS, spring through fall, and soaring TURKEY VULTURES and RAPTORS during migration and in winter may be found in the air over almost any habitat. The odd flock of GEESE, SWANS, and even SANDHILL CRANES may pass over, yodeling. One must learn to identify such birds by silhouette, mode of flight, and calls, as close scrutiny is rarely possible.

3. GUIDE TO BIRDING SITES IN KING COUNTY

I have divided King County into 11 birding areas. These areas follow stream basin boundaries or otherwise natural routes of travel. This should facilitate planning a day's birding to enhance the diversity and interest of what you might find, while limiting the distance traveled and the time spent en route.

We begin in Seattle, focusing on city parks and shorelines (Area 1). We then move to the east side of Lake Washington and the Sammamish Valley, traveling north to south from Kenmore and Bothell to Issaquah and Renton (2). Next we follow the Cedar River southeast to the foothills of the Cascades (3). We then bird the Green River Valley from Renton to Auburn (4) and travel the Puget Sound shoreline to the west (5), followed by a ferry ride across the Sound to Vashon Island (6). Next we jump to the Snoqualmie River Valley, traveling south to north, North Bend to Duvall, exploring the North Fork Snoqualmie River along the way (7). Our final routes lead us into the Cascades, first along the Skykomish River to Stevens Pass (8), then along I-90 to Snoqualmie Pass (9), then up SR-410 from Enumclaw to Greenwater and Naches Pass (10). We conclude with a few tough hikes to alpine areas along the Cascade Crest (11). To encourage "green birding" I have added a description of bus routes to major birding areas for those without a car or for those motivated to burn a bit less gas in pursuit of their passion (12).

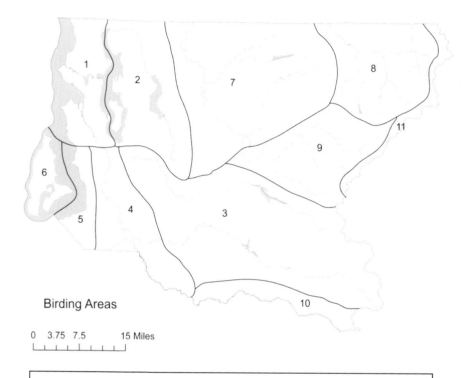

Birding Areas (Map Key)

1. Seattle

2. Eastside of Lake Washington, Kenmore to Renton

3. Cedar and Upper Green River Valleys, Renton to Black Diamond

4. Green River Valley, Renton to Auburn

5. King County South Shore, Seahurst to Dash Point

6. Vashon and Maury Islands

7. Snoqualmie River Valley and North Fork Snoqualmie River, North Bend to Duvall

8. Skykomish River, Baring to Stevens Pass

9. The I-90 Corridor, North Bend to Snoqualmie Pass, plus Middle Fork Snoqualmie River and Stampede Pass

10. White River Corridor, Enumclaw to Naches Pass

11. The Alpine Zone

Opposite page: American Coot, Montlake Fill (© Tim Kuhn).

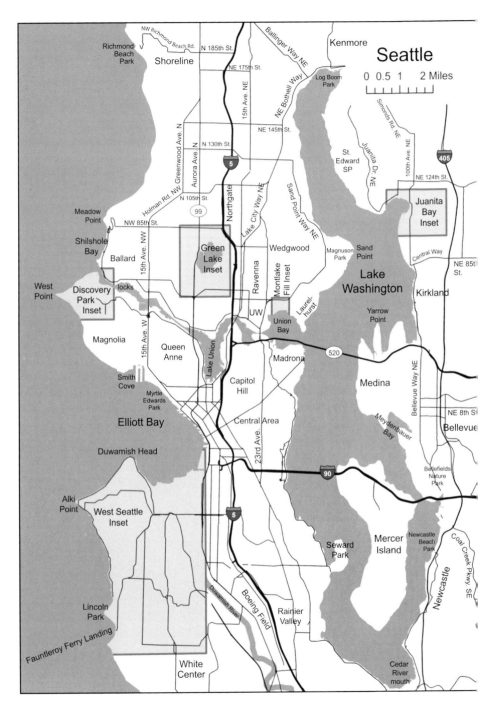

Richmond Beach Park

NW Richmond Beach Rd.

Shoreline

N 185th St.

Ballinger Way NE

Kenmore

NE Bothell Way

Seattle

0   0.5   1   2 Miles

NE 175th St.

15th Ave. NE

Log Boom Park

NE 145th St.

Aurora Ave. N

Greenwood Ave. N

N 130th St.

Holman Rd. NW

Sand Point Way NE

St. Edward SP

Simonds Rd NE

Juanita Dr. NE

100th Ave. NE

NE 124th St.

I-405

Northgate

N 105th St.

Lake City Way NE

99

Juanita Bay Inset

Meadow Point

NW 85th St.

Central Way

NE 85th St.

Shilshole Bay

Ballard

15th Ave. NW

Green Lake Inset

Wedgwood

Magnuson Park

Sand Point

Kirkland

West Point

Discovery Park Inset

locks

Ravenna

Montlake Fill Inset

Lake Washington

Magnolia

15th Ave. W.

Queen Anne

UW

Laurel-hurst

Union Bay

Yarrow Point

Lake Union

Capitol Hill

Madrona

Medina

Bellevue Way NE

Smith Cove

Myrtle Edwards Park

520

NE 8th St

Bellevue

Meydenbauer Bay

Elliott Bay

Central Area

23rd Ave.

Duwamish Head

Bellefields Nature Park

Alki Point

West Seattle Inset

I-5

I-90

Mercer Island

Newcastle Beach Park

Newcastle

Coal Creek Pkwy. SE

Seward Park

Lincoln Park

Boeing Field

Duwamish River

Rainier Valley

Fauntleroy Ferry Landing

White Center

Cedar River mouth

AREA 1. SEATTLE

More than 90 percent of the bird species recorded in King County have been noted within the city limits of Seattle. Urbanization may be incompatible with a true sense of wilderness, but it need not imply a homogenization of birdlife. Still, the vast majority of birds of unusual interest seen in the city are reported from small pieces of wild woodland, canyon, field, and shore set aside for the public to enjoy with minimal benefit of human "improvements." Discovery and Magnuson Parks (both lately released from the military's benign neglect), Seward Park, Lincoln Park, and the University of Washington's Union Bay Natural Area (Montlake Fill) and Washington Park Arboretum are key areas in which to find birds in the city. It is the juxtaposition of these natural remnants and the human hordes that makes Seattle an exciting center of birding activity.

Discovery Park/West Point. West Point guards the northern entrance to Elliott Bay, on which Seattle's port is located. West Point's historic lighthouse is reached by a mile hike from either the North or South Parking Llots at Discovery Park. From this point you can survey Puget Sound for DIVING BIRDS, GULLS, and TERNS in season. Late fall through early spring is best. At these times you may expect to see LOONS, GREBES, SCOTERS, GULLS, and ALCIDS such as COMMON MURRE, PIGEON GUILLEMOT, MARBLED MURRELET, and RHINOCEROS AUKLET. A telescope is helpful, as the birds are often some distance from shore. Look out as well for Harbor Seals and sea lions, Harbor Porpoises, river otters, and the very occasional whale offshore.

Fall migration (beginning in July) brings PARASITIC JAEGERS near shore as they harry COMMON TERNS, BONAPARTE'S GULLS, and HEERMANN'S GULLS. From late October through November you may spot a flock of ANCIENT MURRELETS flying by. In early spring BRANTS are common. Rarities seen from the point include KING EIDER and LONG-TAILED DUCK; NORTHERN FULMAR; SHORT-TAILED and SOOTY SHEARWATERS; FORK-TAILED and LEACH'S STORM-PETRELS; POMARINE and LONG-TAILED JAEGERS; FRANKLIN'S, LITTLE, and SABINE'S GULLS; BLACK-LEGGED KITTIWAKES; FORSTER'S, ARCTIC, and BLACK TERNS; HORNED and TUFTED PUFFINS; and perhaps even a WHITE WAGTAIL on the beach. One year we had an astounding but too brief visit by a EURASIAN HOBBY.

At low tide you may walk south from the point on a broad sandy flat or north to a rocky beach normally submerged. Rocky shorebirds might be expected in season, such as the fall migrant WANDERING TATTLERS seen here in 1979 and 1981, an occasional BLACK TURNSTONE and SURFBIRD, and the displaced BLACK OYSTERCATCHER of the 1980-81 Christmas Bird Count (CBC henceforth). The gravel paths around the lighthouse have seen HORNED LARKS, GRAYCROWNED ROSY-FINCHES, SNOW BUNTINGS, and LAPLAND LONGSPURS, in addition to a variety of sparrows. As compensation for the expansion of the

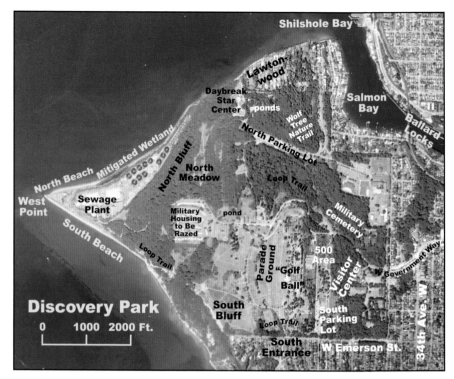

Discovery Park

0   1000   2000 Ft.

sewage plant behind West Point, a willow-bordered freshwater pond was created just behind the seawall along the north beach. The willows often harbor flocks of YELLOW-RUMPED WARBLERS in winter and who knows what in migration.

If you have three hours or more, walk the Loop Trail. You may begin at any of three points: the Visitor Center parking lot at the east entrance (pick up a map and bird list here); the South Parking Lot; or the North Parking Lot near the Daybreak Star Center. From the south lot the Loop Trail traverses the grassy expanse of the South Bluff, then (traveling clockwise) angles through a dry madrone and hazel woods to an overlook above a maple and alder woodland fronting the South Beach. You may continue on the Loop Trail to the North Meadow or branch off on a spur trail to the South Beach and West Point. From West Point a trail follows the breakwater along the North Beach past the sewage plant, then climbs the North Bluff to reconnect with the Loop Trail in the North Meadow. East of the North Meadow, spur roads cross the Loop Trail. These lead north to the Daybreak Star Center and the North Parking Lot. Scouler's Willow (a surprisingly tall tree) forms thickets at seepages near the ponds east of Daybreak Star. North of the North Parking Lot is the Wolf Tree Nature Trail, which loops through a stand of near-virgin Douglas Fir, red cedar, and hemlock. NORTHERN SAW-WHET OWLS have been known to roost along this trail in winter. The wooded ravines above the north lot proved attractive to Seattle's first BARRED OWL in April 1979 and supported a nesting pair of PILEATED WOOD-PECKERS in 1974. Also productive is the plateau at the top of the long staircase that takes you west from the Visitor Center. Cedars and exotic pines here may hide snoozing GREAT HORNED, NORTHERN SAW-WHET, or LONG-EARED OWLS in winter.

ANNA'S HUMMING-BIRDS may be encountered anywhere in the park and at any season. A 1981 survey by David Hutchinson tallied at least 40 resident Anna's in the park and the adjacent neighborhood. The first nesting records in King County for Anna's come from Lawtonwood just north of the park and subsequently from the park itself. The South Bluff supports a substantial SAVANNAH SPARROW population in summer, augmented by migrants, while the broom thickets on the north side of the South Meadow support a half-dozen pairs of nesting WILLOW FLYCATCHERS. Updrafts over the bluffs here aid migrating RAPTORS,

---

Above: A rare male Mountain Bluebird seen at Discovery Park April 9, 2008 (© Marv Breece). Below: More commonly seen at Discovery, a wintering Horned Grebe (© Tim Kuhn).

while the open savanna has attracted rarities such as LAZULI BUNTING, WEST-ERN KINGBIRD, MOUNTAIN BLUEBIRD, and SAY'S PHOEBE.

In the cedar-hemlock forest, check the CHICKADEE flocks carefully. Both BLACK-CAPPED and CHESTNUT-BACKED are common residents and often associate with RED-BREASTED NUTHATCHES, BROWN CREEPERS, KINGLETS, and occasionally YELLOW-RUMPED and TOWNSEND'S WARBLERS in mixed winter flocks. Resident HUTTON'S VIREOS are often in these companies of small birds, though they are always inconspicuous. During spring migration (late April to May) a variety of WARBLERS, VIREOS, and FLYCATCHERS, plus RUFOUS HUMMINGBIRDS, WESTERN TANAGERS, and BLACK-HEADED GROSBEAKS, are common in brush and woods. Metro buses #19, #24, and #33 make Discovery Park accessible from downtown Seattle.

The **Hiram M. Chittenden Locks** (also known as the Government or Ballard Locks), **Shilshole Bay and Marina,** and **Golden Gardens Park** provide additional saltwater shore habitat near Discovery Park. Metro bus #44 is a good connection between the University District and Ballard. At the locks look for BARROW'S GOLDENEYES, GREBES, MERGANSERS, GULLS, and TERNS in season. A TUFT-ED DUCK returned here each winter from 1967 to 1970. Observation windows at the locks provide nose-to-nose views of Chinook, Silver, and Sockeye Salmon and Steelhead in summer and fall—a fine spot to work on your "fish list."

Meadow Point—the sandy prominence in **Golden Gardens Park**—is a good vantage point for ALCIDS, JAEGERS, and diverse DIVING BIRDS. The CROWS here seem particularly small and may represent a relatively pure "NORTHWEST-ERN CROW" stock, though most local birders long ago gave up trying to sort local crows to "species." The consensus is that Puget Sound crows are highly variable and entirely intermediate between the "Northwestern Crow" of the northern coasts and the "American Crows" everywhere else.

Farther north, **Carkeek** and **Richmond Beach Parks, Boeing Creek,** and the grounds of **Shoreline Community College** offer additional wooded bluff and saltwater shore access. **Carkeek Park** encompasses dark second-growth woods in the small deep gorge of Piper's Creek and a bit of Puget Sound beach at the creek's mouth. Enter the park from Greenwood Ave. N via N 110th St. Piper's Creek supports runs of several salmon species and the occasional wintering AMERICAN DIPPER. Metro bus #15 will take you to the south entrance off 8th Ave. NW.

Richmond Beach Park is more open than Carkeek, with grassy slopes, a willow-alder thicket along the railroad tracks, and a sandy beach reminiscent of the beach at Golden Gardens. To get to Richmond Beach Park from I-5, take the N 175th St. exit and go west to SR-99 (Aurora Ave. N), then turn north to N 185th St., and then left (west) on N 185th St., which becomes N (eventually NW) Richmond Beach Rd. From this arterial, turn left (south) on 20th Ave. NW to the park entrance.

A productive vantage point for seabirds is north of Richmond Beach Park just south of the Point Wells pier near the Snohomish County line along Richmond Beach Dr. NW. A postage-stamp park recently opened here, providing parking spaces. Look in season for LOONS, GREBES, BRANT, DIVING DUCKS, GULLS, TERNS, and ALCIDS off the beach. Both Carkeek and Richmond Beach Parks may be overrun on warm summer days. Metro bus #348 will take you from the Northgate Transit Center to within easy walking distance of the park and the beach.

South of Richmond Beach, **Boeing Creek** cuts down through the bluff to the Sound. The area is privately owned, but public access is allowed via NW 166th St. From Greenwood Ave. N, turn west onto NW Innis Arden Way and drive past the Shoreline Community College entrance to NW 166th St. Park at the dead end here and maneuver past the locked gate to walk down an abandoned roadway to the beach at the mouth of Boeing Creek. This is a rich area for spring songbird migrants. WESTERN SCREECH-OWLS and NORTHERN SAW-WHET OWLS have been reported in spring also. Pacific Yew and Grand Fir are native here. **Shoreline Community College** and **Shoreview Park** provide access to bird-rich woods at the head of Boeing Creek. Metro bus #5 will get you there from downtown Seattle via Woodland Park or from Northgate (Sundays excepted).

Green Lake is a favorite of hikers, joggers, bicyclists, and roller-skaters. This is an excellent location for observing GREBES, DUCKS, and GULLS (except in June and July). The local nesting PIED-BILLED GREBES have been studied in detail by Martin Muller (1995, 2000). A three-mile path encircles the lake. EURASIAN WIGEONS are regular, October to April, usually frequenting the northeast bay or the south end. A large flock of COMMON MERGANSERS feeds in the center of the lake November to February. At this time there are usually HOODED MERGANSERS around the sanctuary island near the Bathhouse Theatre, where BALD EAGLES like to perch. The two concrete diving platforms fronting the Bathhouse Theatre are ideal for close study of GULLS in winter. Regularly present October to April are GLAUCOUS-WINGED and GLAUCOUS-WINGED X WESTERN GULL hybrids, and HERRING, THAYER'S, RING-BILLED, and MEW GULLS, with BONAPARTE'S, WESTERN and CALIFORNIA GULLS less regularly noted. GLAUCOUS, BLACK-HEADED, FRANKLIN'S, and LITTLE GULLS and BLACK-LEGGED KITTIWAKES have also been recorded here. Green Lake may also host a variety of exotic waterfowl. Occasionally a MANDARIN DUCK is reported; however, it is most likely just a visitor from Pilling's Pond, located on the property of the late famed aviculturist Charles Pilling. Mr. Pilling's collection is now managed by his son. It is a highly recommended stop on the Green Lake tour. Drive north from Green Lake to N 90th St. and Densmore Ave. N; watch quietly from the sidewalk. You may see EIDERS of all kinds, TUFTED DUCKS, SMEWS, BAIKAL TEALS, and something new each time (Morgan 1981).

Southwest of Green Lake is **Woodland Park** and the **Woodland Park Zoo.** The zoo charges a nominal fee to support its exhibits, which include displays of

Green Lake
and
Woodland Park

0   425   850   1,700 Feet

Northwest marsh birds and a section for rehabilitating injured eagles and owls. A backyard ecology exhibit called "Our Backyard" illustrates the use of native plants to attract backyard wildlife, a joint effort by the Woodland Park Zoological Society and the Seattle Audubon Society. Bald Eagles have nested in the park. During migration, from late April to May and from August through September, Woodland Park is alive with small land birds, particularly east of Aurora Ave. N. Green Lake and Woodland Park may be reached from downtown via Metro buses #16 and #26.

University of Washington Campus and Arboretum. The most productive birding area on campus is **Montlake Fill** (also called Union Bay Natural Area (UBNA), long a Seattle landfill, now "reclaimed." More than 240 species of birds have been recorded here over the years (Sidles 2009). "The Fill" has playing fields, parking lots, swampy woodland, and a large patch of open, weedy grassland with numerous small ponds. Park in the few spaces at the east end of Wahkiakum Lane just west of the Center for Urban Horticulture (3501 NE 41st St.). The ponds have hosted a surprising variety of SHOREBIRDS during migration, and as many as seven species of SWALLOWS may be seen in season. KILLDEER and SPOTTED SANDPIPERS nest, while GREATER and LESSER YELLOWLEGS, LEAST and WESTERN SANDPIPERS, and LONG-BILLED DOWITCHERS are regular migrants. WILSON'S SNIPES are found in winter, and SOLITARY, SEMIPALMATED, BAIRD'S, and PECTORAL SANDPIPERS are rare but regular in season. BLACK-BELLIED PLOVER, BLACK-NECKED STILT, AMERICAN AVOCET, UPLAND SANDPIPER, WHIMBREL, STILT SANDPIPER, WILSON'S and RED-NECKED PHALAROPE, and BUFF-BREASTED SANDPIPER are also on record.

The entire Montlake Fill area provides resting, feeding, and nesting habitat for many ducks. CANADA GEESE, MALLARDS and GADWALLS are conspicuous year-round. EURASIAN WIGEONS are present each winter among the throngs of AMERICAN WIGEONS. Three species of TEAL and RUDDY DUCKS are present each spring. The Eurasian form of the GREEN-WINGED TEAL (formerly COMMON TEAL) is occasionally found wintering with its American cousins. GREATER WHITE-FRONTED, SNOW, and CACKLING GEESE join the local CANADAS from time to time. WOOD DUCKS, HOODED MERGANSERS, PIED-BILLED GREBES, and AMERICAN COOTS nest here.

In the open waters of Union Bay, winter flocks include thousands of GAD-WALLS and WIGEONS, mixed with dozens of NORTHERN SHOVELERS, SCAUPS, RING-NECKED DUCKS, CANVASBACKS (and the occasional REDHEAD), COMMON GOLDENEYES, BUFFLEHEADS, and COMMON and HOODED MERGANSERS, plus PIED-BILLED, HORNED, and WESTERN GREBES, DOUBLE-CRESTED CORMORANTS, and a couple thousand AMERICAN COOTS, as well as the occasional family of SWANS.

A hike along the Loop Trail may flush migrant AMERICAN PIPITS, WESTERN MEADOWLARKS, rarities such as ASH-THROATED FLYCATCHER, and numerous SPARROWS. SONG, LINCOLN'S, FOX, SAVANNAH, WHITE-CROWNED, and GOLDEN-CROWNED SPARROWS are common in season. The list of rare sparrows is quite impressive. There have been one or more reports of vagrant AMERICAN TREE, CHIPPING, BREWER'S, CLAY-COLORED, LARK, VESPER, SAGE, SWAMP, WHITE-THROATED, and HARRIS'S SPARROWS, plus a single CHESTNUT-COLLARED LONGSPUR. LAPLAND LONGSPURS, GRAY-CROWNED ROSY-FINCHES, and SNOW BUNTINGS are additional possibilities.

Raptors of regular occurrence include BALD EAGLES, OSPREYS, ACCIPITERS, RED-TAILED HAWKS, MERLINS, and PEREGRINE FALCONS, with less frequent visits by NORTHERN HARRIERS, AMERICAN KESTRELS, GREAT HORNED and SHORT-EARED OWLS, and once a RED-SHOULDERED HAWK. SNOWY OWLS are possible during invasion winters. Cattail borders support MARSH WRENS, RED-WINGED BLACKBIRDS (with an occasional YELLOW-HEADED BLACK-BIRD straggler in migration), and both VIRGINIA RAILS and SORAS. AMERICAN BITTERNS were once common (see Higman and Larrison 1951) but are now scarce. GREEN HERONS provide partial compensation, as they appear to be on the increase. The first documented evidence of Green Herons nesting in Washington was a young juvenile photographed here in 1939 by Harry Higman. Painted Turtles, and Red-eared Sliders—among other ex-pets—are common introduced species, as are Nutrias and Bullfrogs, while native American Beavers, Common Muskrats, Raccoons, and North American River Otters are still much in evidence.

The upper campus plantings can be productive, especially during spring migration. South of the Montlake Cut, **Foster Island** and **Washington Park Arboretum** (both managed by the University of Washington Botanic Gardens' staff, as is Montlake Fill) host many woodland species. The Arboretum's Waterfront Trail from the Museum of History & Industry (staging point for many Seattle Audubon field trips) to Foster Island offers views of Union Bay waterfowl and access to swampy woods of willow and cottonwood, which attract YELLOW WARBLERS and BULLOCK'S ORIOLES in summer. Vagrants recorded here include DUSKY FLYCATCHER, BLUE-GRAY GNATCATCHER, and BLACK-AND-WHITE WARBLER. BARN, WESTERN SCREECH-, GREAT HORNED, and BARRED OWLS have been found in the Arboretum recently. RED-TAILED HAWKS nested within sight of the Space Needle in Interlaken Park in 1981, and COOPER'S HAWKS nested nearby in Volunteer Park in 2009. Metro bus access from downtown Seattle (Third and Pike) is via #11.

Magnuson Park/Sand Point. Northeast of the University of Washington campus off Sand Point Way NE is Warren G. Magnuson Park, a portion of the decommissioned Sand Point Naval Air Station that has been donated to the city. Enter the park at NE 65th St. or NE 74th St. Magnuson Park's prime attractions are open weedy fields and a substantial stretch of Lake Washington shoreline. The usual DIVING BIRDS and GULLS may be seen along the shore, with an occasional BARROW'S GOLDENEYE or LOON. The diving platform just off the beach attracts roosting gulls in winter, reliably including MEW, RING-BILLED, CALIFORNIA, THAYER'S, HERRING, and GLAUCOUS-WINGED GULLS. CANADA GEESE and GADWALLS roost about the grassy ponds. The fields and thickets may shelter wintering WILSON'S SNIPES, SHORT-EARED OWLS, NORTHERN SHRIKES, WAXWINGS, YELLOW-RUMPED WARBLERS, LAPLAND LONGSPURS, and WESTERN MEADOWLARKS. SHORT-EARED OWLS nested here in 1972—the only such record for the county. BARN OWLS nested in 2010. King County's first TROPICAL KINGBIRD proved cooperative for several days in November 2006, while one or more BOHEMIAN WAXWINGS tantalized observers here during December 2007 and the following January, and a flock of 16 stayed for several days during December 2010.

North of Magnuson Park in the bight at the mouth of Thornton Creek is **Matthews Beach Park.** A mudflat at the creek mouth is good for GULLS in winter, especially the CALIFORNIA GULL, often difficult to find after October. GREAT BLUE HERONS, COOPER'S HAWKS, and BARRED OWLS have nested in recent years. Thornton Creek supports salmon and Coastal Giant Salamanders. Metro bus access to both parks from downtown Seattle is via #74.

Seward Park. Seward Park is a heavily wooded peninsula jutting into Lake Washington from Seattle's southeast side. The northern half of the park is a remnant old-growth forest sheltering some Douglas Firs more than 200 years old. Woods bordering the parking lot at the crest of the hill once hid three pairs of WESTERN SCREECH-OWLS, which seem to have been driven off by invading BARRED OWLS. GREAT HORNED and NORTHERN SAW-WHET OWLS are noted occasionally. OSPREYS and BALD EAGLES have nested on the steep northwest slope. The typical western Washington woodland birds may be expected in season, e.g., resident CHICKADEES, RED-BREASTED NUTHATCHES, HUTTON'S VIREOS, GOLDEN-CROWNED KINGLETS, and PACIFIC and BEWICK'S WRENS. Look for TOWNSEND'S WARBLERS, GOLDEN-CROWNED and FOX SPARROWS, and VARIED THRUSHES in winter. WARBLERS, VIREOS, and FLYCATCHERS are conspicuous in migration. Scan Lake Washington for wintering LOONS and GREBES, in particular the scarce EARED GREBE. A DIPPER wintered at the trout hatchery outlet for several years during the 1980s, probably dying of old age. A flock of feral parrots has frequented the neighborhood since the early 1990s. These

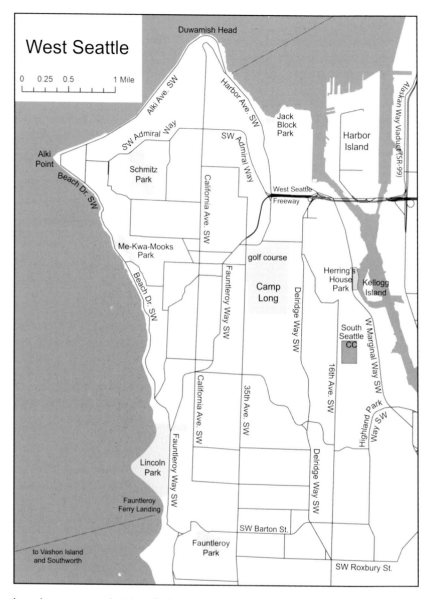

West Seattle

0   0.25   0.5   1 Mile

Duwamish Head

Alki Ave. SW

Harbor Ave. SW

Jack Block Park

Harbor Island

Alaskan Way Viaduct (SR-99)

SW Admiral Way

SW Admiral Way

Alki Point

Beach Dr. SW

Schmitz Park

California Ave. SW

West Seattle Freeway

Me-Kwa-Mooks Park

golf course

Herring's House Park

Kellogg Island

Beach Dr. SW

Fauntleroy Way SW

Camp Long

Deiridge Way SW

South Seattle CC

W Marginal Way SW

California Ave. SW

35th Ave. SW

16th Ave. SW

Highland Park Way SW

Lincoln Park

Fauntleroy Way SW

Deiridge Way SW

Fauntleroy Ferry Landing

to Vashon Island and Southworth

SW Barton St.

Fauntleroy Park

SW Roxbury St.

have been tentatively identified as CRIMSON-FRONTED PARAKEETS *(Aratinga finschi)*, originally from Central America. Metro bus access from downtown Seattle is via #34 and #39.

West Seattle. The best way to bird West Seattle is to do the perimeter; it is most productive between October and April. From the West Seattle Freeway, cross the Spokane Street Bridge (also called the West Seattle Bridge and now formally

the Jeanette Williams Memorial Bridge) and take
Harbor Ave. SW north past an industrial wasteland
toward Duwamish Head. Watch for the entrance
to **Jack Block Park** on your right. Purple Martin gourds here are occupied in summer, and the
high catwalk provides an excellent vantage point
for monitoring harbor activities, human and otherwise. At **Duwamish Head** carefully inspect the
breakwater fore and aft in winter for a large mixed
flock of BLACK TURNSTONES and SURFBIRDS,
reliably present here since the early 1990s. From
here you may watch the Elliott Bay activity, including freighters, ferries, and sea birds, particularly
our three CORMORANT species, three species of
LOONS, and PIGEON GUILLEMOTS, RHINOC-
EROS AUKLETS, and the occasional MARBLED
MURRELET. Nearer Harbor Island BARROW'S
GOLDENEYES and WESTERN GREBES are reg-

ular in winter. GULLS, BLACKBIRDS, and CROWS patrol the bathing beaches
southwest to the Alki Point Lighthouse. Low tide exposes sedimentary rock strata
south of Alki Point along Beach Dr. SW, drawing SHOREBIRDS and sea ducks
such as BLACK SCOTERS and HARLEQUIN DUCKS.

---

*Above: Brown Creepers can be found in the wet coniferous forests of West Seattle parks such as
Schmitz and Lincoln Parks (© Thomas Sanders). Below: Sanderling at sunset, south of Alki
Point (© Kathrine Lloyd).*

A worthwhile side trip is to **Schmitz Park,** off SW Admiral Way a half-mile east of 63rd Ave. SW. These few acres of virgin timber suggest the scene that greeted Seattle's first non-Indian settlers, Arthur Denny's party, when they landed at Alki in November 1851. The park's timber attracts birds of the deepest forest, notably HUTTON'S VIREOS and BROWN CREEPERS. WESTERN SCREECH-OWLS raised a family here in 1982, and PILEATED WOODPECKERS have also nested.

The beaches south of Alki Point are largely privately controlled, but vantage points include the **Emma Schmitz Memorial Overlook** at the Me-Kwa-Mooks Park—still noted for resident WESTERN SCREECH-OWLS—and **Lowman Beach Park.** Beyond is **Lincoln Park,** one of Seattle's largest parks, and one with ample birding potential. Madrones line the sea bluff, with mixed native and exotic conifers in thick copses at the center of the park. BARRED OWLS have been regular here since first noted in 1980. The dense groves are excellent in winter for BAND-TAILED PIGEONS, CHESTNUT-BACKED CHICKADEES, RED-BREASTED NUT-HATCHES, BROWN CREEPERS, RED-BREASTED SAPSUCKERS, and lingering CEDAR WAXWINGS. A stray GRAY FLYCATCHER visited a glade here one sunny spring day in 2008. The Lincoln Park beach promenade is reached from the crown of the bluff. RED-NECKED GREBES and LOONS are common in winter. A rare YELLOW-BILLED LOON was spotted here in the winter of 1979-1980 and the state's first KING EIDER was found here in 1948. Lincoln Park is the only mainland site in the county for Western Fence Lizards. Metro bus access from downtown Seattle is via #37 and #56 (with transfers from various West Seattle locations).

If you are driving, you may take an alternate route back to Seattle by way of the Duwamish River and Kellogg Island. Follow SW Wildwood Pl. up the hill east of the Fauntleroy Ferry Landing to SW Barton St. Continue to Delridge Way SW, then turn left on Delridge to SW Holden St. Go right (east) and continue on 21st Ave. SW/20th Ave. SW to reconnect with SW Holden. Continue east to Highland Park Way SW, then left down the hill to the Duwamish River Valley. Turn left (north) on W Marginal Way SW to SW Alaska St. Park here at the newly revegetated **Herring's House Park** for a view of Kellogg Island, all that is left of the vast salt marshes of the Duwamish River delta. The actual Herring's House was a Duwamish Indian village on what is now Harbor Island. In winter the birds about the north end of Kellogg Island, with its remnant salt marsh, are of interest. BAR-ROW'S GOLDENEYES and many COMMON MERGANSERS and GREAT BLUE HERONS are conspicuous among the varied waterfowl here. The muddy shorelines may attract wintering shorebirds such as LEAST SANDPIPERS, DUNLINS, LONG-BILLED DOWITCHERS, or WILSON'S SNIPES. RED-TAILED HAWKS reside on the hillside to the west, where a few GREAT BLUES may nest. Continue north on W Marginal Way SW to the West Seattle Bridge, then head east for connections to Seattle's freeways. CASPIAN TERNS nested on a roof visible from the bridge in 2008, a King County first.

Right: A Pileated Woodpecker probes for food on a tree in Juanita Bay Park (© Gregg Thompson).

AREA 2. EAST SHORE OF LAKE WASHINGTON, KENMORE TO RENTON

Our route starts at the lake's north end at Log Boom Park (officially Tracy Owen Station at Log Boom Park) in Kenmore. The park lies astride the Burke-Gilman Trail, a bike-and-hike trail which starts at Gas Works Park on Lake Union in Seattle and ends at Marymoor Park on Lake Sammamish in Redmond. For those who enjoy bicycle birding, this bike trail has many possibilities.

Log Boom Park is just south of SR-522 (NE Bothell Way), west of the Kenmore Air Harbor at 61st Ave. NE and NE 175th St. An old loading dock which

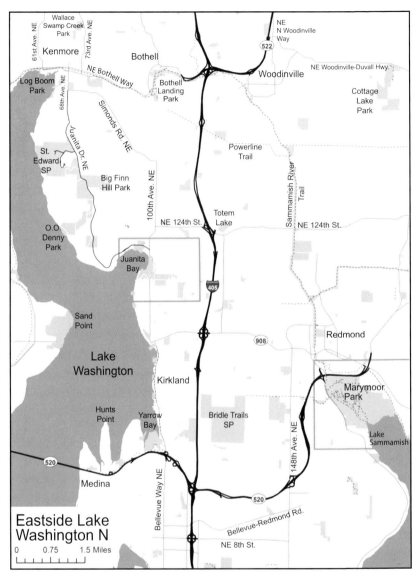

Eastside Lake Washington N

0   0.75   1.5 Miles

has been renovated for the fisher folk is a fine spot to study waterfowl in winter. Several thousand AMERICAN COOTS hang out here all winter in the company of GADWALLS, AMERICAN WIGEONS, NORTHERN SHOVELERS, SCAUPS, CANVASBACKS, BUFFLEHEADS, and MERGANSERS. PURPLE MARTINS quickly discovered the gourds Kevin Li put up here in 2006 and are joined by TREE, VIOLET-GREEN, CLIFF, and BARN SWALLOWS in summer. BLACK SWIFTS often forage over the lake on dark days when they first arrive in early June. An OSPREY fishes in the lake here spring and summer, while BALD EAGLES are present year-round.

Both probably nest nearby. GREEN HERONS and TUNDRA SWANS have also been noted. Rarities are possible, including EURASIAN WIGEON, LONG-TAILED DUCK, REDHEAD, TUFTED DUCK, and CLARK'S and EARED GREBES. Two totally unexpected FORSTER'S TERNS appeared in September 2008.

From Log Boom Park go east on SR-522 to 68th Ave. NE/Juanita Dr. NE and turn right (south) across the Sammamish River. Juanita Dr. continues south past Inglewood Golf Club to the latest prize acquisition of the state park system, **St. Edward State Park,** on what had been the St. Edward Seminary grounds. Enter on NE 145th St., then bear right at the first "Y" to park at the St. Edward chapel and dormitory. Many birds of the deep woods are found here, close to the metropolis. March observations include RUFOUS HUMMINGBIRDS, feeding at the rich pink Salmonberry blooms decorating the bare brambles, and torrents of PACIFIC WREN song from within the sword ferns. PACIFIC-SLOPE FLYCATCHERS return here before mid-April. BARRED OWLS are now resident.

Continue south on Juanita Dr. NE as it curves east around Juanita Bay to **Juanita Beach Park**. RING-NECKED DUCKS and REDHEADS have been reported here, while a female AMERICAN BLACK DUCK of uncertain provenance foraged in the parking lot during several successive winters. Study the GULLS here in winter. RING-BILLED, CALIFORNIA, and MEW GULLS roost in close proximity. Turn right (south) on 98th Ave. NE and park in the **Juanita Bay Park** lot on the right at the intersection with Forbes Creek Dr. The trail leaves the lot for three lakeshore boardwalks. The old highway bridge is to your right, parallel with the

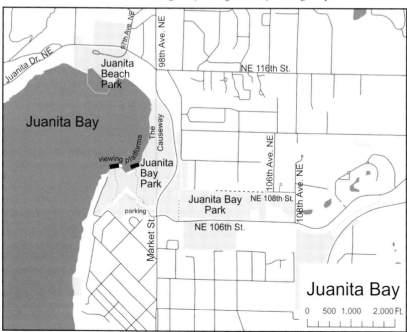

highway. From this pedestrian causeway you have an excellent chance for close-up views of VIRGINIA RAILS and possibly a SORA. GREEN HERONS have nested in the dense willow thickets bordering the causeway. Rarities noted here include an AMERICAN REDSTART and both SWAMP and WHITE-THROATED SPARROWS. The westernmost boardwalk overlooks a muddy bay favored by WOOD DUCKS and wintering GREEN-WINGED TEALS, among other waterfowl. If you drive across Juanita Dr. NE onto Forbes Creek Dr. and park just past the fire station at a gravel road, you can walk in north past the gate to explore this patch of wooded swamp. You may access the north edge of Forbes Creek by continuing east on Forbes Creek Dr. to 108th Ave. NE. Turn left here, then left again on NE 108th St. Park at the end and walk the trail west. At night you might hear WESTERN SCREECH-OWLS and BARRED OWLS here.

For a change of scene you might explore **Bridle Trails State Park,** an entire square mile of undulating, wooded terrain crisscrossed by bridle trails (naturally). The forest is primarily second-growth Douglas Fir. A GREAT GRAY OWL skulked about the margins of the park during February 1997. To get here from Juanita Bay Park in Kirkland, follow Market St. south to the jog east onto Central Way, which becomes NE 85th St. Continue to I-405 and enter the freeway going southbound. Take the NE 70th Pl. exit off I-405 and go right (south) just east of the freeway on 116th Ave. NE to the northwest park entrance at NE 60th St.

Back in downtown Kirkland you may continue south on Lake St. S/Lake Washington Blvd. NE, which skirts marshy willow thickets at the south end of

In the marshes of Juanita Bay Park and Mercer Slough, you may find Sora (this page, © Gregg Thompson) and American Bittern (opposite page, © Thomas Sanders).

Yarrow Bay, a remnant wetland proposed for condominium development. **Yarrow Bay Wetlands** is a 73-acre conservancy park that provides public access to the western fringe of Yarrow Bay marsh lands, an area rich in RAILS. Look for WOOD DUCKS and the occasional REDHEAD here in winter. To reach the park, approach from Lake Washington Blvd. NE and drive to NE Points Dr. (immediately north of the SR-520 freeway). Turn west (right) on NE Points Dr. to 92nd Ave. NE, then right (north) to NE 40th St. Turn right again (east) to 95th Ave. NE and take a short jog north to the park entrance.

Our route continues south on 92nd Ave. NE directly to tiny **Clyde Beach Park** on Bellevue's Meydenbauer Bay. An AMERICAN BLACK DUCK recorded here in 1973 was the first ever for Seattle's CBC. It was judged to have strayed from the now-defunct introduced populations near Everett.

Lake Washington Blvd. NE/Bellevue Way SE may be pursued southward to the mouth of **Mercer Slough Nature Park** (Kelsey Creek) in the shadow of I-90. Just north of the freeway ramparts, opposite 113th Ave. SE, turn left at a bike symbol to reach **Sweyolocken Park,** terminus of bike-and-hike paths across Mercer Slough, and then west under the freeway to **Enatai Beach Park,** which provides views of the Newport Yacht Basin. Mercer Slough is best examined from a canoe or kayak—there is a launching facility at Sweyolocken Park. **Bellefields Nature Park** provides access to Mercer Slough from the east via a network of trails through a tangle of underbrush beneath a tall cottonwood "gallery forest" and across a wet grassy savanna.

From Sweyolocken Park, retrace your route north to 112th Ave. SE, thence north to SE 8th St., connecting east to 118th Ave. SE/Lake Washington Blvd. SE. This arterial leads south past the Bellefields Trailhead at Mercer Slough Nature Park, which provides access to the east side of Mercer Slough. RUFFED GROUSE—perhaps no longer—and RED-EYED VIREOS achieve a close approach to the city here. GREEN HERONS, WILLOW FLYCATCHERS, MARSH WRENS, and COMMON YELLOWTHROATS are notable summer residents. Unusual trees include both exotic Paper Birch and native swamp birches. Further south on 118th Ave. SE, just under the I-90 bridge, is a pipeline; park opposite and climb out on the pipe. From this vantage you may spy HERONS, BITTERNS, RAILS, even perhaps an introduced Red Fox. The next right turn off of 118th Ave. SE/Lake Washington Blvd. SE onto SE 40th St. leads to the Newport Yacht Basin. Little is left of this once-rich wetland.

Phantom Lake in east Bellevue is reputed to be worth more attention from birders than it has received to date. Go east on I-90 toward Issaquah from the I-405 interchange, and exit to the north at the Bellevue Airfield (150th Ave. SE). Go right (east) on SE Eastgate Way, then left on 156th Ave. SE, which continues past the airfield to the park entrance on SE 20th Pl. A fine male TUFTED DUCK spent the winter here in 2005-2006.

A variety of alternatives are available for further exploration east of Lake Washington. If you choose to return to Seattle via I-90, you might visit **Luther Burbank Park** on Mercer Island en route. Go west on I-90, exit to 80th Ave. SE via N Mercer Way. Take the first right turn onto SE 26th St., then a left on 84th Ave. SE to the park. Explore a half mile of waterfront, brushy thickets, and a pocket-sized marsh. BALD EAGLES and OSPREYS pay frequent visits in season.

The **Sammamish River Trail** links with the Burke-Gilman Trail just east of downtown Bothell. It provides a paved, motor-free bike-and-hike route to Marymoor Park in Redmond on the shore of Lake Sammamish. The path follows the diked Sammamish River through the broad, bucolic Sammamish Valley. The valley remains largely devoted to agricultural pursuits, thanks in part to the King County farmlands initiative accepted by voters in 1979. However, residential development is evident as the trail approaches Redmond.

The Sammamish Valley is a haven for DUCKS in all seasons. Droves of WIGEONS feed in the flooded fields from October through April. A close inspection of the flocks should produce a EURASIAN WIGEON or two also. RAPTORS are conspicuous: RED-TAILED HAWKS, NORTHERN HARRIERS, and AMERICAN KESTRELS are regular. On warm spring days the air is abuzz with the conversations of SWALLOWS, COMMON YELLOWTHROATS, AMERICAN GOLDFINCHES, and SAVANNAH SPARROWS.

If you must drive your motor vehicle, from north Seattle take SR-522 (Lake City Way NE/NE Bothell Way) to I-405 and go south on I-405, or travel north on

I-405 from Bellevue. Exit I-405 at Totem Lake (Exit 20B) and follow NE 124th St. east, then go south on Willows Rd. NE along the west side of the valley. The field east of Willows Rd. between NE 124th and NE 116th Sts. is worth a scan for NORTHERN HARRIERS or AMERICAN KESTRELS. A ROUGH-LEGGED HAWK spent all winter here in 2008-2009. **Sixty Acres Park** off NE 116th St. offers walking trails with access to meadow and hedge habitats. Continue south on Willows Rd. NE under the SR-520 overpass (you're now on W Lake Sammamish Pkwy. NE) to the Marymoor Park entrance on your left.

Marymoor Park. The grove of Douglas Fir surrounding Clise Mansion harbors flocks of GOLDEN-CROWNED KINGLETS and CHESTNUT-BACKED CHICKADEES. HUTTON'S VIREOS may join them. Look for DOWNY and HAIRY WOODPECKERS and the occasional RED-BREASTED SAPSUCKER in winter. I have seen VAUX'S SWIFTS use the museum's chimney as a migratory roost. BARN OWLS often roost in or near the windmill. Note that a $1 parking fee is required to park. A trail leads south along the Sammamish River through open grassy fields. This trail cuts through the dog-run area, so be forewarned. COMMON YELLOW-THROATS, MARSH WRENS, and SAVANNAH SPARROWS are common breeding species of these fields. GREEN HERONS, VIRGINIA RAILS, and SPOTTED SAND-PIPERS frequent the river margin. The trail continues through a swampy thicket to an observation platform built out from the cattails of the lake margin. Martin gourds were installed here in 2008 and soon attracted nesting PURPLE MARTINS as well as TREE SWALLOWS. BULLOCK'S ORIOLES and RED-EYED VIREOS nest in the tall cottonwoods. King County's only BALTIMORE ORIOLE sang here for several days in June 2007.

Michael Hobbs leads a weekly census of Marymoor Park on Thursday mornings. Hobbs's crew usually starts at sunrise at Lot G (a parking fee of $1 is payable at the ticket machines) on the northeast edge of the dog-run area. To begin, scramble up the dirt piles to your east to scan East Meadow, and in winter check the SPARROWS in the adjacent blackberry thickets. This vantage point has been exceptionally productive. At dawn you might observe a BARN or SHORT-EARED OWL patrolling the fields. Rarities spotted from the dirt piles or in the nearby meadow and soccer fields include BURROWING and LONG-EARED OWLS; SAY'S PHOEBE; LEAST and ASH-THROATED FLYCATCHERS; EASTERN KINGBIRD; SAGE THRASHER; AMERICAN TREE, BREWER'S, CLAY-COLORED, SAGE, and VESPER SPARROWS; HORNED LARK; and LAPLAND and SMITH'S LONG-SPURS. The trail leading south from the east edge of Lot G along the west edge of East Meadow continues through a tall forest of cottonwood and ash trees, then through a willow swamp to the observation platform described above. You may complete this hike as a loop if you wish.

A section of Marymoor Park lies west across Sammamish Slough at the rowing boat house. Return to the west entrance at W Lake Sammamish Pkwy. NE and bear left. Keep an eye out for the parking lot on the left. Walk toward the slough

past forested ponds that host WOOD DUCKS and GREEN HERONS. Expect WARBLERS and FLYCATCHERS in spring and summer.

From Marymoor Park go north on W Lake Sammamish Pkwy. NE to SR-520, then proceed east to Redmond-Fall City Rd. (SR-202). Bear right (southeast) to 196th Ave. NE, and turn left (north). Paving soon gives way to red brick. Follow the Red Brick Road! Stop at the small bridge over Evans Creek.

Red Brick Road (196th Ave. NE) Marsh. VIRGINIA RAILS are resident. COMMON YELLOWTHROATS and WILSON'S SNIPE nest in the marsh grass, and WILLOW FLYCATCHERS sneeze their notes in the streamside willows. Foraging OSPREYS are often overhead. Northwestern Salamanders live here also. In

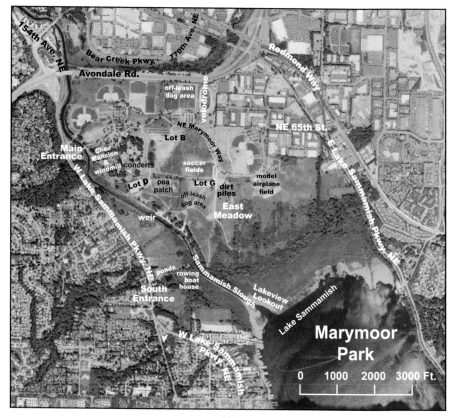

migration and winter, SPARROWS flock just north of the bridge in the blackberry tangle on the hillside west of the road. What sounds like guerrilla warfare is just target shooters practicing at a nearby rifle range.

Return to the Redmond-Fall City Rd. (SR-202) and continue southeast to the traffic light at Sahalee Way NE. Follow Sahalee Way NE/228th Ave. NE south to NE Inglewood Hill Rd./ NE 8th St. Go east 1.5 miles on NE 8th to **Llama Lake,** on your left at 235th Ave. NE. Depending on water levels you may hope to find SHORE-BIRDS here with a variety of DUCKS. A WHITE-FACED IBIS turned up in May 2008. SOLITARY, SEMIPALMAT-ED, and PECTORAL SANDPIPERS have been recorded as well.

Continue east on NE 8th St. to 244th Ave. NE to return to SR-202, or return via 228th Ave. NE/Sahalee Way NE to SR-202. If you take the latter route, you can avoid hectic traffic by turning at NE 50th St. just shy of the highway. NE 50th cuts across a swamp to rejoin SR-202. The swamp harbors summering RUFOUS HUMMINGBIRDS, YELLOW WARBLERS, and BLACK-HEADED GROSBEAKS.

At this point you may choose to continue via SR-202 to NE Ames Lake Rd. or NE Tolt Hill Rd., which leads east to the Snoqualmie Valley at Carnation (Area 7), or you may continue on SR-202 directly to Fall City, Snoqualmie, and North Bend. Our route turns southwest off SR-202 at SE Duthie Hill Rd., which becomes SE Issaquah-Fall City Rd., past the SE Issaquah-Beaver Lake Rd. junction to SE 58th St. Turn right here and drop down the hill to E Lake Sammamish Pkwy. SE. Turn right (north) here to the boat launch parking lot on the southeast corner of Lake Sammamish. SWAMP SPARROWS have

Marymoor Park has a way of producing mega-rarities such as the ones shown here. Opposite page: Sage Sparrow, April 7, 2007 (© John Tubbs). This page, above: Baltimore Oriole, June 5, 2006 (© Ollie Oliver). This page, left: Smith's Longspur, August 30, 2006 (© Ollie Oliver).

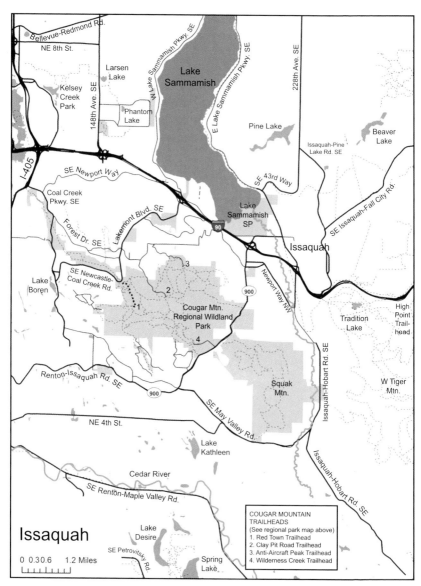

0 0.3 0.6   1.2 Miles

COUGAR MOUNTAIN
TRAILHEADS
(See regional park map above)
1. Red Town Trailhead
2. Clay Pit Road Trailhead
3. Anti-Aircraft Peak Trailhead
4. Wilderness Creek Trailhead

wintered in the flooded Reed Canary Grass fields south of the boat launch. Alternatively, go west on SE 56th St./NW Sammamish Rd. to the main entrance of Lake Sammamish State Park.

Lake Sammamish State Park provides excellent birding at the lake's marshy southern extremity and along the lower reach of Issaquah Creek, the lake's major tributary stream and a salmon superhighway. The park is crowded on summer weekends, but a measure of solitude is possible across the footbridge over Issaquah

Creek north of the parking lots. Thick swampy woods here may shelter roosting BARN and GREAT HORNED OWLS by day. GREAT BLUE HERONS gather in numbers in winter, clattering about in the bare cottonwoods. Some stay on to nest. GREEN HERONS apparently also nest nearby. A hike across the grassy expanse eastward in winter might turn up a NORTHERN SHRIKE or ROUGH-LEGGED HAWK. A small colony of NORTHERN ROUGH-WINGED SWALLOWS nests in the creek bank, and HOUSE WREN and YELLOW-BREASTED CHAT sightings in summer suggest possible breeding. Scan the skies for SWIFTS and OSPREYS in summer and for BALD EAGLES any time. Brushy thickets about the picnic areas have produced both a HARRIS'S and SWAMP SPARROWS.

South of Issaquah are the mountain outliers known locally as the **Issaquah Alps,** rising progressively west to east from Cougar to Squak to Tiger Mountain summits. Cougar Mountain is the centerpiece of a regional park. A substantial piece of Squak Mountain has been set aside as **Squak Mountain State Park,** a gift of the Bullitt family. The main route to the summit is via Squak Mountain Rd. SE, which can be reached by going south on Renton-Issaquah Rd. SE (SR-900) to SE May Valley Rd. and turning left (southeast) to Squak Mountain Rd.

Cougar Mountain Regional Wildland Park. The north and west slopes of Cougar Mountain have been transformed by suburban developments. However, 3,000 acres of the summit plateau and south and east slopes have been set aside for wildlife habitat, accessible via 32 miles of hiking trails. There are four main

trailheads that access the park: Red Town on the west, Clay Pit Road and Anti-Aircraft Peak on the north, and the Wilderness Creek Trailhead at the eastern base of the mountain off Renton-Issaquah Rd. SE (SR-900).

The Red Town Trailhead may be reached from I-405 by taking Exit 10. Go right (southeast) on Coal Creek Pkwy. SE, which climbs through Coal Creek Park, site of early coal mining operations. NORTHERN SAW-WHET OWLS have been reported calling in this ravine in March and April in recent years. Turn left off Coal Creek Pkwy. SE onto Forest Dr. SE and drive southeast to Lake-

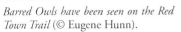

Barred Owls have been seen on the Red Town Trail (© Eugene Hunn).

mont Blvd. SE/SE Newcastle-Coal Creek Rd. Turn right and park where Lakemont Blvd. SE bends right to become Newcastle Golf Club Rd. This is the trailhead for the Red Town Trail. A network of trails leads through mixed second-growth and swampy woods. WESTERN SCREECH-OWLS, GREAT HORNED, BARRED, and NORTHERN SAW-WHET OWLS have been heard between the trailhead and Red Town, but the park is closed after dark. The park administration fears nocturnal hikers might fall into an abandoned mine shaft.

To reach the upper trailheads on the north side of Cougar Mountain, return up Lakemont Blvd. SE to SE 63rd St./SE Cougar Mountain Way. Turn right and climb to the intersection with 166th Way SE. Go right here to the gate at the Klondike Swamp Trailhead or left following SE Cougar Mountain Way/168th Pl. SE/SE 60th St. to SE Cougar Mountain Dr. Turn right up SE Cougar Mountain Dr. to the parking lot at Anti-Aircraft Peak. The peak offers fine views by day and WESTERN SCREECH-OWLS by night. NORTHERN PYGMY-OWLS and SNOWY OWLS are also on record. To descend from Anti-Aircraft Peak to Issaquah and Lake Sammamish State Park, follow Lakemont Blvd. SE to the northeast (or trace this route in reverse if you are coming from Issaquah). The still-wild east side of the mountain is accessible from Renton-Issaquah Rd. SE (SR 900) at the Wilderness Creek Trailhead.

Tiger Mountain has been designated a state forest. Though it has been heavily logged over the years, the summit area attracts montane birds west of their normal

Common species of the Tiger Mountain area include Pacific Wren (this page, © Gregg Thompson) *and Chestnut-backed Chickadee (opposite page,* © Kathrine Lloyd).

haunts. These birds have included TOWNSEND'S SOLITAIRES, GRAY JAYS, and HERMIT THRUSHES. Pacific Silver Fir and Mountain Hemlock extend west from the high Cascades to this point.

West Tiger Mountain's several summits are reached by a network of trails starting from the Preston-High Point exit (Exit 20) off I-90. The usual line-up of parked cars along SE 79th St. at the trailhead attests to the popularity of these trails. The climb up through dense coniferous forest is not particularly birdy, though you may count on resident forest species such as HAIRY and PILEATED WOODPECK-ERS, CHESTNUT-BACKED CHICKADEES, RED-BREASTED NUTHATCHES, BROWN CREEPERS, PACIFIC WRENS, GOLDEN-CROWNED KINGLETS, and VARIED THRUSHES. A family of GRAY JAYS is resident near the bald top of West Tiger #3, which offers as well outstanding views to the south and west.

Tiger's highest summit (East Tiger, at 3049 feet) is reached via a five-mile hike up Tiger Mountain Rd. SE. Take Exit 25 from I-405 and head south on SR-18 for 4.1 miles. Park in the lot on the right. A network of logging roads provides hikers access to much of the mountain, which hides pockets of near wilderness.

Tradition Lake, just east of Issaquah at the foot of West Tiger Mountain

summit, is well worth the four-mile round-trip hike. The trail begins behind the high school stadium on 2nd Ave. SE in Issaquah. BALD EAGLES and PI-LEATED WOODPECK-ERS are characteristic resident birds. BROWN CREEPERS and RED-EYED VIREOS nest here, while HUTTON'S VIREOS and VARIED THRUSHES are present all year. Tradition Lake can also be reached by a level trail and an easy hike from the West Ti-ger Mountain Trailhead at Exit 20 off I-90.

As you head south from downtown Is-saquah, the Issaquah-

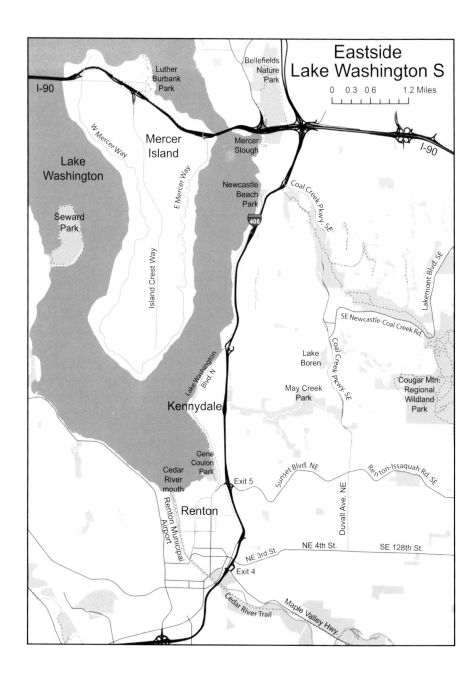

Eastside
Lake Washington S

0   0.3 0.6   1.2 Miles

I-90

Luther
Burbank
Park

Bellefields
Nature
Park

Mercer
Island

Mercer
Slough

I-90

W Mercer Way

Lake
Washington

E Mercer Way

Newcastle
Beach
Park

Coal Creek Pkwy. SE

405

Seward
Park

Lakemont Blvd. SE

Island Crest Way

SE Newcastle-Coal Creek Rd.

Lake
Boren

Coal Creek pkwy. SE

Cougar Mtn.
Regional
Wildland
Park

May Creek
Park

Lake Washington Blvd N

Kennydale

Gene
Coulon
Park

Sunset Blvd. NE

Renton-Issaquah Rd. SE

Cedar
River
mouth

Exit 5

Duvall Ave. NE

Renton Municipal Airport

Renton

NE 4th St.

SE 128th St.

Exit 4

NE 3rd St.

Cedar River Trail

Maple Valley Hwy.

Hobart Rd. SE squeezes between cliffs on Squak and Tiger Mountains. These cliffs support a complex of plants of more southern affinities, such as Garry Oak, manzanita, and Rocky Mountain Maple. At SE May Valley Rd. you may go west to Renton and Seattle, or you may continue to Cedar Grove Rd. SE, which connects with SR-169 in Area 3.

For additional access points on Lake Washington, return west from Issaquah on I-90 to I-405, drive one exit south on I-405 to Lake Washington Blvd. SE (Exit 9), and keep right (north) on 106th Ave.SE/Lake Washington Blvd. SE to **Newcastle Beach Park,** which offers swampy woodland, a resident pair of BALD EAGLES, and a pier excellent for DUCKS in winter. A large flock of CANVASBACKS favors the shoreline here or across the channel at Mercer Island.

Continue south on I-405 to SR-900 at Exit 5 (NE Park Dr./Park Ave. N), which takes you to Renton near Lake Washington's south end. Keep right onto Park Ave. N, then make a sharp right onto Lake Washington Blvd. N to the entrance to **Gene Coulon Memorial Beach Park**. Coulon Park and the nearby Cedar River mouth are best November through March for DUCKS, GEESE, GREBES, and above all, GULLS. Gulls that forage at the Cedar Hills Regional Landfill 10 miles east drift in throughout the afternoon to bathe and roost for the night. Many line up on the Coulon Park log booms, while others gather on the gravel bars at the mouth of the Cedar River just north of the Renton Municipal Airport runway.

To reach the Cedar River mouth return to Park Ave. N, head south to N 6th St., then west to N Riverside Dr. Park at the north end and walk over the bridge to the Cedar River Boathouse overlook. MEW, RING-BILLED, CALIFORNIA, THAYER'S, HERRING, GLAUCOUS-WINGED, and WESTERN GULLS and hybrids of the last two are reliable here.

Be forewarned! The airport periodically blasts recordings of birds being tortured. It is thought the sounds scare off the gulls, preventing the birds from interfering with the comings and goings of small planes. Somewhat more effective are periodic displays of fireworks. Between blasts, one may study the gulls at close range. Rare gulls spotted here include GLAUCOUS, ICELAND, SLATY-BACKED, and Washington's first and only GREAT BLACK-BACKED, as well as a variety of puzzling hybrids. A flock of several hundred WESTERN GREBES often hides a CLARK'S. EARED GREBES are regular, as are both of the GOLDENEYES and COMMON and HOODED MERGANSERS. You might also walk south along the Cedar River Trail, checking the streamside alders for wintering warblers, mostly YELLOW-RUMPED but with the occasional PALM.

A visit to these Renton gull mobs may cap a productive day exploring the lower Green River Valley, from Auburn to Kent (Area 4).

AREA 3. CEDAR & UPPER GREEN RIVER VALLEYS, RENTON TO BLACK DIAMOND

SR-169 is the rib of this route. It is a busy arterial running east then south from Renton through Maple Valley and Black Diamond to Enumclaw. Here it joins SR-410 and the White River Valley routes (Area 10) on the way to Mt. Rainier National Park's north gate, with access to the Naches Pass high country. SR-169 closely parallels the Cedar River as far as Maple Valley. About two miles east of Renton on the south side of the highway is **Riverview Park**. Grassy fields abut the

Willow Flycatchers come to King County lowlands to nest every summer. They are especially easy to find along Soos Creek (© Thomas Sanders).

cottonwood-bordered Cedar River. RED-EYED VIREOS may be expected in summer. BARROW'S GOLDENEYES, DIPPERS, and SPOTTED SANDPIPERS frequent the river in winter. A fine Sockeye Salmon run attracts GULLS and an occasional BALD EAGLE in late fall. Along the top of the dike is a riverside path, the **Cedar River Trail,** which you can follow downstream to the mouth of the river or upstream past the Maplewood Golf Course to Cedar River Park. This hike-and-bike trail continues to Maple Valley and beyond.

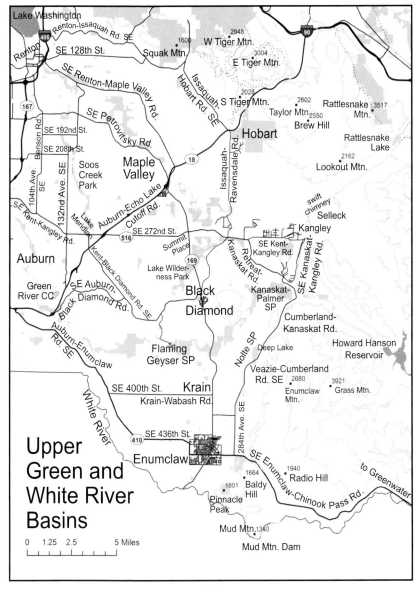

SE Jones Rd. parallels SR-169 along the north bank of the river for several miles, providing some respite from the hectic pace of the main highway. Farther north, skirting the south margin of Cougar Mountain, is SE May Valley Rd. (see also Area 2). This meanders through a wet valley full of cows and GULLS. The gulls roost here after feeding at nearby Cedar Hills Regional Landfill, then move down to Lake Washington to the Cedar River mouth.

Continue south on SR-169 1.5 miles past the Cedar River Bridge at Maple Valley to the **Lake Wilderness Park** turnoff, a right turn on Witte Rd. SE. A small county park at the lake allows views of SCAUPS and MERGANSERS in season and a variety of common birds of the mixed lowland woods of western Washington. Other accessible lakes in this vicinity worth inspection include Meridian, Desire, Shady, Otter (Spring Lake on some maps), Shadow, Morton, and Sawyer. Look for RUFFED GROUSE.

At Summit Place, a junction between Maple Valley and Black Diamond, you can go east on SR-516 to Kanaskat and Kangley at the edge of the montane zone. COMMON MERGANSERS and AMERICAN DIPPERS nest at the **Kanaskat Fish Hatchery** and Kanaskat-Palmer State Park. BALD EAGLES gather when the salmon spawn near Cumberland, south of Palmer near Nolte State Park. East of Kanaskat are the upper basins of the Cedar and Green Rivers, closed to public access because they serve municipal water needs. Two large reservoirs, Chester Morse Lake on the Cedar River (serving Seattle) and Howard Hanson Reservoir on the Green River (serving Tacoma), are large enough and sufficiently free of disturbance to support breeding COMMON LOONS and BARROW'S GOLDENEYES. The Cedar River watershed shelters one of the few SPOTTED OWL nest sites known for King County.

From Summit Place at the junction of SR-169 and SR-516, you may continue south on SR-169 through Black Diamond to SE Green Valley Rd., then turn right (west) to **Flaming Geyser State Park.** The park is deep in a partly cleared, broad, curving canyon bottom. RED-BREASTED SAPSUCKERS are common. HARLEQUIN DUCKS breed on the river just above the park and might drift down.

From Summit Place you may also go west on SR-516 (SE Kent-Kangley Rd.) to **Lake Meridian,** or you can explore the valley of the Big Soos, a densely wooded, still partly wild creek bottom. The **Gary Grant Soos Creek Park** offers a paved greenbelt trail that follows this creek south from SE 192nd St. nearly to SE Kent-Kangley Rd./SE 272nd St., where it connects with Lake Meridian Park at 152nd Way SE. Parking for the Soos Creek Trail is available in three areas: at the north end of the trail off 124th Ave SE just south of SE 192nd St., off SE 208th St., and off 148th Ave. SE just north of SE 256th St. You can reach the northern terminus of the trail more directly from SR-169 three miles southeast of I-405 in Renton. Take 140th Way SE south to SE 192nd St., then go right (west) on SE 192nd St. to the parking lot off 124th Ave SE. GREEN HERONS, RED-TAILED HAWKS, and VIRGINIA RAILS nest along the creek, and WESTERN WOOD-PEWEES, WILLOW FLYCATCHERS, RED-EYED VIREOS, COMMON YELLOWTHROATS, and PURPLE FINCHES sing in summer from the big cottonwoods and Hardhack thickets along the trail. GREAT HORNED OWLS are calling by early January, most often from the woods north of SE 244th St.

South of Black Diamond, SR-169 crosses the yawning Green River Gorge on a high bridge, then drops into farmland and pasture north of Enumclaw. A NORTHERN MOCKINGBIRD spent some time at Krain, just west of the junction of SR-169/264th Ave. SE and SE 416th St. during January 2008. If you are headed into the mountains southeast from Enumclaw, you can take a shortcut around downtown Enumclaw by jogging east off SR-169 on SE 416th St. to 284th Ave. SE/Farman St. N, then south to SR-410, then left on SR-410 toward Greenwater.

Left: Juvenile Red-tailed Hawks are common throughout the lowlands of King County (© Thomas Sanders).

Area 4. Lower Green River Valley, Tukwila to Auburn & Enumclaw

Samuel F. Rathbun described the Green River Valley in 1902 as "a beautiful, fertile and cultivated valley" extending for many miles up the river. However, the Howard Hanson Dam on the upper Green River has so reduced the threat of flooding that development of the floodplain along the lower river has proceeded apace. Today the Green River Valley's once productive wetland habitat is reduced to remnant ponds such as those on the Black River Slough and at Tukwila, Kent, and Auburn. These represent a fall-back defensive line for wildlife advocates, patches preserved for floodwater retention and wetland mitigation. Still, what remains of the Green River Valley today is a haven for WATERFOWL and RAPTORS.

The Duwamish Tribe long occupied a large communal house-village at a place the people called Sbabadid near what is now downtown Renton. The site has been excavated by archaeologists from the University of Washington. It was located on the Black River below what was once its confluence with the Cedar River. When the Ship Canal was cut, lowering the level of Lake Washington and redirecting the lake's outlet through Lake Union, the Black River was cut off and reduced to the status of slough (Thrush 2007).

The Black River Slough still supports patches of Black Cottonwood and Oregon Ash forest but is hemmed in by development. A still-impressive remnant has been preserved as the **Black River Riparian Forest,** in large part due to the efforts of Herons Forever, a nonprofit organized by Suzanne Krom in 1989 to save the local heron colony from being destroyed by development. As of 2006, the Black River Riparian Forest hosted one of the largest heronries in the state, with 121 active nests fledging 300 young. Since then, however, a pair of Bald Eagles has moved in to feast on the nestlings. The colony persists despite the predation but is much reduced in size, an ironic outcome of the dramatic recovery of our Bald Eagles from the brink. The dense riparian thickets along the slough are excellent for migrant land birds. To explore the Black River Riparian Forest, go west from downtown Renton on SW Grady Way to Oakesdale Ave. SW, turn right (north) past the Springbrook Trail crossing to the parking lot on your right. Alternatively, from I-5 south of Boeing Field take Exit 156 just after crossing the Duwamish River onto Interurban Ave. S, continue past Foster Golf Links and Fort Dent Park to Southcenter Blvd./SW Grady Way. Turn left (east) to Oakesdale Ave. SW, then left (north) to the entrance.

Next stop on our tour is the **Foster Golf Links** off Interurban Ave. S. Back-track from the Black River Riparian Forest via Oakesdale Ave. SW and Southcenter Blvd. In winter large numbers of THAYER'S GULLS congregate on the club-house roof or just to the south on the highway maintenance sheds, an excellent opportunity to study this challenging species. Continue south on Interurban Ave. S to **Fort Dent Park.** Bicycle enthusiasts may ride south from here along the Green

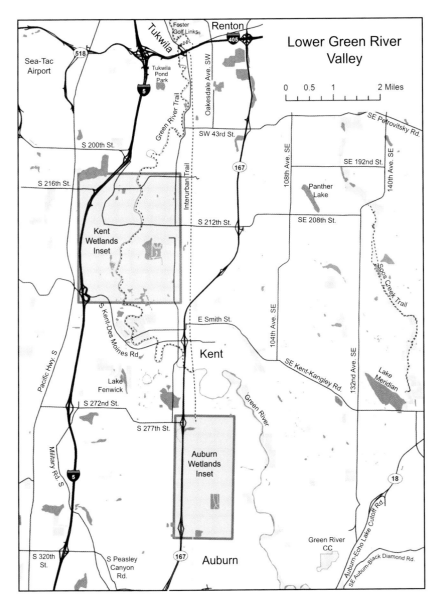

River and Interurban Trails all the way to Auburn, with convenient access just off these trails to several of the sites described below.

Next stop on our tour of Area 4 is **Tukwila Pond Park** just south of the Westfield Southcenter Shopping Mall complex. Southbound from Seattle on I-5 exit and turn left at Southcenter Blvd., go under I-5, turn right on 61st Ave. S, cross over I-405 to Tukwila Pkwy., then go right (west) to Southcenter Pkwy. If south-

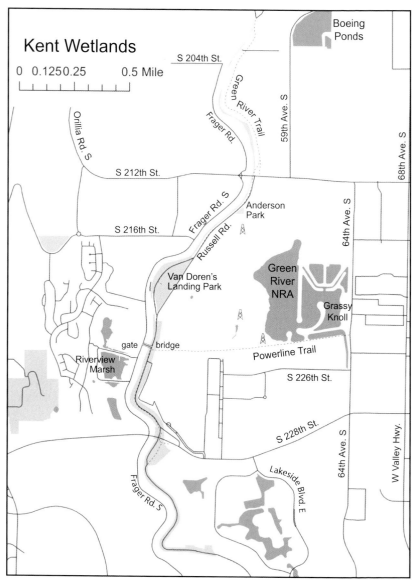

Kent Wetlands

0 0.125 0.25   0.5 Mile

S 204th St.

Green River Trail

Frager Rd.

Orilla Rd. S

59th Ave. S

68th Ave. S

S 212th St.

Frager Rd. S

Russell Rd. S

Anderson Park

S 216th St.

64th Ave. S

Van Doren's Landing Park

Green River NRA

Grassy Knoll

gate   bridge

Powerline Trail

Riverview Marsh

S 226th St.

S 228th St.

64th Ave. S

W Valley Hwy.

Lakeside Blvd. E

Frager Rd. S

Boeing Ponds

bound on Interurban Ave. S/W Valley Hwy. (SR-181), go right (west) on Strander Blvd. to Southcenter Pkwy. and turn left (south). The park is east of the mall just south of Strander Blvd. Two places to park are behind the Half Price Books outlet (16828 Southcenter Pkwy.) or between the DoubleTree Guest Suites and the Outback Steakhouse (16510 Southcenter Pkwy.). From October through April you will find GADWALLS, NORTHERN PINTAILS, GREEN-WINGED TEALS, NORTHERN SHOVELERS, CANVASBACKS, RING-NECKED DUCKS, BUFFLE-

HEADS, RUDDY DUCKS, PIED-BILLED GREBES, and COOTS. PECTORAL and LEAST SANDPIPERS and LONG-BILLED DOWITCHERS have been recorded during fall migration.

Our next stop is at the **Boeing Ponds** and the fields—flooded in winter—along S 204th St. between Orillia Rd. S on the west and the Frager Rd. S spur that goes north from S 212th St. From I-5 take Exit 152 at S 188th St./Orillia Rd. S, cross left under the freeway, and continue down the hill to S 200th St. Go left (east) on S 200th St./Russell Rd./S 196th St. to 62nd Ave. S, then right on 62nd Ave. S to S 199th Pl./59th Ave. S. Park at the barrier at this "T" junction. To reach the Boeing Ponds from the Westfield Southcenter Shopping Mall, go east on Strander Blvd. to W Valley Hwy., turn right (south) on W Valley to S 199th Pl., then right (west) to 62nd Ave. S. Park out of traffic at the barrier and walk south along the east margin of the main pond, then southwest along the dike between the main pond and a smaller, shallow, southeastern pond. An alternative parking spot is at the southwest corner of the ponds off 59th Pl. S. Boeing Company guards occasionally warn birders off the section of the dike adjacent to the Boeing facility fence, but for the most part, birders are tolerated.

A WHITE-FACED IBIS visited the Boeing Ponds briefly in 2007. GREAT BLUE and GREEN HERONS are regular residents on the main pond, joined occasionally by a GREAT EGRET or two. SHOREBIRDS are not abundant here, but both GREATER and LESSER YELLOWLEGS, SOLITARY and PECTORAL SAND-

---

"Bob," a controversial white-winged gull, shown here in a temporary pond in the Kent wetlands, January 30, 2006. Bob returned each winter from 2004 to 2009. Some birders (including myself) are convinced Bob was an adult male Iceland Gull of the nominate Greenland race, while others think Bob was a runt Glaucous Gull (© Marv Breece).

PIPERS, PEEPS, and WILSON'S PHALAROPES are noted with some regularity in season. SPOTTED SANDPIPERS nest. The willow borders welcome nesting PIED-BILLED GREBES, AMERICAN COOTS, DUCKS, YELLOW WARBLERS and COMMON YELLOWTHROATS and wintering YELLOW-RUMPED WARBLERS. Rarities noted here include a PALM WARBLER in October 2007 and a decidedly out-of-place GREEN-TAILED TOWHEE in October 2006.

The notorious small, adult, white-winged gull that came to be known as "Bob" foraged in nearby fields during January 2006 and again in January 2009. I believe "Bob" was first noted the previous winter (December 2004) at the gull concentration in Renton and reappeared there in subsequent winters until at least 2008. While some judged "Bob" to be a runt Glaucous Gull, it was a dead ringer for an adult ICELAND GULL, either an individual of the nominate Greenland-nesting race or a Kumlien's Iceland Gull with immaculate white wing-tips.

Continue south on 59th Pl. S to S 212th St., turn right and cross the Green River to Frager Rd. S, then turn right (north) on Frager Rd. S to S 204th St. The weedy margins along Frager Rd. are excellent SPARROW habitat. The fields south of S 204th St. west of the Green River and north of S 212th St. may have KILLDEER, YELLOWLEGS, SOLITARY SANDPIPERS, PEEPS, and LONG-BILLED DOWITCHERS in spring before the fields dry out. Winter flocks of geese may include CACKLING GEESE, GREATER WHITE-FRONTED GEESE, the occasional SNOW GOOSE, and perhaps even a stray ROSS'S GOOSE. DABBLING DUCKS are common, and there have been sightings of REDHEAD and TUFTED DUCK.

To continue to our next hot spot, the **Green River Natural Resources Area** (GRNRA), it is best to continue west on S 204th St. to Orillia Rd. S, then turn left onto Orillia Rd. S, which curves east at the bottom of the hill and becomes S 212th St. A right turn just east of the Green River onto Russell Rd. leads to tiny **Anderson Park** on the left, and a parking area just south with access to the northwest observation tower at the GRNRA. Climb this tower for a commanding view of the area east and south, including meadows patrolled by NORTHERN HARRIERS by day, SHORT-EARED OWLS at dusk in winter, and BARN OWLS by night. The snags offer perches for BALD EAGLES, ACCIPITERS, RED-TAILED HAWKS, AMERICAN KESTRELS, MERLINS, and PEREGRINE FALCONS. Rarer raptors include occasional ROUGH-LEGGED HAWKS. An immature RED-SHOULDERED HAWK—one of the first ever recorded in King County—moved in during the fall of 2006 and remained through spring 2009, molting meanwhile into full adult plumage. In years past, a WHITE-TAILED KITE, several GYRFALCONS, and a PRAIRIE FALCON have been reported.

A hike-and-bike trail—the Powerline Trail—skirts the southern border of the GRNRA beneath the powerlines. You may park along Russell Rd. by the footbridge opposite the west end of this trail and walk east to the gate for the southeast observation tower. From this point on Russell Rd. you may also walk west over the

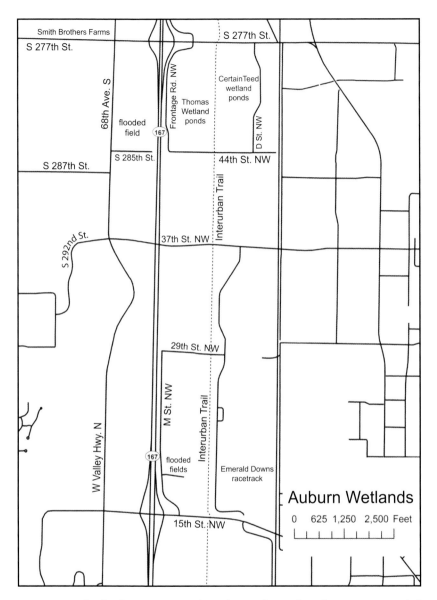

Green River footbridge to Frager Rd. S, then walk south and west on a wooded loop trail that circles a pond and swamp known to local birders as the **Riverview Marsh**. Lots of VIRGINIA RAILS are here year-round.

You may also access the Powerline Trail from cul-de-sacs off S 226th St. or from the tiny pull-off along 64th Ave. S, south of the animal shelter (access point for the eastern overlook known as the "Grassy Knoll"). The Grassy Knoll provides a vantage point over the GRNRA impoundments to the east. For a better look at the impoundments, it is necessary to hike the Powerline Trail west to the southeast tower for a clear view. AMERICAN BITTERNS are often seen or heard from here, and a persistent male YELLOW-BREASTED CHAT has called from an island northeast of the tower during the past several nesting seasons, but without finding a mate. Also regular in late spring and summer near the southeast tower are WESTERN KINGBIRDS and LAZULI BUNTINGS, in addition to the abundant SAVANNAH SPARROWS and WILLOW FLYCATCHERS. A variety of SPARROWS may be found in winter. Most of the waterfowl species of normal occurrence in western Washington may be noted here in season. A secretive male BAIKAL TEAL drew hundreds of listers to this tower in late winter of 2004, hoping for a glimpse of this mega-rarity. Metro bus service to the GRNRA from downtown Seattle is via #150. Get off the bus at S 220th St. along W Valley Hwy. and walk the few blocks west.

Continue south from the Green River Natural Resources Area on W Valley Hwy./68th Ave. S to downtown Kent. Turn right on W Meeker St. and go west across the Green River, then immediately turn south (left) on Frager Rd. S. This southernmost segment of Frager Rd. passes a small pond just south of W Meeker St., then winds past weedy lots and fields before intersecting the W Valley Hwy. south of downtown Kent. Look for WESTERN SCRUB-JAYS along Frager Rd. at the underpass beneath SR-516.

Below: White-faced Ibis foraging at Boeing Ponds, May 20, 2007 (© Ruth Sullivan). *Opposite page, top: Male Gadwall in flight* (© Tim Kuhn). *Opposite page, bottom: Pectoral Sandpiper flanked by two Sharp-tailed Sandpipers at Auburn Wetlands, October 5, 2009* (© Gregg Thompson).

Continue south on W Valley Hwy. to the Smith Brothers Farms dairy operation at the junction with S 277th St. Examine the large blackbird flocks here in winter. Who knows? There could be a YELLOW-HEADED or even a RUSTY BLACKBIRD in these restive flocks. Scan the bare fields north of S 277th St. in winter for GEESE and SWANS. Both TRUMPETER and TUNDRA SWANS have been noted here with some regularity in recent years. BLACK-BELLIED PLOVERS and WHIMBRELS have been noted in early spring before the fields dry out and are planted. Be careful to park out of traffic, which can be wicked through here.

Next go east from W Valley Hwy. on S 277th St. over the SR-167 freeway, then south on the eastside frontage road to **Thomas Wetland**, a mitigated wetland

just south of the Toysmith warehouse. This was a magnet for SHOREBIRDS during the fall of 2008, but it has been planted with willows and other marsh vegetation, which may limit shorebird opportunities there in future. Nevertheless, that property plus the marshy ponds at the bend onto 44th St. NW are worth checking for SHOREBIRDS, AMERICAN BITTERNS, GREEN HERONS, and VIRGINIA RAILS. Continue east on 44th St. NW across the railroad tracks to D St. NW, turn left (north) to another mitigated wetland, this one adjacent to the CertainTeed warehouse. A walk around the cattail-bordered ponds, particularly with a rail recording, should produce at least vocal evidence of VIRGINIA RAILS and, in spring, SORAS. AMERICAN BITTERNS are also possible here. Keep an eye out for resident Long-Tailed Weasels.

Continue north on D St. NW back to S 277th St., go left (west) back over SR-167 to W Valley Hwy. once again, and continue south. At S 285th St. turn left toward the freeway. The field north of S 285th St. is flooded in winter and spring and may have an excellent selection of GEESE, DABBLING DUCKS, and SHOREBIRDS, including DUNLINS, LONG-BILLED DOWITCHERS, and WILSON'S SNIPES in winter and YELLOWLEGS and PEEPS in spring.

A short dogleg south on W Valley Hwy. to S 287th St. takes you west past marshy tracts and weedy fields to a dead end against the hillside. The local residents may be a bit suspicious of strangers, so be cautious, explain yourself if given the opportunity, and stay on the road. A YELLOW-BELLIED SAPSUCKER foraged in the ornamental cedars along S 287th St. one winter, and a pair of TROPICAL KINGBIRDS foraged along this road for several days in November 2007. A HARRIS'S SPARROW hung out with DARK-EYED JUNCOS along S 287th St. in December 2008. BARN OWLS roost in the area.

Continue south on W Valley Hwy. past 37th St. NW to 15th St. NW. Turn left (east) here over SR-167, then left (north) on M St. NW, which serves here as a frontage road along the east side of the freeway. You will soon notice two large fields west of the **Emerald Downs** race track. You may park here and walk east along the southern edge of the larger field, which is bordered by a slough. These fields are partially flooded from late fall through spring and attract SWANS, GEESE, DABBLING DUCKS, and SHOREBIRDS. AMERICAN AVOCET and BLACK-NECKED STILT have put in cameo appearances in recent springs, and a juvenile AMERICAN GOLDEN-PLOVER spent a few fall days here in 2008. An INDIGO BUNTING joined several LAZULIS here in June 2008. During migration look for an assortment of SPARROWS and flocks of AMERICAN PIPITS. The slough where M St. NW curves into 29th St. NW attracted an AMERICAN REDSTART during early winter 2005 and a BLACK PHOEBE for two summers in 2005 and 2006.

If you're now ready to return to Seattle, try the Green River Rd. north from Auburn to Kent for a change of scene. This road is a greenbelt park along the Green River's east bank, flanked by steep, wooded hills. Consult a county map for the complex street connections in Auburn. From Kent you may use the SR-167 freeway for the return trip, though be forewarned that traffic on SR-167 approaching Renton is nasty during rush hours.

If you're not yet ready for home, an alternate route of special interest during breeding season leads south from Auburn via SR-164 to Enumclaw through the **Muckleshoot Prairie.** The "prairie" is now open farm country with scattered copses of alder, ash, and maple. Exit busy SR-164 southeast of Auburn onto SE 368th Pl. (eastbound), which, after several twists, turns, and name changes, becomes SE 384th St. At 176th Ave. SE is a sparse stand of Quaking Aspen, scarce in the county. Continue east to 188th Ave. SE, go left (north), and continue downhill to the end of the road on SE 364th St. A trail here takes you down through **O'Grady Park** to the Green River. A colony of BANK SWALLOWS was discovered here in 2001, the first for King County. In late spring and summer, RED-EYED VIREOS are common, and LAZULI BUNTINGS nest near the river.

Return to SE 384th St., then continue east to 212th Ave. SE. Turn right (south) here to SE 424th St., jog west to 208th Ave. SE, then go south. A substantial flock of EURASIAN COLLARED-DOVES was located here in the vicinity of the Degroot Brothers Dairy in 2009. Continue south to Auburn-Enumclaw Rd. SE/SE 436th St. (SR-164). Go right (west) on SR-164 to 196th Ave. SE, then head south on 196th Ave. SE to viewpoints on bluffs overlooking the canyon of the White River. Listen for OLIVE-SIDED FLYCATCHERS and RED-EYED VIREOS singing from the dense woodland below. Angle east on SE 456th Way/SE 452nd St. to 244th Ave. SE/Osceola St. S, then turn right to join SR-410 southbound. Stop just short of the White River Bridge (the county line) at the entrance to a gravel quarry on your right. A rough track leads into dense floodplain forest for a short distance. Civilization seems miles away. (It isn't.) Return north on SR-410 to SE Mud Mountain Rd. The isolated hill you see ahead is **Pinnacle Peak** (also known as Mt. Peak or Mt. Pete). Look for LAZULI BUNTINGS about the farms just west of Pinnacle Peak. SE Mud Mountain Rd. skirts the south side of Pinnacle Peak through a stretch of forest with a distinctly east-of-the-Cascades feel, with CASSIN'S VIREOS, WESTERN TANAGERS, and HAMMOND'S FLYCATCHERS present in summer.

Continue to the **Mud Mountain Dam** picnic area and the White River corridor/Naches Pass routes of Area 10. If you wish to return to Seattle, you may go north on 284th Ave. SE to Enumclaw and then, still on 284th Ave. SE/Veazie-Cumberland Rd. SE, go north to Nolte State Park, Cumberland, Kanaskat, and Georgetown, thence via Maple Valley to Seattle. You may also return to Seattle via SR-169 north from downtown Enumclaw. SR-169 connects with Area 3 routes at Black Diamond. SR-410 runs east through Greenwater, the gateway to the Naches Pass high country, and on to Mt. Rainier National Park and points east of the Cascades (when Chinook Pass is open).

Area 5. King County South Shore, Seahurst to Dash Point

A wooded plateau extends south from West Seattle between Puget Sound and the Kent (Duwamish/Green River) Valley. It is now largely devoted to suburban sprawl, with Sea-Tac Airport as the centerpiece, but public access to the Puget Sound shoreline and assorted patches of native forest in various stages of regeneration have been preserved in county and state park properties. Saltwater species are best observed from natural promontories or about bays and marinas. Numerous small lakes, most with civilized borders, might be profitably inspected for their wintering waterfowl.

Seahurst Park offers typical birds of mixed, second-growth woodland, with VARIED THRUSHES common in winter. The cobbled shoreline provides a good vantage point for observing LOONS, GREBES, SCOTERS, and GULLS during migration and in winter.

In West Seattle, you can approach the park via Ambaum Blvd. SW. If you're coming from Sea-Tac or downtown Seattle via I-5 or SR-99/SR-509, go west on SR-518, which becomes SW 148th St. before it intersects Ambaum Blvd. SW. A sign for the park entrance is at SW 144th St. on Ambaum Blvd. SW.

Just south of Seahurst Park is **Eagle Landing Park,** at the junction of SW 149th St. and 25th Ave. SW. This bit of shoreline bluff hosts nesting GREAT HORNED and WESTERN SCREECH-OWLS. Exit Ambaum Blvd. SW going west on SW 152nd St., then jog right (north) on 22nd Ave. SW to SW 149th, then west to the park entrance.

Lake Burien is nearby. Viewpoints are limited, as most of the lakeshore is privately owed, but you may scan most of the lake from a street-side pullout at the

Red-throated Loon in basic (winter) plumage, swimming in the waters between Seattle and Vashon Island (© Kathrine Lloyd).

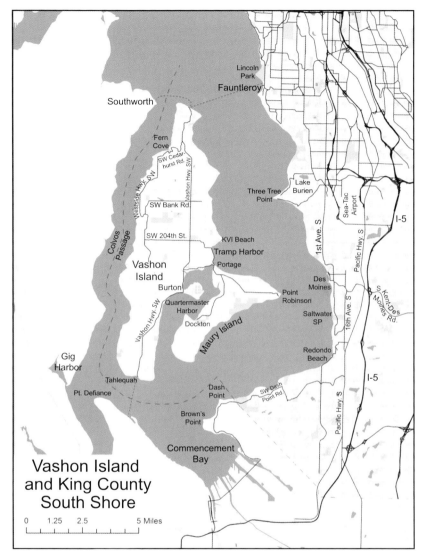

Vashon Island and King County South Shore

0   1.25   2.5   5 Miles

southeast corner of the lake, where SW 156th St. bends south at 12th Ave. SW. You can find SW 156th off Ambaum Blvd. SW four blocks south of SW 152nd St.

Next stop is the **Des Moines Marina,** reached by continuing south on Ambaum Blvd. SW to 1st Ave. S, thence south to where—at a sharp left bend—1st Ave. S morphs into S 216th Place/S 216th St., then into Marine View Dr. S. A right turn on S 223rd St./Cliff Ave. S to Dock St. leads to the parking lot at the base of the long pier at the entrance to the marina. Des Moines Beach Park at the mouth of Des Moines Creek is worth checking in winter for the stray AMERICAN

DIPPER. Scan the harbor and offshore in winter for LOONS, GREBES, CORMORANTS, ALCIDS, SCOTERS, GOLDENEYES, and other diverse DIVERS.

From here you may proceed south on Marine View Dr. S to **Saltwater State Park**, a smaller version of Seahurst Park, with shoreline access via the ravine of McSorley (formerly Smith) Creek. Point Robinson on Maury Island is directly opposite across the Sound and just two miles away. Campsites are tucked away in the deep woods.

South of Saltwater State Park is **Redondo Beach** on Poverty Bay. in winter, this stretch of waterfront is rich in SEA DUCKS and other DIVERS, which can be readily observed along Redondo Beach Dr. S. The county's first AMERICAN WHITE PELICAN record is of two birds here in 1946. To reach Redondo Beach, follow SR-509's tortuous course via Marine View Dr. S, up Woodmont Dr. S to 16th Ave. S, then south along 16th Ave. S to S 272nd St. Turn right on 12th Ave. S/Marine View Dr. S (it reappears)/10th Ave. S/S 281st St. to Redondo Beach Dr. S. To continue to Dumas Bay and Dash Point State Park, regain SR-509, now SW Dash Point Rd., via Redondo Beach Dr. S/1st Ave. S. Dumas Bay Park is currently accessible off SR-509 at 44th Ave. SW; Dash Point State Park is accessible directly from SR-509.

Undeveloped **Dumas Bay Park** contains a wide tract of beach exposed at low tide and a tiny freshwater marsh with SORAS, a colony of some eight nesting pairs of GREAT BLUE HERONS, and GREEN HERONS spring through fall.

Dash Point State Park, with its 300 acres, three quarters of a mile of sandy beach, and camping facilities in a rich woodland setting, is the high point of this route. In late spring FLYCATCHERS, WARBLERS, FINCHES, and four species of VIREOS challenge your ear with song. A singing male ROSE-BREASTED GROSBEAK—the second recorded in the state—paused here briefly in June 1979. Follow the trail south from the beach parking area up a wet ravine of huge moss-decked maples and cedar snags. WILLOW FLYCATCHERS breed in this rather atypical habitat, and PILEATED WOODPECKER work marks the snags (look for large rectangles chiseled in the trunks). On the north bluff, check for HUTTON'S VIREOS in the madrones, one of their favorite trees. In winter you may find the full complement of Puget Sound ALCIDS here, including ANCIENT MURRELETS from October to December. Dash and Brown's Points, just south of the county line in Pierce County, are equally productive.

If you wish to extend your route, you may continue on SR-509/Marine View Dr. south past Dash and Brown's Points to the north shore of Commencement Bay and thence to I-5. TURNSTONES are often noted on log booms here, though they are difficult to find in King County.

The most direct return route from Dash Point State Park to I-5 is via 47th Ave. SW and SW 320th St., which traverses Weyerhaeuser's "West Campus" tract.

This Federal Way high country is studded with small lakes, many with public boat access. Lake Lorene and Lake Jeane just east of Dash Point are both worth a check. Lake Lorene hosted a REDHEAD and Lake Jeane a EURASIAN WIGEON in December 2008.

For additional birding sites, continue east from Dash Point State Park on SW Dash Point Rd. to 47th Ave. SW. Turn right (south) to SW 320th St. Continue east on SW 320th St. to 21st Ave. SW, take a right here to SW Campus Dr., and go left past the Weyerhaeuser King County Aquatic Center to **Panther Lake Park.** A trail circles the lake. ORANGE-CROWNED, YELLOW, and BLACK-THROATED GRAY WARBLERS are in full song here by mid-April. The Cascara, Oregon Crabapple, and Hardhack swamp at the lake's northeast end is an interesting wetland variant. A mile southeast of Panther Lake on SW Campus Dr./S 348th St. is **West Hylebos Wetlands Park,** likewise worth investigation. **Steel Lake** is good for HOODED and COMMON MERGANSERS and PINTAILS in winter. Go east on SW Campus Dr./S 348th St. to Pacific Hwy. S (SR-99) and turn left on SR-99 to S 312th St., which cuts through Steel Lake Park. Return to I-5 via SR-99 and S 320th St.

AREA 6. VASHON & MAURY ISLANDS

Vashon Island (and its appendage, Maury Island) is 12 miles long by 7 miles wide. It is a rural district set off from the urban hustle of Seattle and Tacoma by a mile or two of deep saltwater. Ferries serve Vashon Island from Fauntleroy in West Seattle (just south of Lincoln Park), from Southworth on the Kitsap Peninsula, and from Tacoma to Tahlequah on Vashon's southern tip.

Ed Swan has published *The Birds of Vashon Island* (2005). His book is not only a detailed, annotated account of all known Vashon Island bird species but also provides habitat accounts, historical analysis, a description of key birding areas, and an excellent map. Consult Swan's book for more detail. Briefly, Vashon's west shore is steep and largely inaccessible, with the exception of Fern Cove. However, east shore saltwater vantage points, from Ellisport to Point Robinson and south along the west side of Quartermaster Harbor to Tahlequah, are prime.

When crossing the Sound from Fauntleroy, keep a wary eye out for RED-NECKED PHALAROPES and PARASITIC JAEGERS in September and for pelagic species driven inshore after storms. Check the **ferry dock area** at Point Vashon in season for SCOTERS, LOONS, GREBES, CORMORANTS, GULLS, and ALCIDS. From the dock at Point Vashon, drive south on Vashon Hwy. SW/106th Ave. SW to Cedarhurst Rd. SW. Turn right (west) and continue past SW 144th St. to the gravel drive on your right, signed for the **Fern Cove** reserve. Park outside the gate and hike down to the beach. At low tide an extensive mudflat, the delta of Shingle Mill Creek, is exposed. Here Gulls loaf and SHOREBIRDS may be common during migration. Loons and Grebes form rafts offshore in Colvos Passage.

From Fern Cove you may continue south on Westside Hwy. SW to Thorsen Rd. SW, then turn left (uphill) to where Thorsen Rd. SW bends east to become SW Bank Rd. Drive 1.2 miles to **Fisher Pond**. Alternatively you may return on SW Cedarhurst Rd. to Vashon Hwy. SW, then continue south to the town of Vashon. Turn right onto SW Bank Rd. Fisher Pond is on the north side of SW Bank Rd. 1.2 miles from the town. At the bottom of the hill on SW Bank Rd. is a pullout on the north side that affords a peek into the swamp that is Fisher Pond. A second vantage point is at the west end of the pond, accessible by a trail that circles the pond. WOOD DUCKS and KILLDEER are resident. In fall, as the pond recedes, shorebirds such as WILSON'S SNIPE, YELLOWLEGS, and an occasional SOLITARY SANDPIPER may be expected. Winter brings NORTHERN PINTAILS, GREEN-WINGED TEALS, BUFFLEHEADS, HOODED MER-GANSERS, and once brought a TRUMPETER SWAN! TREE SWALLOWS may nest here, a species rare on the island.

Another marshy spot is the **Island Center Forest,** which includes Meadow-lake. This area is accessible from SW Bank Rd. to the south via 115th Ave. SW a short distance east of Fisher Pond. Rare trees here include Shore Pine (a form of Lodgepole Pine) and Quaking Aspen. The woods here are particularly produc-tive for SONGBIRDS in late spring. On one trip I found Long-toed Salamanders

under a log at the lake shore. An extensive network of tracks intertwines in the woods surrounding Meadowlake, affording hours of meandering. This is nearly the entire extent of Vashon's freshwater habitat available for public scrutiny. In summer there are VIRGINIA RAILS, MARSH WRENS (rare on Vashon), and COMMON YELLOW-THROATS. A half-mile west of Fisher Pond on SW Bank Rd. is **Agren Memorial Park,** with trails through dense coniferous timber. Check under rocks and things for Ensatinas, our commonest salamander.

For saltwater birds, go south from downtown Vashon on Vashon Hwy. SW to SW Cemetery Rd./SW 196th St., then east and south to **Ellisport.** Between Ellisport and Portage, from the narrow neck of land connecting Vashon to Maury Island, you can look over **Tramp Harbor.** LOONS, CORMORANTS, GOLDEN-EYES, GREBES, and SCOTERS are common in season, as are BRANTS in spring passage. EURASIAN WIGEONS are regular here in winter, while PURPLE MARTINS nest in boxes and gourds mounted on offshore pilings. Just north of Ellisport is a small sandy point with a single radio tower, called Point Heyer on some maps but known here as **KVI Beach,** for the radio station that owns the tower. There is a minute estuary here with a patch of salt marsh worth inspecting for migrating shorebirds. This spot is best as the tide comes in. Shorebirds gather here at high tide, scattering on the falling tide to feed elsewhere. During fall migration you may expect PEEPS, including perhaps the odd SEMIPALMATED, BAIRD'S, or PECTORAL SANDPIPER. In September 2007 a single juvenile SHORT-BILLED DOWITCHER dropped in, a species that is quite rare in King County. SEMIPALMATED PLOVERS are also regular in migration.

East from Portage is **Point Robinson Park** and a Coast Guard post. The deep waters off the point produced a sighting of SHORT-TAILED SHEARWATERS during their 1977 Puget Sound invasion. PARASITIC JAEGERS may pass close to the point in fall. The regular species of LOONS, GREBES, SCOTERS, and ALCIDS are to be expected in winter. Also on record for Point Robinson are LONG-TAILED DUCK, FRANKLIN'S GULL, and SNOW BUNTING.

South of Portage is the shallow north end of Quartermaster Harbor, officially designated a National Audubon Society Important Bird Area. Studies here indicate

---

Opposite page, top: Lewis's Woodpecker perching in the yard of John and Ellie Friars above KVI Beach on Vashon Island, October 10, 2005. Opposite page, bottom: Juvenile Short-billed Dowitcher feeding in the salt marsh at KVI Beach, September 3, 2007. This page: White-breasted Nuthatch in the yard of Alan and Amy Huggins on Vashon (all photos © Steve Caldwell).

that as many as 8 to 10 percent of Washington's wintering WESTERN GREBES forage here. It is an excellent spot for BARROW'S GOLDENEYES and one of the few spots on Vashon where RUDDY DUCKS are regularly found.

The **marina at Burton** is worth checking. PEEPS and DOWITCHERS have been spotted here at low tide. For a pleasant and productive stroll, hike uphill from Burton toward the west, returning via Shawnee, south of Burton. There are brushy thickets and fields alongside these little-traveled back roads.

The main portion of **Quartermaster Harbor** is south of Burton and may be scanned from several turnoffs along Vashon Hwy. SW. Here is your best chance to find good numbers of LOONS in King County in winter. Look also for EARED GREBES and BLACK SCOTERS.

Our route ends at **Tahlequah,** where a ferry will take you to Point Defiance Park in Tacoma and a return to Seattle via I-5. Dalco Passage off the ferry dock is busy with wildlife. It is the most likely spot in the county for Harbor Seals and—with great good fortune—Orcas. JAEGERS, GULLS and ALCIDS are common at appropriate times. An alternate return route is via **Wax Orchard Rd. SW,** which peels off Vashon Hwy. SW heading north. Wax Orchard Rd. SW follows the crest of a ridge through more open pastureland. Look for raptors here such as AMERICAN KESTRELS. Wax Orchard Rd. SW ends at SW 220th St. A left turn here leads down to Lisabeula Park on the west shore. A right jog on SW 220th St. leads to Westside Hwy. SW, which you may follow north all the way to Fern Cove and then via SW Cedarhurst Rd. to Vashon Hwy. SW just south of the dock for ferries from Vashon to Southworth and Fauntleroy.

AREA 7. SNOQUALMIE RIVER VALLEY, NORTH BEND TO DUVALL

The three forks of the Snoqualmie River join just north of North Bend. Mt. Si's northwest face looms overhead. A careful inspection of Mt. Si's high cliffs here may reveal Mountain Goats or cruising BLACK SWIFTS in summer. The land about the three forks is patchy woods and farms. North Bend is the gateway to the North Fork and Middle Fork Snoqualmie River Valleys. COMMON and HOODED MERGANSERS nest along the river banks in cottonwood cavities, and GREEN HERONS patrol the banks in summer. Near the town of Snoqualmie, the river plunges over Snoqualmie Falls, which, at 272 feet, is higher than Niagara.

The jewel of this area is the **Three Forks Natural Area,** which offers prime spring and summer birding. Exit I-90 at North Bend. Jog two blocks east in downtown North Bend to Ballarat Ave. N/NE and follow its peregrinations out of town north as SE 420th Ave./SE 108th St./428th Ave. SE. In short order you will cross the Middle Fork and then the North Fork just above their union. The bridges offer convenient vantage points, but beware of traffic. Continue to SE Reinig Rd. and

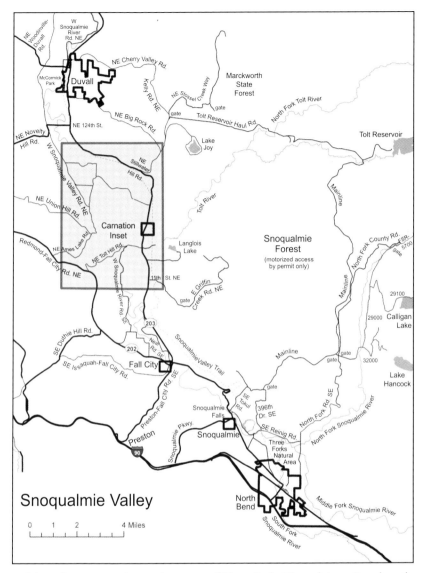

park here for access to the northern part of Three Forks Natural Area. Rough trails under tall cottonwoods lead from the parking lot to the river shore.

There is more extensive habitat across the river accessible from SE Park St. Continue on SE Reinig Rd. to Meadowbrook Way SE, cross the river, then turn left (east) off Meadowbrook Way SE on SE Park St. Continue 0.4 miles to a small gravel parking lot opposite Centennial Fields Park. A trail from here crosses an off-leash dog area, then leads over the Snoqualmie Valley Trail to a large meadow bordering the riparian forest beside the Snoqualmie River. In late spring 2009 an

INDIGO BUNTING, a LEAST FLYCATCHER, and a GRAY CATBIRD joined local LAZULI BUNTINGS and RED-EYED VIREOS at the meadow's edge. This prime area may be reached more directly from Exit 27 off of I-90 via SE North Bend Way and Meadowbrook Way SE, crossing Railroad Ave. SE (SR-202) to SE Park St. Turn right to the parking area opposite Centennial Fields Park.

To access the **Snoqualmie Forest** via Weyerhaeuser Mainline Rd., go back to Meadowbrook Way SE and backtrack across the bridge over the Snoqualmie River to the three-way junction with SE Reinig Rd., Meadowbrook Way SE, and 396th Dr. SE. Take 396th Dr. SE to SE 53rd St. and turn right (east) on SE 53rd St. to the Mainline. Park at the gate to your left. Entry is by bicycle or on foot only. The Mainline connects to North Fork County Rd. at the Spur 10 Gate in four miles. This affords a peaceful walking tour of a network of gravel roads through the second-growth woodland and wetlands of the Snoqualmie Forest, now managed by Hancock Timber Resource Group. In spring and summer expect WARBLING VIREOS; PACIFIC WRENS; SWAINSON'S and VARIED THRUSHES; CEDAR WAXWINGS; ORANGE-CROWNED, BLACK-THROATED GRAY, and WILSON'S WARBLERS; WESTERN TANAGERS; BLACK-HEADED GROSBEAKS; PURPLE FINCHES; and EVENING GROSBEAKS. This foothill region east of the Snoqualmie Valley is also accessible via Griffin Creek, Lake Joy, and Stossel Creek (described a bit later in this section) and from North Fork County Rd.

North Fork County Rd. to FSR-57—maintained by the county as far as the national forest boundary—may be approached either from Snoqualmie via SE Reinig Rd. or from North Bend via Ballarat Ave. N. The lower portion of the county road is known locally as Lake Hancock Rd. or Ernie's Grove Rd., and is popular with local teens and ORV (off-road vehicle) enthusiasts. North Fork County Rd. is fed by a complex of logging roads—more than 20,000 miles' worth—so beware of logging trucks on working days. You are free to hike or bike these roads. However, vehicular access to the Weyerhaeuser road system—also managed by the Hancock Timber Resource Group—requires an annual permit. The permit costs $225 and includes a Snoqualmie Forest Recreation Access Map and a key to the gates. To obtain a permit, contact Hancock Timber Resource Group at 800-782-1493.

The main access point from North Fork County Rd. is at the **Spur 10 Gate,** with access east and north to Lake Hancock and Calligan Lake. COMMON LOONS nest on Calligan Lake, and a nesting pair of SPOTTED OWLS was reported from above Lake Hancock as recently as 2006.

West of the Spur 10 Gate is a trail that leads around **Fuller Mountain** (the conspicuous hump northwest of this junction) to Klaus and Boyle Lakes, picturesque ponds attractive to fishermen. These foothill woodlands abound with PACIFIC-SLOPE FLYCATCHERS and BLACK-THROATED GRAY WARBLERS following their late April arrival. The Mainline Rd. north from the Spur 10 Gate parallels the North Fork County Rd. on the west for several miles. Where the county road curves east, the Mainline continues north past the South Fork Tolt Reservoir. The Spur 30 road system (#29400 on the Hancock map) runs east from the Mainline past **Fitchener Slough**—a promising birding area—to join North Fork County Rd. just west of the Mt. Phelps Campground. A mile beyond the campground, the road becomes FSR-57 and enters the national forest, then continues up Lennox Creek. A left branch (FSR-5730) follows the North Fork several miles farther.

A rare beetle of the Carabidae family, Beller's Ground Beetle (*Agonum belleri*), is known from Sunday Creek, south from North Fork County Rd. on spur #29300/29370/29372. Tailed frogs live in **Lennox Creek**. GOLDEN EAGLES nested in this vicinity in 1980. Both VAUX'S and BLACK SWIFTS and RUFFED and SOOTY GROUSE are common. MOUNTAIN BLUEBIRDS find the North Fork clear-cuts to their liking in fall migration, and the possibility of their nesting should encourage further exploration.

To reach our next stop, Snoqualmie Falls, from the three-way intersection of SE Reinig Rd., Meadowbrook Way SE, and 396th Dr. SE, follow Meadowbrook Way SE past SE Park St. to SR-202/Railroad Ave. SE. A right turn on SR-202/Railroad Ave. SE/1st Ave. SE leads through the town of Snoqualmie to Snoqualmie Falls. (From the Meadowbrook Way SE intersection with SR-202, you may also continue on Meadowbrook Way SE and SE North Bend Way to I-90, or you may turn left on SR-202 to return to North Bend.)

Snoqualmie Falls is sacred to the local Snoqualmie Indian Tribe and is an impressive sight, particularly at high water. A pair of PEREGRINE FALCONS nests

Adult American Dipper feeding its young at Tokul Creek, April 6, 2010 (© Gregg Thompson).

on cliffs at the falls. The progress of their nesting efforts is carefully monitored from public viewpoints not far from the lodge. Hike the trail down through dense young conifers to the river at the foot of the falls. AMERICAN DIPPERS nest here. Look for them in the concrete nooks of the old powerhouse, Plant 2.

Dippers are also reliably spotted at the Tokul Creek Hatchery just off SR-202 on your left at 372nd Ave. SE. Park at the fishing access at the bridge just downstream from the hatchery and check the tumbling stream above and below the bridge. Then you may follow **SE Fish Hatchery Rd.** along the Snoqualmie River toward Fall City, avoiding the traffic on SR-202. A small cattail marsh along this road has VIRGINIA RAILS. COMMON MERGANSERS nest along the river. Just past the golf course (which may be worth a detour) you will turn left back onto SR-202 and continue to a traffic circle across the river from Fall City.

You may follow Fall City-Carnation Rd. SE (SR-203) north to Carnation and beyond to Duvall. Neal Rd. SE off SR-203 at the traffic circle is a quiet dead end through farmlands and may be productive of SPARROWS and BLACKBIRDS in winter. However, our standard route takes us back through Fall City via SR-202 toward our next stop at **Carnation Marsh Sanctuary** and on to Carnation via NE Tolt Hill Rd.

Proceed northwest from Fall City on SR-202. One mile west of Fall City, turn right onto 324th Ave. SE. After several zigs and zags (SE 31st St./SE 28th St./316th Ave. SE/SE 24th St.), join the W Snoqualmie River Rd. SE, heading north. Continue past the Tall Chief Golf Course and Jubilee Farm to two 90-degree bends. Park at the second bend. There should be a Carnation Marsh Sanctuary sign. A muddy trail leads a short distance west. The thickets here may be full of SPARROWS in winter, with WHITE-THROATED SPARROWS sometimes almost common. Continue north on W Snoqualmie River Rd. NE to the Carnation Golf Course entrance. A quick side trip into the golf course may be productive, with views into a lush oxbow lake where you might spot WOOD DUCKS and GREEN HERONS. You may also park just north of the entrance and hike up the road to a bridge and beyond, around a gentle curve to an open marshy tract. This is the core of the Carnation Marsh. Brooding Western Red Cedars and Sitka Spruce—some drowned recently behind beaver dams—frame a roadside view of an OSPREY'S nest on a broken snag. RUFFED GROUSE and AMERICAN BITTERNS might be heard in early spring, WOODPECKERS are conspicuous, and all four Washington VIREOS sing in season. MARSH WRENS and COMMON YELLOWTHROATS sing all summer. In winter a stray SWAMP SPARROW might lurk in the roadside marsh. BARRED and NORTHERN SAW-WHET OWLS have been heard here in May. As of 2008, Black Bear was reported in the vicinity.

Continue north on W Snoqualmie River Rd. NE to NE Tolt Hill Rd. A dirt track opposite this junction and just west of the Snoqualmie River Bridge leads to an overlook of the confluence of the Tolt and Snoqualmie Rivers, framed by Tolt-

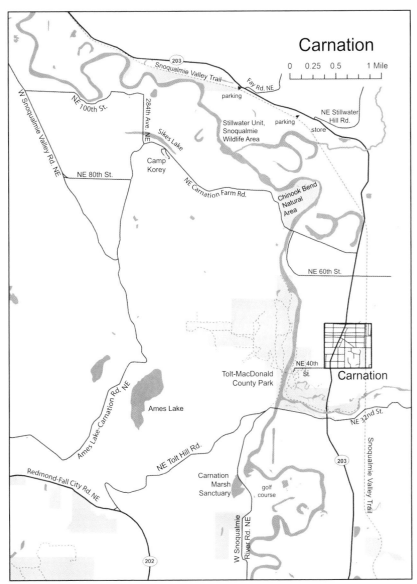

Carnation

0   0.25   0.5   1 Mile

203 Snoqualmie Valley Trail
Fay Rd. NE
parking
NE 100th St.
284th Ave. NE
W Snoqualmie Valley Rd. NE
Sikes Lake
NE Stillwater Hill Rd.
parking
store
Stillwater Unit, Snoqualmie Wildlife Area
Camp Korey
NE 80th St.
NE Carnation Farm Rd.
Chinook Bend Natural Area
NE 60th St.
NE 40th St.
Carnation
Tolt-MacDonald County Park
Ames Lake-Carnation Rd. NE
Ames Lake
NE 32nd St.
Snoqualmie Valley Trail
NE Tolt Hill Rd.
203
Redmond-Fall City Rd. NE
Carnation Marsh Sanctuary
golf course
W Snoqualmie River Rd. NE
202

MacDonald Park. This dirt track is a back door to the park. Note in particular the small NORTHERN ROUGH-WINGED SWALLOW colony in the bank behind you. To reach the more commonly used entrance to this park, drive across the river on NE Tolt Hill Rd./NE 32nd St. to SR-203 (Fall City-Carnation Rd. NE), then left (north) across the Tolt River Bridge into Carnation on what is now Tolt Ave. Immediately north of the Tolt River Bridge on the left is a parking area on the Tolt River, a staging area for kayaking and Steelhead fishing. AMERICAN DIPPERS have nested under the highway bridge and frequent the Tolt's shore in winter. Alternatively you may continue on SR-203 to NE 40th St. for the main entrance to Tolt-MacDonald Park. Turn left at the sign at the south edge of Carnation.

Tolt-MacDonald Park—especially the Wilderness Camp section west of the Snoqualmie River across the suspension footbridge and west of the main parking area—is exceptional birding habitat. Its variety of breeding species rivals eastern Washington's Wenas Creek campground. In season five species of SWALLOWS can be closely observed from the swinging bridge. NORTHERN ROUGH-WINGED SWALLOWS nest in the sand bank just upstream from the suspension bridge, not far from nesting BARN OWLS and BELTED KINGFISHERS. COMMON MERGANSERS range up and down the river at all seasons, while KILLDEER and SPOTTED SANDPIPERS raise families on gravel bars at the river's edge.

From the west end of the swinging bridge you may proceed in three directions. To the left (south), the dirt road under the Northern Rough-Winged Swallow colony leads out to NE Tolt Hill Rd., as noted above. Straight ahead (west) from the footbridge you may climb through a grassy swale past rental yurts to reach the Railroad Grade Trail. WILLOW FLYCATCHERS, COMMON YELLOWTHROATS, and MACGILLIVRAY'S WARBLERS are found in and about this field in summer. BLACK-HEADED GROSBEAKS and BLACK-THROATED GRAY and WILSON'S WARBLERS sing from the wooded slopes above. The Railroad Grade Trail ducks into forest, curving north under moss-draped old maples at the base of a steep slope of Douglas Fir. The bank above the trail oozes ferns and bustles with

PACIFIC WRENS. With luck, a RUFFED GROUSE might cross your path. Branch trails climb steeply through second-growth timber full of resident GOLDEN-CROWNED KINGLETS and CHESTNUT-BACKED CHICKADEES, with PACIFIC-SLOPE FLYCATCHERS, BLACK-THROATED GRAY WARBLERS, and WESTERN TANAGERS present in spring and summer. High above the river you emerge into clear-cuts and an extensive tangle of logging roads stretching west toward Ames Lake.

A right turn (north) at the footbridge leads downstream along a broad, sandy path under giant cottonwoods to the North

Camp area and beyond to the park boundary. Listen here to HAMMOND'S FLYCATCHERS singing from the high deciduous canopy, allowing a close comparison with their cousins, the PACIFIC-SLOPE FLYCATCHERS, also common here. The association here of Hammond's Flycatchers and BULLOCK'S ORIOLES is odd, as Hammond's are characteristic birds of deep coniferous forests in the mountains, orioles of hot, lowland river margins. Expect all four Washington VIREOS. In June 1980 a VEERY'S song joined the chorus of SWAINSON'S THRUSHES at Big Maple Camp, while in June 1983 a CHESTNUT-SIDED WARBLER joined the regular chorus of ORANGE-CROWNED, BLACK-THROATED GRAY, YELLOW, MACGILLIVRAY'S, and WILSON'S WARBLERS here.

Jaunts east from Carnation include Entwistle St./Tolt River Rd. NE/NE 45th St. departing downtown Carnation. This road leads five miles up the Tolt River to a Steelhead fishing spot. Look for RUFFED GROUSE and AMERICAN DIPPERS, with SWIFTS overhead. Just south of the Tolt River Bridge on SR-203, you may turn east on Tolt-Bunker Rd./NE 32nd St. Check the fields southeast of the SR-203 intersection with NE 32nd St. in winter for SWANS, SPARROWS, and BLACKBIRDS. A flock of MOURNING DOVES hangs out nearby. Further south of SR-203 you may turn east on NE 24th St./Langlois Lake Rd. Langlois Lake is another favored site for SWANS in winter.

Two miles south of Carnation is **Griffin Creek.** Turn east off SR-203 on 11th St. NE, then south on E Griffin Creek Rd. NE to a locked gate. Vehicle access beyond the gate is by permit from the Hancock Timber Resource Group (see page 82 for details on how to get a permit) or on foot or bicycle. Road #26000 connects to miles of logging spurs through second-growth timber, clear-cuts of varied ages, and wetlands in the heart of the Snoqualmie Forest.

A large blackbird flock just north of Carnation included three RUSTY BLACKBIRDS in January 2007. Winter blackbird flocks here move about, so it is nec-

Birds such as Black-headed Grosebeak (left, © Thomas Sanders) *and Belted Kingfishers (above,* © Gregg Thompson) *nest in Tolt-MacDonald Park.*

essary to patrol the area via NE 60th St./310th Ave. NE to locate them. One mile north of Carnation is **NE Carnation Farm Rd.**, which leads west across the Snoqualmie River. On the east side of the river at the Snoqualmie River Bridge, a short spur to the north along the river is worth checking in winter for SPARROWS. CLIFF SWALLOWS nest under the bridge in summer, where they may be joined by VIOLET-GREEN, NORTHERN ROUGH-WINGED, BARN, and a few BANK SWALLOWS. On the west side of the bridge is a parking spot for the **Chinook Bend Natural Area.** Hike north along the river through a stand of planted pines, then through a tall riparian forest to a sandy beach. WILLOW FLYCATCHERS nest here in summer, and a flock of WESTERN BLUEBIRDS found here in spring 2008 might return to nest. BALD EAGLES nest nearby.

From the Snoqualmie River Bridge continue northwest on NE Carnation Farm Rd. to the complex of buildings now known as **Camp Korey** at Carnation Farm, previously the Nestle Training Center/Carnation Research Farm. Scan the fields across the road from the buildings in winter for GEESE. Hundreds of CANADA GEESE winter here. These large flocks often hide a few GREATER WHITE-FRONTED and CACKLING GEESE and an occasional SNOW GOOSE, joined in recent years by TRUMPETER SWANS.

Just past the Camp Korey buildings is **Sikes Lake,** best viewed from the bridge on 284th Ave. NE. WOOD DUCKS nest here, and CINNAMON and BLUE-WINGED TEAL may also. Sikes Lake and the fields nearby are excellent for migrating and wintering WATERFOWL, with recent reports of TRUMPETER and TUNDRA SWANS, and even the stray SANDHILL CRANE. SAY'S PHOEBES and WESTERN KINGBIRDS are occasionally reported in spring. Continue north on 284th Ave. NE, which winds past farms close to the Snoqualmie River and bends west as NE 100th St. before intersecting W Snoqualmie Valley Rd. NE. The weedy fields south of NE 100th St. are prize SPARROW habitat in winter. A HARRIS'S SPARROW joined the abundant SONG, LINCOLN'S, FOX, GOLDEN-CROWNED, and WHITE-CROWNED SPARROWS here in 2008. Go north on W Snoqualmie Valley Rd. NE past **"Pepper's Pond,"** but be careful of the traffic. It is barely possible to pull off opposite the ponds to scan the WIGEONS for EURASIAN WIGEON or some other less common duck. Continue north to the junction with NE Novelty Hill Rd. (an alternate return route to Redmond), then on past NE 124th St. (an alternate route east to Duvall or Carnation via SR-203) to NE Woodinville-Duvall Rd. (a return route to Seattle via Woodinville and Bothell). Turn right (east) here to cross the valley toward Duvall.

Just west of Duvall, before the Snoqualmie River Bridge, turn left onto **W Snoqualmie River Rd. NE,** a quiet three-mile spur that follows the west bank of the river toward the Snohomish County line. This short spur has proved quite productive in recent years. NORTHERN HARRIERS and AMERICAN KESTRELS nest near the road. Temporary wet spots may have SHOREBIRDS in spring, including WILSON'S PHALAROPES and nesting WILSON'S SNIPES. WESTERN

KINGBIRDS have nested on a power pole along the road each spring since 2007. TRUMPETER SWANS are increasingly common here November through February.

Our route now loops back through Duvall along the eastern margin of the Snoqualmie River Valley. Busy SR-203 (Carnation-Duvall Rd. NE) is the main artery. The **Snoqualmie Valley Trail,** a gravel-surfaced hike-and-bike trail that follows the old Chicago, Milwaukee, St. Paul and Pacific Railroad tracks, provides a scenic alternative to the highway from Duvall to Snoqualmie Falls and beyond. Access to the trail in downtown Duvall is at **McCormick Park.** Park by the police station down NE Stephens St. west of Main St. NE., and walk south on the trail. At the swamp, look or listen for WOOD DUCKS, HOODED MERGANSERS, AMERICAN BITTERNS, VIRGINIA RAILS, and SORAS. In spring and summer the tall cottonwoods may seem almost tropical, filled with RED-BREASTED SAP-SUCKERS, RED-EYED VIREOS, YELLOW WARBLERS, WESTERN TANAGERS, BLACK-HEADED GROSBEAKS, and BULLOCK'S ORIOLES.

North from Duvall, SR-203 passes the **Cherry Valley Unit** of the Snoqualmie Wildlife Area. The fields east of the highway here attract hundreds of BLACK-BIRDS in winter, mixed with COWBIRDS and PIPITS. In summer AMERICAN BITTERNS and SORAS may be vocal. You may explore the Wildlife Area from the Washington Department of Fish & Wildlife (WDFW) public access lot off SR-203 (parking permit required).

At the north edge of Duvall, NE Cherry Valley Rd. peels off to the east above the southern margin of the Cherry Valley Unit. NE Cherry Valley Rd. bends south as Kelly Rd. NE, continues past an extensive cattail swamp, and eventually passes Swan Mill Rd. before looping back to SR-203 as NE Stillwater Hill Rd., described below. Before the intersection with NE Big Rock Rd. are two spur roads providing access east into the foothill country. The first is **NE Stossel Creek Way.** At the end of the pavement, Stossel Creek Way enters **Marckworth State Forest** and carries on rough and winding for several miles east and north, past bogs and gated spur roads, eventually joining Ben Howard Rd. southwest of Sultan in Snohomish County. At the first gated spur, 1.4 miles past the end of the pavement, you may park and walk south to where the road crosses Stossel Creek. NORTHERN PYG-MY-OWLS toot here in early spring, and COMMON NIGHTHAWKS "peent" and boom in summer. RUFFED and SOOTY GROUSE nest in appropriate habitat here.

One may also enter this area at **Moss Lake,** reached by a spur road off E Lake Joy Dr. NE, reached in turn off Kelly Rd. NE two miles south of the NE Stossel Creek Way junction. NORTHERN PYGMY-OWLS and forest species such as RED CROSSBILLS and EVENING GROSBEAKS are birds of special interest here.

South of Duvall on SR-203, just north of the Stillwater Store and the junction with NE Stillwater Hill Rd., is the **Stillwater Unit** of the Snoqualmie Wildlife Area. You have three parking alternatives: two WDFW lots (permit required), one just north of the Stillwater Store and another further north opposite Fay Rd. NE;

and a turnoff at a gated spur between the two (no permit required). A trail heads southwest from this last gate across the Snoqualmie Valley Trail, past a marshy pond, over a dike, alongside a broad meadow, and through a patch of riparian woodland to the Snoqualmie River. BANK SWALLOWS nest here in the cutbank of the river, while BELTED KINGFISHERS and COMMON MERGANSERS patrol the currents. KILLDEER and SPOTTED SANDPIPERS nest on the banks and sandbars in midstream. These woods, ponds, marshes, and fields are well worth a visit after the hunters have gone. Mink and bear have been seen here. A pair of WESTERN BLUEBIRDS nested in a snag near this trail in 2007. Nesting species include WOOD DUCKS, AMERICAN BITTERNS, RED-BREASTED SAPSUCKERS, WESTERN WOOD-PEWEES, WILLOW FLYCATCHERS, WARBLING and RED-EYED VIREOS, BLACK-HEADED GROSBEAKS, LAZULI BUNTINGS, and BULLOCK'S ORIOLES. One or two YELLOW-BREASTED CHATS set up territories in 2007 and 2008 along the Snoqualmie Valley Trail at the first bridge south of the parking lot at the Stillwater Store. An AMERICAN REDSTART sang at the next bridge south in June 2007, and in 2009 two male American Redstarts defended territories at the end of the spur track that runs west from the northern parking access opposite Fay Rd. NE.

Continue south on SR-203 to Carnation and Fall City, or return north on SR-203 to the roundabout at NE 124th St. to cross the valley and connect with the W Snoqualmie Valley Rd. NE to return to Redmond or Woodinville.

AREA 8. SKYKOMISH RIVER, BARING TO STEVENS PASS

This isolated section of the county is reached from Everett via US-2 or from Seattle via SR-522 through Bothell and Monroe. US-2 closely follows the South Fork Skykomish River through Sultan, Startup, Gold Bar, and Index to Skykomish, then goes up the Tye River to its head at Stevens Pass (4061 feet). The valley is narrow and the river swift, hedged in by the imposing peaks of Baring Mountain (6125 feet) on the north and Mt. Index (5979 feet) on the south. U.S. Forest Ser-

---

Above: Male American Redstart singing at the Stillwater Unit of the Snoqualmie Wildlife Area, June 14, 2010 (© Gregg Thompson).

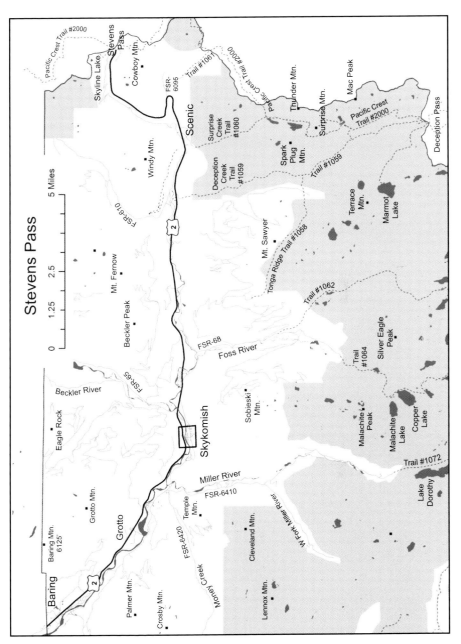

vice roads provide access to tributary streams such as Money Creek (FSR-6420), East Fork Miller River (FSR-6410), and Foss River (FSR-68), with spurs to Tonga Ridge (FSR-6830) and Sobieski Mountain (FSR-6840), all south of US-2. FSR-65 runs north to the county line along the Beckler River.

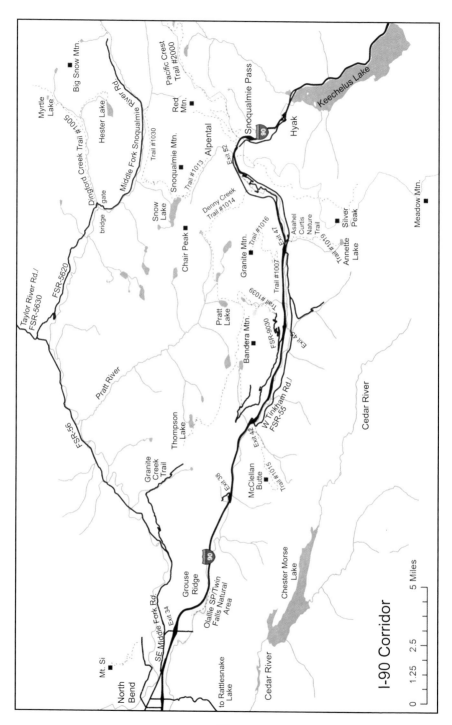

I-90 Corridor

0   1.25   2.5   5 Miles

FSR-6420 (along Money Creek) provides trail access to the high country about the Tolt-Snoqualmie divide (consult F. Beckey, *Cascade Alpine Guide: Climbing & High Routes, 1: Columbia River to Stevens Pass,* pp. 220-224, for climbing routes on Lennox Mountain, Mt. Phelps, Red Mountain, and Crosby Mountain). SPRUCE GROUSE are rumored to occur above 4000 feet in this area. East Fork Miller River Rd. ends at the Lake Dorothy Trailhead, a backcountry link to Taylor River Rd. up the Middle Fork Snoqualmie River (Area 9). Foss River Rd.,via the West Fork Foss River Trail, leads to Malachite Lake, Copper Lake, and the Heart Lakes, and fine alpine country on the Middle Fork Snoqualmie divide. A trail up the East Fork Foss ascends to the Necklace Valley and PTARMIGAN country (Area 11).

King County's first recorded BARRED OWL was a road kill found near **Skykomish** in 1973. The elusive and threatened SPOTTED OWL has also been recorded in this area. Two 1980 reports came from the Surprise Creek Trail 0.5 mile south of Scenic (to get here, turn right immediately west of the bridge over the Tye River on US-2 at Scenic) and from near Lake Clarice off Deception Creek Trail. Beckler River supports breeding HARLEQUIN and WOOD DUCKS, while nesting GOLDEN EAGLES, LEWIS'S WOODPECKERS, MOUNTAIN BLUEBIRDS, and AMERICAN THREE-TOED WOODPECKERS have all been reported on Huckleberry Mountain just north of the county line. BALD EAGLES gather in late fall and winter to feed on spawned-out salmon along the Skykomish and Tye Rivers.

High-country denizens of special interest include AMERICAN DIPPERS, which are common all year, GRAY-CROWNED ROSY-FINCHES on Malachite Peak, MOUNTAIN CHICKADEES in summer on Tonga Ridge and Surprise Mountain, and CLARK'S NUTCRACKERS along the Pacific Crest Trail just east of the crest between Trap and Hope Lakes. This area can be reached via a short, steep hike up Tunnel Creek Trail #1061 off US-2 just above the big horseshoe curve before the final climb to Stevens Pass (take FSR-6095 and Spur 115 to the trailhead.)

In years when there is a big cone crop, **Stevens Pass** is well worth checking in winter for such rarities as WHITE-WINGED CROSSBILLS and COMMON REDPOLLS. During January and February of 2008—a year with an exceptional cone crop—snowshoe hikers who climbed the steep **Skyline Lake Trail** north from the pass met large flocks of both CROSSBILL species, CASSIN'S FINCHES, PINE and EVENING GROSBEAKS, REDPOLLS, and resident GRAY JAYS.

Area 9. I-90 Corridor, North Bend to Snoqualmie Pass, plus Middle Fork Snoqualmie River & Stampede Pass

I-90 shows off Washington's timber industry at its most efficient. My 1982 text read as follows: "The super-highway traverses a scene of devastation: hills trimmed like green poodles, with logging-road Marks-of-Zorro staggering up the denuded

slopes. Yet trails depart this desolation for tracts of mountain forest." Nearly 30 years have passed since, and the massive clear-cuts of that era have healed somewhat. Here it is almost possible to forget that this is the 21st century, except for the dull background roar of freeway traffic that pursues the hiker for miles from the trailheads.

The climb up **Mt. Si** (4167 feet) begins just east of North Bend. Locating the trailhead is a bit tricky. Exit I-90 at 436th Ave. SE (Exit 32). Jog northwest on SE Cedar Falls Way to SE Mt. Si Rd., turn right (north) across the Middle Fork Snoqualmie River Bridge, then continue east for 2.3 miles to a large parking lot at the trailhead. It is four miles and 3500 vertical feet up to the haystack summit. Along the trail, you graduate from BLACK-THROATED GRAY WARBLERS to TOWNSEND'S WARBLERS buzzing and wheezing in the treetops. Attempting to identify which it is you are hearing is excellent exercise for both ear and neck! Generally, the Black-Throated Gray Warbler's songs are buzzier and more emphatically syncopated, with a rising inflection. The Townsend Warbler's songs are "spiritless," with a couple of lower-pitched, clear "zee" notes at the end. However, each individual sings a unique variant of its species's tune. HERMIT WARBLERS or HERMIT X TOWNSEND'S WARBLER hybrids are possible. Be alert for a jauntier variant of the Townsend Warbler's song. GRAY JAYS may visit you at the summit, and SWIFTS may pirouette overhead. A ROCK WREN sang from the rocks near the summit in 2007. Mountain Goats also frequent the summit cliffs.

Follow 436th Ave. SE south from I-90 to get to **Rattlesnake Lake Recreation Area;** 436th Ave. soon becomes Cedar Falls Rd. SE. Drive 3.1 miles from I-90 to the trailhead parking lot and a bit further to road's end. Trails lead around the lake and climb west up to Rattlesnake Ledge (where PEREGRINE FALCONS nest) then lead another 3.6 miles to the east peak of Rattlesnake Mountain (3480 feet). Check Rattlesnake Lake for LOONS and DIVING DUCKS, and search the swampy woods nearby for RUFFED GROUSE. A NORTHERN WATER-

THRUSH sang briefly here in late May 2007. The end of Cedar Falls Rd. SE is also the eastern end of Snoqualmie Valley Trail (see Area 7), as well as the western terminus of John Wayne Pioneer Trail, a trail reserved for hikers, bicyclists, and equestrians that follows an abandoned railway east through the Snoqualmie Tunnel then down to the Columbia River east of Ellensburg.

To continue on our route, take I-90 to SE Edgewick Rd./468th Ave. SE (Exit 34, four miles east of North Bend) and cross the freeway to Ken's Gas & Grocery. Here pick up SE Middle Fork Rd., which, at the entrance to the national forest, becomes FSR-56, signed Taylor River Campground. This road is good gravel for 15 miles to the Taylor River junction. Here you have the option of two rough tracks, usually passable if you go slowly. Taylor River Rd. (FSR-56) continues six miles to the trailhead connecting, via Lake Dorothy, to East Fork Miller River Rd. in Area 8. Middle Fork Rd. (FSR-5620) goes six miles up the Middle Fork Snoqualmie River to a trailhead at Dingford Creek. A Forest Service Pass is required to park here. The road was gated here in 2008 following serious washouts upstream.

Dingford Creek Trail (#1005) takes you to Myrtle Lake (3777 feet). From here you may struggle to the summit of **Big Snow Mountain** (6680 feet), a proven haunt of WHITE-TAILED PTARMIGANS. This climb involves tricky route selection, considerable stamina, and a long day's hike under the best of circumstances.

A second option from the Middle Fork Rd. gate is to hike or bike the old road to its end at the trailhead for Dutch Miller Gap. An alternative trail parallels the road along the south side of the Middle Fork Snoqualmie River. Cross the river here on a footbridge and proceed upstream to **Goldmyer Hot Springs.** A long soak at the hot springs is inspirational but requires advance reservations via Goldmyer's website. SPOTTED OWLS are rumored to be here as well.

From Goldmyer you may rejoin the old Middle Fork Rd. and continue to the Dutch Miller Gap Trailhead at road's end. Follow Trail #1030 to an alpine

---

Typical birds of the montane region include Townsend's Warbler (opposite page, © Paul Bannick) and Rufous Hummingbird (this page, © Doug Parrott).

wonderland that rivals Yosemite Valley, beneath the sheer cliffs of Chimney Rock (7634 feet). The trail cuts through dense thickets of bracken and Slide Alder, overpowering, virgin stands of Pacific Silver Fir, Douglas Fir, Western Hemlock, and Western Red Cedar, and high boggy terrain characterized by groves of Yellow Cedar and Subalpine Fir. HAMMOND'S FLYCATCHERS are heard in June from every dark forest nook, and LINCOLN'S SPARROWS nest on bog margins. VARIED and HERMIT THRUSHES replace SWAINSON'S THRUSHES after the first mile or two of trail. Other birds found here are typical of wet coniferous forest habitat: CHESTNUT-BACKED CHICKADEES, GOLDEN-CROWNED KINGLETS, BROWN CREEPERS, and TOWNSEND'S WARBLERS at neck-breaking heights, and PACIFIC WRENS scurrying like mice among the sword ferns of the forest floor. GRAY JAYS drop in unexpectedly. It's a land of Douglas Squirrels and Townsend's Chipmunks by day and pack-raiding deermice by night. Cascades Frogs swarm in the higher streams and bogs.

True alpine terrain is accessible above **La Bohn Gap** on the slopes of Mt. Hinman (7490 feet). GRAY-CROWNED ROSY-FINCHES and WHITE-TAILED PTARMIGANS may reward the determined scrambler. From La Bohn Gap you can look north down the Necklace Valley and the East Fork Foss River toward Skykomish (Area 8).

Back on I-90, you can make connections south to the Twin Falls Trail and Olallie State Park, scenic options along the South Fork Snoqualmie River. Drive south on 468th Ave. SE for 0.6 mile to SE 159th St., then left another 0.6 mile to the trailhead. Beyond SE Edgewick Rd., I-90 ascends the ancient moraine of the Puget Lobe of the last ice advance. Above the moraine (labeled Grouse Ridge on maps), the silver snags of Bandera and Granite Mountains are visible on the left, the prow of **McClellan Butte** (5162 feet) on the right. From I-90 take Exit 42 (W Tinkham Rd.) for the McClellan Butte Trailhead (Trail #1015, 4.4 miles and 3800 vertical feet to the summit). A SPOTTED OWL once sat beside the trail toward the crest, providing a rare Breeding Bird Atlas report, and CLARK'S NUTCRACKERS have strayed to the summit rocks, from which the view is stupendous. FSR-55—a pot-holed gravel road—parallels I-90 south of the South Fork Snoqualmie River. Here you can poke and putter.

The Bandera exit (Exit 45) from I-90 leads to FSR-9030, which slices across Bandera Mountain to trailheads to Talapus Lake (Trail #1039, 2.2 miles in) and beyond. I once found a HERMIT WARBLER singing where the Talapus Lake Trail first enters forest. The E Tinkham Rd. exit (Exit 47) provides access north of I-90 to the trailhead for Pratt Lake (Trail #1007, 5.7 miles in) and **Granite Mountain** (Trails #1007 and #1016, 4.3 miles and 4000 vertical feet to the summit lookout). SOOTY GROUSE and FOX SPARROWS nest among the blueberries near Granite Mountain's summit. GRAY-CROWNED ROSY-FINCHES forage here in late spring on their way to higher ground to breed, and two families of WHITE-TAILED PTARMIGAN raised young near the summit in the 1980s.

South of I-90 at Exit 47 is the Annette Lake Trailhead (Trail #1019, 3.5 miles in) and the Asahel (pronounced ACE-ull) Curtis Picnic Ground and Nature Trail. The **Asahel Curtis Nature Trail** shows off a postage-stamp-sized pocket of virgin timber barely screened from the highway. A short trail loops through gothic timber past extraordinary examples of Noble, Pacific Silver, and Douglas Firs and a patch of the rare Round-leaved Bog Orchid *(Platanthera orbiculata)*, each neatly labeled. In spring and summer, expect typical deep forest birds.

At **Snoqualmie Pass** in summer expect VAUX'S SWIFTS, YELLOW and MAC-GILLIVRAY'S WARBLERS, and LINCOLN'S and WHITE-CROWNED SPARROWS (the latter represented by the race *pugetensis,* a recent arrival from the lowlands of western Washington). Resident species include GRAY and STELLER'S JAYS, AMERICAN CROWS, CHESTNUT-BACKED CHICKADEES, and GOLDEN-CROWNED KINGLETS. The Snow Lake Trail (#1013, 3 miles in) begins at the end of the Alpental spur road just north of the pass. NORTHERN PYGMY-OWLS are frequently encountered along this trail. A hard-to-find second trail, hidden by tall willows north across the access road opposite the parking lot and very steep, leads up to the Guye Peak-Snoqualmie Mountain saddle and then up the south spur of Snoqualmie Mountain to its summit at 6278 feet. GRAY-CROWNED ROSY-FINCHES and WHITE-TAILED PTARMIGANS may be expected at the summit or on the alpine terrain of the east ridge. TOWNSEND'S SOLITAIRES serenade along the summit ridge.

The **Denny Creek Trail** (#1014) leaves from Denny Creek Campground. The campground can be reached from the old highway that parallels the freeway west of Snoqualmie Pass, which is accessible from I-90 via either Exit 47 or 52. The trail goes under the westbound freeway lanes and passes several dramatic cascades before climbing to Melakwa Lake (4551 feet, 4.5 miles in). An AMERICAN THREE-TOED WOODPECKER, a county first, was spotted up this trail in October 1981.

The **Pacific Crest Trail** (#2000) intersects I-90 at Snoqualmie Pass. The trail heads south up the marshy ski slopes toward Lodge Lake and beyond. The trail-head for the northern extension is on a short spur road east off the Alpental road, just past the I-90 underpass at Exit 53. Four miles up the trail, down a short spur at the foot of Red Mountain, is a bog campsite where GRAY JAYS join you for dinner. Nesting HAIRY WOODPECKERS and mixed pairs of RED-BREASTED and RED-NAPED SAPSUCKERS have been noted in snags about the bog. SOOTY GROUSE and OLIVE-SIDED FLYCATCHERS may call along the trail above, en route to Red Mountain Pond.

If you continue on the Pacific Crest Trail to the Kendall Peak ridge and beyond to the Kendall Katwalk (5.5 miles in), you may hope to find GRAY-CROWNED ROSY-FINCHES and CLARK'S NUTCRACKERS, and might perhaps hear the complex song of the TOWNSEND'S SOLITAIRE, sounding rather like an alpine thrasher. You might also surprise a Black Bear rooting amongst the huckleberries.

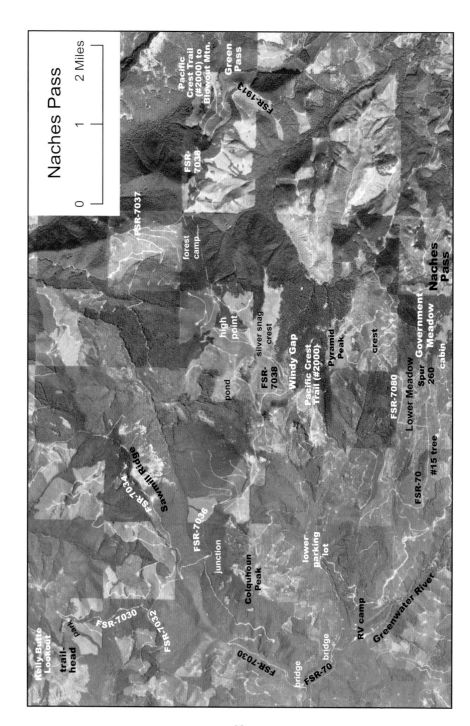

Naches Pass

0 1 2 Miles

Kelly Butte Lookout
trail-head
park
FSR-7030
FSR-7032
FSR-7034
Sawmill Ridge
FSR-7036
junction
Colquhoun Peak
FSR-7030
bridge
FSR-70 bridge
RV camp
Greenwater River
lower parking lot
FSR-70
#15 tree
Lower Meadow
Spur 260
Government Meadow
cabin
Naches Pass
FSR-7080
crest
Pyramid Peak
Pacific Crest Trail (#2000)
Windy Gap
FSR-7038
silver snag
crest
pond
high point
forest camp
FSR-7037
FSR-7038
FSR-7913
Pacific Crest Trail (#2000) to Blowout Mtn.
Green Pass

Snoqualmie Pass is also of interest during migration. For example, WESTERN BLUEBIRDS have been reported in September and May, GRAY-CROWNED ROSY-FINCHES in April, and COMMON REDPOLLS in November. CASSIN'S FINCHES may be abundant a mile or two east at Hyak but are uncommon within King County. Fall should bring strays to the crest.

A slightly drier portion of the Cascade Crest is accessible at **Stampede Pass** at the head of the Green River. The middle reach of the Green River is closed to the public to protect urban water supplies, but the headwaters can be reached by leaving I-90 just past Keechelus Lake at Exit 62 and heading south on FSR-54. Stampede Pass is scarred with clear-cuts and powerlines, destroying any semblance of wilderness. However, these same clearing operations have created opportunities for GOLDEN EAGLES. The first confirmed King County nest came from this area in 1975 (C. Servheen, 1978). The eagles feed on Mountain Beaver (*Aplodontia rufa),* which abound in clear-cuts. Stampede Pass is also a good area to look for woodpeckers, including both RED-BREASTED and RED-NAPED SAPSUCKERS.

Area 10. White River Corridor, Enumclaw to Naches Pass

SR-410 dives into the hills southwest of Enumclaw, heading for Mt. Rainier National Park. (SE Mud Mountain Rd. south and east of Enumclaw has been described in Area 4.) Follow SR-410 17 miles to **Federation Forest State Park,** a strip of virgin timber left along the highway to provide an illusion of the past. The interpretive center features a native plant garden and natural history displays. Trails loop through the forest between the road and the river, which are never out of earshot. HERMIT WARBLERS were regularly noted here through 1980 but not since. The Federation Forest is at or near the Hermit Warbler's northern range limit in the Cascades. Since both TOWNSEND'S and BLACK-THROATED GRAY WARBLERS also occur here, and hybrid HERMIT X TOWNSEND'S WARBLERS are more likely than "pure" Hermits, a careful comparison of songs is essential. HAMMOND'S and PACIFIC-SLOPE FLYCATCHERS, HAIRY WOODPECKERS, RED-BREASTED SAPSUCKERS, and VARIED THRUSHES nest here also, as do GRAY JAYS, though the elevation is but 1650 feet. WILSON'S and MACGILLIVRAY'S WARBLERS are conspicuous in brushy habitat near the river. A clump of the rare Phantom Orchid (*Cephalanthera austinae)* was in bloom here in July 2008.

At the village of **Greenwater** (gas station, store, resort) the highway enters Pierce County. Two miles beyond, turn left on FSR-70 (the Greenwater River Rd.). Pursue this well-maintained logging access route 8.5 miles to where it crosses the Greenwater River back into King County. The Greenwater River Valley here is another scene of devastation, and the parking area at the Pyramid Creek Trailhead is an ORV lek. (A lek is a dance-ground where male birds, such as Sage-Grouse and Ruffed Grouse, compete to win the females' favors.)

Trail bikes and jeeps now claim the historic **Naches Pass Wagon Trail** as their own. Not much scenery has been lost to them, however, as all the little white squares on the Forest Service map have been shaved bare, including Naches Pass itself (at 5000 feet). However, Government Meadow just below is on U.S. Forest Service land, as yet spared from clear-cutting. The meadow is hemmed in by a fine stand of virgin Pacific Silver Fir.

To reach Naches Pass and adjacent meadows, continue on FSR-70 for five miles past the end of the pavement to a patch of tall timber and a tree with a large number 15 painted on the trunk. This spot has produced nesting RED-NAPED SAPSUCKERS and sightings of both WILLIAMSON'S SAPSUCKER and AMERICAN THREE-TOED WOODPECKER in recent years. SOOTY GROUSE boom within earshot of the road in spring. Look and listen for HERMIT WARBLERS or HERMIT X TOWNSEND'S WARBLER hybrids here or along the road below. Continue past a left-hand junction marked FSR-7080. This branch climbs two miles to the Cascade Crest just south of Pyramid Peak, then connects down the east slope to the Little Naches (as FSR-9014), but it is closed by snow from late fall through early summer most years. Two WHITE-CROWNED SPARROW subspecies, *pugetensis* and *gambelii,* nest at the crest here in close proximity. *Pugetensis* is characteristic of the lowlands to the west, while gambelii is a subalpine breeder at the southern limit of its nesting range here. Each subspecies sings distinctive songs, and there is evidence that each breeds only with its own kind (Dave Beaudette, personal communication). If this could be confirmed, it would provide a strong case for splitting this complex into two species.

FSR-70 continues straight ahead past FSR-7080 to a rough left-hand spur, Spur 160. Park here, or, if your vehicle has the clearance, continue up the spur to park at the Naches Pass Wagon Trail crossing. An extensive network of wet subalpine meadows borders the wagon trail for a mile or two to the west, excellent habitat for FOX and LINCOLN'S SPARROWS. A NORTHERN SAW-WHET OWL was found here in September 2008, and there are reports of possible BOREAL OWLS in the vicinity in late fall (Dave Beaudette, personal communication), though visual confirmation is desired.

Follow the Naches Pass Wagon Trail east into a patch of virgin timber that embraces a series of wet meadows. One mile up, the Naches Pass Wagon Trail crosses the Pacific Crest Trail (#2000). A cabin provides shelter here at the western edge of the main **Government Meadow.** If you continue east up the Naches Pass Wagon Trail another mile, you will come to a historic marker at a high point of the trail. Beyond the marker, you will descend slightly, and, a short distance past the Upper Meadow, you will arrive at Naches Pass itself, surrounded by clear-cuts. Here four counties join: King, Pierce, Kittitas, and Yakima.

The Naches Pass Wagon Trail continues east into the Little Naches River Valley. Pioneers, following Indian trails, fought their way over this route in 1853. Today the route challenges off-road vehicle enthusiasts, at least after mid-July, when the often-snowbound and/or muddy trail is officially open to vehicular traffic.

Birds of special note in the forest and around the meadows include AMERICAN THREE-TOED and BLACK-BACKED WOODPECKERS, both of which appear to be permanent residents, though often hard to locate. RUFOUS HUMMINGBIRDS; HAMMOND'S, PACIFIC-SLOPE, WILLOW, and OLIVE-SIDED FLYCATCHERS; GRAY JAYS; CLARK'S NUTCRACKERS; MOUNTAIN CHICKADEES; MOUNTAIN BLUEBIRDS; TOWNSEND'S and YELLOW-RUMPED WARBLERS; FOX and LINCOLN'S SPARROWS; PINE GROSBEAKS; CASSIN'S FINCHES; RED CROSS-BILLS; and EVENING GROSBEAKS are to be hoped for in summer. NASHVILLE WARBLERS may be regular in late summer.

Back at the Greenwater River, FSR-7030 branches north just west of where FSR-70 crosses back into King County. Look for AMERICAN DIPPERS at the bridge where FSR-7030 crosses from Pierce into King County. From here, climb 4.0 miles up FSR-7030 to a "T" junction on the ridge dividing the Greenwater and Green River watersheds. Here FSR-7030 angles left (west) to Kelly Butte. The right (east) branch, FSR-7036/7038, continues 3.0 miles to the Cascade Crest in an old silver-snag burn just north of **Windy Gap.** Watch for TOWNSEND'S SOLITAIRES on the way up FSR-7036. This high and lonesome ridge offers fantastic views south to Mt. Rainier, north to Mts. Stuart and Daniel and Chimney Rock (see Area 11), and west to the Olympics. If the winds are favorable, a significant raptor migration follows the crest south in fall. TURKEY VULTURES; BALD and GOLDEN EAGLES; NORTHERN HARRIERS; SHARP-SHINNED, COOPER'S, and RED-TAILED HAWKS; AMERICAN KESTRELS; and PEREGRINE FALCONS might be seen in transit. NORTHERN GOSHAWKS and MERLINS likely nest nearby. WESTERN and MOUNTAIN BLUEBIRDS nest in the silver snags, while CHIPPING, FOX, and both forms of WHITE-CROWNED SPARROW nest in brushy areas. In late summer and fall, the open ridge may be alive with migrating sparrows, including a post-breeding dispersal of BREWER'S, VESPER, and SAVANNAH SPARROWS, and AMERICAN PIPITS, HORNED LARKS, and even the occasional LAPLAND LONGSPUR. An odd sparrow here in September 2007 was most likely a "TIMBERLINE" SPARROW, considered to be a northern form of BREWER'S SPARROW but possibly a distinct species. FSR-7038 follows the Cascade Crest north for five miles nearly to Green Pass, where it becomes FSR-1913 and drops down the east side to the Little Naches River. From here you may go east via FSR-19 and SR-410 to Yakima. The Pacific Crest Trail continues east and north along the crest to Blowout Mountain and beyond to Tacoma, Stampede, and Snoqualmie Passes.

Kelly Butte (5400 feet) stands out five miles east of the Cascade Crest on the Green-Greenwater divide. A new trail was carved up the west face of this basaltic mesa in 2007, replacing the precarious rope climb of prior years. On the summit is a historic fire lookout, currently being restored. Mountain Goats and Hoary Marmots favor rocky points near the summit. The south slopes are a floral garden in summer and appear to attract birds normally limited to the drier east slopes of the Cascades. ROCK WRENS may be common here some summers (for example, in 2006) but absent in others (such as 2007 and 2008). There is a record of CANYON WREN here also. BLACK-CHINNED and CALLIOPE HUMMINGBIRDS have been reported, though they are most likely post-breeding wanderers. GOLDEN EAGLES likely nest somewhere on the butte, as they are often seen soaring past.

AREA 11. ALPINE ZONE

Alpine terrain can be found along the Cascade Crest as it ascends above timberline along a 25-mile stretch between Snoqualmie and Stevens Passes bordering Kittitas and Chelan Counties. More alpine terrain can be found on scattered peaks west of the Cascade Crest in the Alpine Lakes Wilderness Area, such as Big Snow Mountain, mentioned in Area 9. These areas of alpine and subalpine habitat are accessible only by trail or by bushwhack and scramble. The most extensive area harboring that alpine prize, the WHITE-TAILED PTARMIGAN, is around La Bohn Gap, a gentle saddle of heather and boulder between the head of Necklace Valley and the headwaters of the Middle Fork Snoqualmie River. Necklace Valley is a 10-mile hike from the trailhead on East Fork Foss River Rd. out of Skykomish (Area 8). The river headwaters lie some 10 trail miles from the end of rough-and-tumble FSR-5620 via the trail to Dutch Miller Gap (the old Cascade Crest Trail).

This page: White-tailed Ptarmigan in summer plumage, Snoqualmie Peak, June 28, 2006 (© George Gerdts). Opposite page: Pacific race of the Gray Jay, showing extensive dark color on the head (© Paul Bannick).

Seasoned day-hikers might ascend Snoqualmie Mountain (6278 feet, Area 9) from Alpental at Snoqualmie Pass. The first 1000 feet of the ascent are the worst, as the trail that winds up through trees and brush to the Guye Peak-Snoqualmie Mountain saddle is hard to locate. In mid-June 1980, A. Richards and I found ROSY-FINCHES, AMERICAN PIPITS, TOWNSEND'S SOLITAIRES, NORTHERN PYGMY-OWLS, and WHITE-TAILED PTARMIGANS near the summit. Hoary Marmots, American Pikas, Yellow-pine Chipmunks, and Mountain Goats were also present. This high country might support an impressive raptor migration in late August or early September.

AREA 12. BIRDING BY BUS

This site guide generally presumes that you have a car at your disposal and that you are not averse to filling the tank and enlarging your carbon footprint while admiring nature's bounty. However, for those of you who lack wheels or who would like to explore the possibilities of greener birding, I offer these Metro and Sound Transit bus route suggestions. Detailed route maps and schedules are available at the King County Metro Transit website. Fares as of 2011 were $2.25 for adults during off-peak hours; $2.50 for one zone, peak hours; and $3.00 for two zones, peak hours. Children to age 5 may ride for free anytime. Youth to age 17 and seniors 65 and over may ride for $0.75 anytime. The great majority of the routes listed below start from downtown Seattle. A few cross-town routes are noted, as well as some that require transfers from suburban transit centers.

Mark Vernon has been a leader in promoting birding by bus. Here are a few of his favorite routes, downloaded with his permission from his Tweeters postings:

Tweeters, August 18, 2008: Here is an interesting bus-and-birds place, the Kent Ponds area. I arrived on the #150 bus and got off on W Valley Hwy. close to the Boeing Ponds [at S 196th St.]. I had coffee nearby before walking west to the Boeing Ponds. Here I found a Lesser Yellowlegs. I also found two broods of Pied-billed Grebes and a Green Heron. From the Boeing Ponds I kept walking west until I connected with the Green River Trail. On the Green River Trail I walked south to the Kent Ponds and [then] walked the loop in the interior of the place. An Osprey was flushing a duck....From here I reconnected with the Green River Trail at Van Doren's Landing Park.

From Van Doren's Landing Park I kept going south until I came to the foot-bridge crossing the Green River, which I crossed [to get to the west side]. From here it is just a hop and a skip to the Riverview Marsh. I counted a large flock of swallows perched on electrical wires—124 Violet-green Swallows with some Barn and Cliff Swallows mixed in....Next I crossed back over the Green River and walked east on the paved trail that goes along the south border of the Kent Ponds. I climbed the south tower and then continued east until I returned to W Valley Hwy. The #150 bus comes every 15 minutes, so it is very handy. In this last stretch I heard the cry of a Western Scrub-Jay.

Tweeters, August 20, 2008: This morning between rain showers I did my regular Emerald Downs bus trip. I like to start at the Auburn Station, but there are numerous variations of this walk. I came to Auburn on the #180 route, but there are many buses that use this station....From the Auburn Station I walked west on W Main St. until I intersected the Interurban Trail. On this trail I proceeded north. There is a lot of good birding…[at] several well-known marshes. I heard a Yellow Warbler calling just before I walked under SR-18. From this point, continuing north, it is only a short way to Emerald Downs. This is such a good birding spot, in the past featuring rarities such as the Black Phoebe….Today I had some luck with warblers. I found four juvenile Common Yellowthroats. There was also a[n] Orange-crowned Warbler. Because of the rain there was some water in the sometimes flooded fields. There was a large flock of Canada Geese, but I could find no shorebirds except for the usual Killdeers. I did find one juvenile Red-winged Blackbird. An accipiter made an appearance. There was a lot of American Goldfinch and Cedar Waxwing activity; the two species seemed to be in mixed flocks. As the weather was threatening, I made my escape walking east on 37th St. NW and going to Auburn Way N, where I caught a northbound #180 bus.

Tweeters, September 2, 2008: This morning I did another one of the easy birding-by-bus trips, Marymoor Park in Redmond. I have been doing this one for the past three years. I use Sound Transit #545. I either catch it in downtown Seattle or meet it at the Overlake Transit Center [in Bellevue]....The #545 runs frequently....Arriving in Redmond, I got off at the very first stop, at the corner of W Lake Sammamish Pkwy. NE and Leary Way NE. I walked a short distance east on Leary Way NE and jumped onto the Sammamish River Trail. This goes under Leary Way NE, then under SR-520 and on to Marymoor Park. It is a pleasant walk, not very far, and I was able to bird the whole way. I like to do a loop around the park. Usually I start near the windmill. If there is something interesting at the playfields I will sometimes start there. The dog walkers are always asking me where my dog is! Today was a really good warbler day. I saw Black-throated Gray Warblers, Townsend's Warblers, Yellow Warblers, Wilson's Warblers, and some young Common Yellowthroats. Western Tanagers and Warbling Vireos were also about....Sometimes, if I have the time, I like to add this to a Montlake Fill or Mercer Slough walk. Usually I walk back north to Redmond along the Sammamish River Trail. The river bank was restored a short time ago. In July I found Green Herons, Wood Ducks, [and] Spotted Sandpipers along the bank.

Tweeters, October 10, 2008: Today I tackled various West Seattle locations by bus. To sum up, I arrived from downtown Seattle by bus #54 and started at Lincoln Park. Then I went to the Alaska Junction by Sound Transit route #560. From there I used Metro bus #128 to go to the Admiral Junction and walked down to the Duwamish Head by way of Fairmount Gulch. From Alki I returned to downtown Seattle on Metro bus #56. Yes, I made a big day out of it!…(I would suggest doing either Lincoln Park or the Alki/Duwamish Head areas separately. Either are extremely easy to access by bus. The #56 is a really good way to get to Alki, and then you can walk along the waterfront to Duwamish Head. It is a very worthwhile walk.) I found all of my target birds today. At Lincoln Park I found a Common Loon and lots of Harlequin Ducks. Varied Thrushes were singing in the upper forest, which is always wonderful to hear. I found a Townsend's Warbler in a flock of Black-capped Chickadees.

Walking down to the Duwamish Head from the Admiral District I used an interesting trail that starts from the northwest side of the Admiral Way Bridge and descends into Fairmount Gulch. This saves a lot of time if you are on foot.

At Duwamish Head, my goal was to find the Black Turnstones and Surfbirds. I did not find [them] around the head itself but found them when I turned west on my way to Alki. There was a low tide this morning, so not all of their rocks were being splashed by waves. I counted 29 Black Turnstones and 4 Surfbirds.

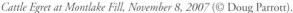

Cattle Egret at Montlake Fill, November 8, 2007 (© Doug Parrott).

Suggested Bus Trips to Prime Birding Spots

Trip 1: Discovery Park. From downtown Seattle (3rd Ave.), the #19 and #24 both go to the South Entrance, and the #33 goes to the North Parking Lot.

Trip 2: Woodland Park and Green Lake. From downtown Seattle (3rd Ave. or the Seattle Ferry Terminal) take the #16 or #26.

Trip 3: Carkeek Park. For Carkeek Park catch the #15 bus on 1st Ave. in downtown Seattle, or take the #48 from the University District and transfer to the #15 at 15th Ave. NW. Get off at 8th Ave. NW and NW 105th St. for the south entrance to the park. The #15 runs every half hour on weekdays and hourly on weekends.

Trip 4: Richmond Beach Park (NW 196th St. and Richmond Beach Dr. NW). Catch the #348 at the Northgate Transit Center. Get off at 20th Ave. NW and walk south to enter Richmond Beach Park, or continue to the end of the line and walk north to reach observation points south of Point Wells. The #348 runs approximately every half hour.

Trip 5: Montlake Fill (officially known as Union Bay Natural Area) at the University of Washington. From downtown Seattle (3rd Ave.), take the #25. Other

---

This page: Wilson's Phalarope at Montlake Fill, May 24, 2008 (© Doug Parrott). *Opposite page: Loggerhead Shrike at Montlake Fill, March 4, 2009* (© Gregg Thompson).

buses—the #43 (4th Ave.); or #71, #72, or #73 (3rd Ave.)—take you to the west side of the UW campus, from where it is a short hike across campus to Montlake Fill. You may wish to make a day of it and combine a morning at Discovery Park with mid-day birding at the Fill. From the North Parking Lot at Discovery Park, walk to the Hiram M. Chittenden Locks, cross over to NW Market St. in Ballard to catch the #44 or #46 to the UW campus, and hike over to Montlake Fill. Extend this route to Magnuson Park by catching the #75 on NE 45th St. just north of the Fill. Another extension is via the #48 to Green Lake from 15th Ave. NE on the northwest corner of the UW campus.

Trip 6: Vashon Island. Take the #118 or #119 from downtown Seattle (3rd Ave.), but note there is no service on Sundays.

Trip 7: Seward Park. Take the #34 from downtown Seattle.

Trip 8: Cedar River Trail and Cedar River mouth. Ride the #240 from the Bellevue Transit Center to the corner of Park Ave. N. and N 6th St. in Renton and walk west on N 6th St. to reach the Cedar River Trail, which you may follow to the Cedar River mouth. This is an excellent spot for gulls and various waterfowl from November through February.

Trip 9: Green River Natural Resource Area (GRNRA) and Auburn. Take the #150 from downtown Seattle (3rd Ave. or Convention Place Station), then walk west from W Valley Hwy./68th Ave. S. This bus stops near Fort Dent Park in Tukwila and continues to Auburn, passing a bit south of Emerald Downs. You may hike north up the bike trail from Auburn to bird the fields west of Emerald Downs.

Trip 10: Log Boom Park and Juanita Bay Park. Take the #522 from downtown Seattle (3rd Ave.). Buses #306 and #312 (2nd Ave., weekdays only) also go past your stop at 61st Ave. NE in Kenmore, the best access point for Log Boom Park. To continue to Juanita Bay Park, transfer at the Kenmore Transit Station to the #234. You may also reach Juanita Bay Park directly from downtown Seattle (4th Ave.) via Kirkland on the #255.

Trip 12: Marymoor Park. Take the #250 from downtown Seattle (5th Ave.).

Trip 13: Red Town Trailhead, Cougar Mountain Regional Wildland Park. Take the #219 from the Factoria Square Mall in Bellevue. Get off at the stop where Newcastle Golf Club Rd. turns into Lakemont Blvd. SE.

Trip 14: Lake Sammamish State Park. Take the #217 from downtown Seattle (Convention Place Station).

Trip 15: Three Forks Natural Area. Take the #215 from downtown Seattle (4th Ave.), or take the #209 from Issaquah Transit Center every day except Sunday.

Killdeer displaying at Montlake Fill (© Doug Parrott).

4. PATTERNS OF OCCURRENCE OF KING COUNTY BIRDS

The distribution patterns of birds in time and space depend on a number of complex variables, including not merely habitat and season—and whether the birds are migrating or nesting—but also large-scale fluctuations in weather and human activities. In this chapter I discuss the distribution of birds observed in King County, organized according to the family groupings used by ornithologists and most field guides, and listed in the order of the "Check-list of North American Birds," 7th edition. This list, compiled by the American Ornithologists' Union (AOU), is updated annually by supplements published in *The Auk*.

In addition to noting all species ever seen in King County in the last 120 years, according to the records available, I present charts that organize visually the information I have compiled about the distribution of each species throughout the year. This information will be useful to the beginning birder who wants to know what to look for and when, or what a certain briefly glimpsed bird might be, given habitat and season. The charts are also valuable for historical comparisons and many other scientific purposes. I have made an effort to annotate precisely all sightings of "rarities," and to provide the interested person with select references for further study. However, if you are not interested in these details, you may skip over them and take what you will from the notes and charts to help you find and identify the birds.

The official AOU checklist is a work in progress. Familiar names are changed regularly to accommodate current evolutionary understanding, which is often driven by DNA analysis.

I deviate from the AOU listing in one case: I "lump" the crows. The NORTH-WESTERN CROW is here treated as a subspecies of the AMERICAN CROW, because it intergrades with the western race of the American Crow throughout the

Puget Sound region (Johnston 1961). In addition to the 377 species of birds definitely recorded in King County as of 2010, some well-marked subspecies are listed under the species name.

Some species that have been attributed to the county's avifauna in previously published lists or reports are not included here. These include birds that have most likely escaped from captivity, such as the following:

BLACK SWAN
EGYPTIAN GOOSE
NENE
BARNACLE GOOSE
MANDARIN DUCK
RINGED TEAL
CHUKAR
GRAY PARTRIDGE
WHITE STORK
CHILEAN FLAMINGO
BLACK VULTURE
RINGED TURTLE-DOVE
MONK PARAKEET
CRIMSON-FRONTED PARAKEET
RED-MASKED PARAKEET
MITRED CONURE
ROSE-RINGED PARAKEET
CRESTED MYNA
GREAT TIT
NORTHERN CARDINAL
ORANGE BISHOP

Other species were included in Earl J. Larrison's 1947 *Field Guide to the Birds of King County, Washington,* apparently on the basis of their occurrence nearby. I have found no convincing evidence for the occurrence in King County of the following species listed by Larrison:

NORTHERN HAWK OWL
WHITE-HEADED WOODPECKER
PYGMY NUTHATCH

Additional sightings have been reported with inadequate substantiating details or vague locality data insufficient to identify either the species or the county where the sighting occurred. These include:

CRESTED CARACARA
YELLOW RAIL
LAUGHING GULL
LESSER BLACK-BACKED GULL
WHITE-THROATED SWIFT

ALDER FLYCATCHER
SEDGE WREN
ARCTIC WARBLER
BLACK-THROATED GREEN WARBLER
BLACKPOLL WARBLER
BAIRD'S SPARROW
TRICOLORED BLACKBIRD

A few additional species have been carefully documented, but due to their difficulty of identification and a lack of corroborating evidence, they are listed here as "interesting possibilities" or birds "that got away." Some of these species may be found in the future but are best left off the current list:

MANX SHEARWATER: Nigel Ball spotted one from the Bainbtridge Island ferry but cannot locate his notes specifying the date.

RED-FACED CORMORANT: One report reconstructed after the fact.

FERRUGINOUS HAWK: Three reports, but none definitive.

XANTUS'S MURRELET: One report, but the very similar though somewhat less likely Craveri's Murrelet could not be ruled out.

BOREAL OWL: Two reports of "skiew" calls heard but the bird not seen.

GRASSHOPPER SPARROW: One report of a bird heard but not seen.

I have also attempted to determine which species have nested within the county. The starting point for this list is the 135 species confirmed as nesting during the King County Breeding Bird Atlas surveys conducted between 1987 and 2000.

In addition, 16 species have been confirmed before, since, or apart from the atlas surveys. Another seven species nested in the past but presumably do so no longer. MOUNTAIN QUAIL and NORTHERN BOBWHITE were introduced in the 19th century, but these introduced populations died out decades ago. YELLOW-BILLED CUCKOOS apparently nested in small numbers in the riparian margins of Lake Washington until at least 1930, but they were doomed early on by habitat loss throughout the Pacific states. LEWIS'S WOODPECKERS nested in cut-over land east of Seattle until the 1940s, while "STREAKED" HORNED LARKS no doubt nested on the Duwamish delta in pre-settlement days. To this short list might be added SHORT-EARED OWLS, which nested or attempted to nest at Sand Point in 1972 and 1973, and HOUSE WRENS, nearly or quite absent in recent decades as a nesting species.

Ten species have not yet been confirmed as nesting in the county but are presumed to do so. These species, such as the MARBLED MURRELET, BLACK SWIFT, and RED CROSSBILL, are particularly elusive. Finally, three species are known or strongly suspected to have hybridized with more common local breeders: A male ROSE-BREASTED GROSBEAK, paired with a female BLACK-HEADED GROSBEAK near Issaquah in 1991, subsequently was observed feeding a juvenile grosbeak. Territorial HERMIT X TOWNSEND'S WARBLERS and the occasional apparently "pure" singing male HERMIT WARBLER support the inclusion of the

Hermit Warbler as a presumptive nester. Finally, an apparent CLARK'S GREBE or hybrid Western X Clark's Grebe was associated with a group of WESTERN GREBES that raised young at Juanita Bay on Lake Washington in 2006.

Thus, 168 species are likely to nest or to have nested in the county. These are noted as such on the species checklist, and dates of nesting activity are indicated on the bar charts when available. Another dozen species might nest or have nested, but positive evidence to include them is lacking at present.

DECODING THE DISTRIBUTION CHARTS

The charts indicate overall status, habitat preferences, seasonal patterns of abundance, documented periods of breeding activity, confirmed nesting, and unusual records of occurrence. Overall status is coded in the first column, as follows:

p   permanent resident
w   winter
s   summer
m   migrant
mf   fall migrant
v   vagrant
a   accidental
x   extirpated
i   introduced
b   breeds
h   hybrid nesting only
[]   rarely or sporadically
<>   presumably
/   separates historical from contemporary patterns

The bar graphs indicate by the width of the line the relative abundance of the species as this changes throughout the year. Four levels of abundance are recognized in the graphs:

No line   Absent
Thin line   Rare
Medium line   Uncommon
Thick line   Common

These abundance ratings do not precisely reflect the actual numbers of individuals of each species; that goal is both unattainable at present and unnecessary. Abundance ratings reflect, rather, the likelihood of encounter. Large birds are thus more likely to be rated as common than are small species, when both are equally numerous. Secretive species, nocturnal species, and species of inaccessible habitats, such as marshes and alpine meadows, are also less likely to be noted than their conspicuous, diurnal, and more accessible fellows. To a certain extent, the bias of habitat and habit has been taken into consideration—as in rating owls—but no doubt there remains a sizeable and indeterminate distortion of actual abundance as charted.

Thus a bird is common if it is seen on most field trips to appropriate habitat at the season indicated and, especially when smaller species are involved, if numerous individuals are seen on a day's outing. Species are considered uncommon if they are regularly found in appropriate habitat at that season but in relatively small numbers, or if the species may be missed if not specifically searched for. Some species that are common in a few restricted localities or in habitats poorly represented in King County may be rated as uncommon. Species are counted as rare if careful search and a measure of luck are normally required to find them, even though they may be expected to be in the appropriate habitat annually at the season indicated. Species that are uncommon but highly restricted also may be cited as rare.

Extraordinary records are indicated by a dot at the date of occurrence. These include individual records of casual or accidental species (those with status "v" or "a") or records for regularly occurring species at a time the species is normally absent. "Accidentals" are the most extreme rarities, having occurred just once or twice to date. "Casuals" include species that have turned up with some regularity in the region and are thus more to be expected in the future. Most such extraordinary sightings are discussed in the annotations for each species. Occasionally an individual or flock of such an unexpected species remains for some time; in such cases, a fine dotted line connects the extreme dates reported. An example is the HOODED WARBLER that remained in Seattle's Discovery Park from December 31, 1975, until April 8, 1976. It was found regularly during this period but had not been reported from anywhere in Washington before and only a very few times since.

Certain species are notably irregular in abundance. They may be common one winter but then absent for the next five or ten. SNOWY OWLS, for example, were common around Seattle during the irruption winters of 1973-74 and 2005-2006 but are rare most other years. Such species are indicated by a dashed line of the appropriate width.

Extreme dates cited for positive breeding activity—treated here to include nest construction, egg laying, the feeding of young in the nest, and care of recently fledged young—are indicated by an open rectangle superimposed on the bar graph. If there is only one such breeding record, a minimal rectangle bracketing the date indicates the known nesting date. In a few instances, species that were once much more common as nesting birds are now rare or absent. In such cases, the charts reflect the situation since 1950, and the change of status is annotated. I wish to stress that our knowledge of breeding dates is still far from complete; thus, the periods indicated are provisional.

LOCAL BIRDING RECORDS

These species accounts are based on a survey of all published records, my personal records (which began in 1972), and interviews and solicited comments from individuals with particularly detailed knowledge of the county's avifauna or of bird distributions in some portion of the county. Published sources of particular value include *Audubon Field Notes* (abbreviated *AFN* in the annotations) and its successors, *American Birds* (abbreviated *AB*) and *Field Notes (FN)*. These journals were the National Audubon Society's summary of bird distributions in North America, region by region. In 2000 the American Birding Association took over publication of these quarterly regional reports, now entitled *North American Birds (NAB)*. Volume numbers have run consecutively from volumes 3 (1948) to 65 (2011). *The Murrelet* (volume 1, 1920, through volume 91, 2011) is the journal of the Pacific Northwest Bird and Mammal Society. *The Auk* and *The Condor* (selected references) published some important early reports and summaries. Jewett, Taylor, Shaw, and Aldrich in *Birds of Washington State* (1953) and Dawson and Bowles in *The Birds of Washington* (two volumes, 1909) cited records in a statewide context. Seattle Audubon Society's earlier Trailside Series volumes by Larrison and his associates provide valuable historical perspective.

An updated "Checklist of the Birds of Washington State, with Recent Changes Annotated" by Mattocks, Hunn, and Wahl (1976) summarized status changes of species statewide since Jewett et al. More recently, *Birds of Washington: Status and Distribution,* edited by Wahl, Tweit, and Mlodinow, detailed the status of all species recorded for the state as of 2005 (cited in the following pages as WTM). The *Seattle Audubon Society Notes* (abbreviated *SAN*), now *EarthCare Northwest* (abbreviated *ECNW*), summarized many local observations not otherwise documented. The primary task of summarizing noteworthy statewide bird observations has now devolved to the Washington Ornithological Society's publication, *WOSNews*, ably collated first by Russell Rogers (1992-2000), then by Tom Aversa (2000-2009). Ryan Merrill now collates all the state's records, as he has done since 2009. Additional sightings mentioned in the following pages are based on personal communications. All of these records were collated by species and date of occurrence, with notes on breeding activities. Sightings were evaluated by the likelihood and adequacy of the documentation.

Despite the mass of records, distributional patterns are often poorly reflected in the frequency of reports, so the construction of these charts involved a fair amount of educated guessing. The data are clearly biased in at least two respects. First, well over 90 percent of all King County records are from the immediate vicinity of Seattle. We know much less about the status of birds in the montane zone, particularly with respect to dates of arrival and departure. The charts thus represent the situation in the lowland part of the county much more accurately than they do that of the montane zone. When these regional distribution patterns are known to be distinct, separate charts are included and the difference is noted in the accompanying text. Second, there is an understandable tendency to take the commonplace for granted. Thus, unusual species are noted more frequently "for the record." For example, I have positive reports of far more Mountain than Black-capped Chickadees and next to none of the American Robin.

Waterfowl

GREATER WHITE-FRONTED GEESE have increased in number and frequency, with small flocks wintering at established locations (such as Gene Coulon Memorial Beach Park in Renton and the fields near Sikes Lake northwest of Carnation) and larger flocks noted during spring and fall migration. An individual of the larger, darker subspecies, the "TULE" WHITE-FRONTED GOOSE, was found near Carnation on January 19, 2010, and stayed for the winter (Ryan Merrill, Marv Breece, *WOSNews* 129).

SNOW GEESE are encountered only as individual stragglers or in small groups in flight overhead. Their numbers increase during migration. "BLACK" BRANT exhibit an asymmetrical migratory pattern, passing directly south from Alaska, much of the way over the Pacific Ocean, to winter in a few widely scattered refugia from Baja California north to Washington's Padilla Bay (a distinct population, "GRAY-BELLIED" BRANT, comes from the central Arctic in Canada). In spring Brants eat their way north, spreading all along the Puget Sound shoreline, where hundreds may be seen on the beaches of Discovery, Lincoln, and Golden Gardens Parks from mid-March through early May. A few also winter in the county.

CANADA GEESE were recently split into two species. The Canada Goose proper (*Branta canadensis*) now includes seven subspecies, while the four smallest forms of Canadas are now known as the CACKLING GOOSE (*Branta hutchinsii*), named for its higher-pitched vocalizations. The largest and smallest geese of each species are easy to identify in the field, but the smallest Canada Goose (*B. c. parvipes*) may be indistinguishable from the largest Cackling Goose (*B. h. taverneri*).

	status	Jan	Feb	Mar	Apr	May	Jun	Jul	Aug	Sep	Oct	Nov	Dec
Greater White-fronted Goose	w												
Emperor Goose	v												
Snow Goose	w												
Ross's Goose	v												
Brant	w												
Cackling Goose	w												
Canada Goose	pb												
Mute Swan	[pbx]vi												
Trumpeter Swan	w												
Tundra Swan	w												

Our nesting Canada Geese were introduced, most likely from the "Great Basin" population (*Branta canadensis moffitti*), a large, pale-breasted, nonmigratory form native to eastern Washington. Winter visitors of several races of Canada and Cackling Geese (Mlodinow et al. 2008) have been noted with increasing frequency, including substantial flocks of "MINIMA" CACKLING GEESE (*Branta hutchinsii minima*), very small and dark. Canada-type Geese intermediate in size and coloration may be either "LESSER" CANADAS (*Branta canadensis parvipes*) or "TAVERNER'S" CACKLING GEESE (*Branta hutchinsii taverneri*). A very few "DUSKY" CANADAS (*Branta canadensis occidentalis*), medium-sized and dark, have also been noted. This form normally winters on the outer coast from southern Washington to northern California. The "ALEUTIAN" CACKLING GOOSE (*Branta hutchinsii leucopareia*), an endangered form, has been reported several times. The "Aleutian" Cackling Goose is small and dark-breasted, with a white neck-collar. However, many "Minima" Cacklers also have white neck-collars, so one can't rely on that feature alone.

SWANS are reported nearly every year, with both TRUMPETER and TUNDRA SWANS likely. Sightings are concentrated in November and December in fields in the lower river valleys, for example near Carnation and Kent. Free-flying MUTE SWANS could be local escapes or birds dispersing from the established breeding population on southern Vancouver Island. Three adults donated to the city in 1980 raised young on Green Lake in 1981. Due to traffic conflicts, they were captured and released on Union Bay, where they continued to produce young each year until eliminated by the Washington Department of Fish & Wildlife around 1995.

Thirty species of DUCKS have been recorded in the county. All but three, BAIKAL TEAL, TUFTED DUCK, and KING EIDER, occur regularly. In addition, the AMERICAN BLACK DUCK has occurred as a straggler from the now extirpated introduced population north of Everett. Twelve species of ducks nest on a regular basis in the county, six more have been recorded breeding here once or twice, and one additional species (BUFFLEHEAD) might nest, but this has not yet been confirmed. A survey by W. English and I. Morgan (personal communication) of waterfowl nesting at the Kent Ponds (now incorporated into the Green River Natural Resources Area) during the late 1970s recorded numerous broods each year of MALLARDS, GADWALLS, CINNAMON TEALS, NORTHERN SHOVELERS, and RUDDY DUCKS.

GADWALLS first nested in western Washington as recently as 1967 at Sand Point (*AFN* 21.5) but are now widespread. In 1980 AMERICAN WIGEONS and CANVASBACKS were reported to have raised broods in Kent, the first western Washington nesting record for the latter. In 1981 LESSER SCAUPS and RING-NECKED and RUDDY DUCKS nested there. In 1982 GREEN-WINGED and BLUE-WINGED TEALS and NORTHERN PINTAILS nested. In July 1988 I found a REDHEAD brood at these ponds, an extraordinary west-side record. BUFFLEHEADS remain all summer but are not known to nest.

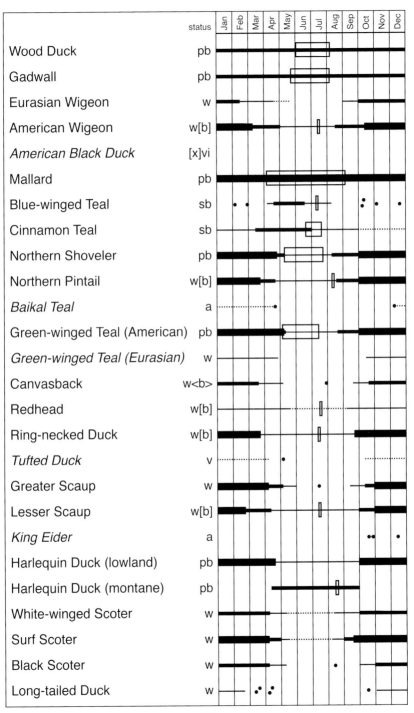

	status	Jan	Feb	Mar	Apr	May	Jun	Jul	Aug	Sep	Oct	Nov	Dec
Wood Duck	pb												
Gadwall	pb												
Eurasian Wigeon	w												
American Wigeon	w[b]												
American Black Duck	[x]vi												
Mallard	pb												
Blue-winged Teal	sb												
Cinnamon Teal	sb												
Northern Shoveler	pb												
Northern Pintail	w[b]												
Baikal Teal	a												
Green-winged Teal (American)	pb												
Green-winged Teal (Eurasian)	w												
Canvasback	w<b>												
Redhead	w[b]												
Ring-necked Duck	w[b]												
Tufted Duck	v												
Greater Scaup	w												
Lesser Scaup	w[b]												
King Eider	a												
Harlequin Duck (lowland)	pb												
Harlequin Duck (montane)	pb												
White-winged Scoter	w												
Surf Scoter	w												
Black Scoter	w												
Long-tailed Duck	w												

117

	status	Jan	Feb	Mar	Apr	May	Jun	Jul	Aug	Sep	Oct	Nov	Dec
Bufflehead	w[s]												
Common Goldeneye	w												
Barrow's Goldeneye (lowland)	w												
Barrow's Goldeneye (montane)	p[b]												
Hooded Merganser	pb												
Common Merganser	pb												
Red-breasted Merganser	w												
Ruddy Duck	pb												

The Snoqualmie River and its associated sloughs between Carnation and Fall City harbor nesting WOOD DUCKS and HOODED and COMMON MERGANSERS, while HARLEQUIN DUCKS nest further up the North Fork Snoqualmie and along the Green River above Flaming Geyser State Park. Green-winged Teals nested in 1979 on Fitchener Slough up the North Fork Snoqualmie in the company of Mallards, Wood Ducks, Hooded Mergansers, and nonbreeding Ring-Necked Ducks (S. Sweeney, personal communication). BARROW'S GOLDENEYES are known to nest on at least two mountain lakes in the county.

Blue-winged Teals may outnumber Cinnamon in late May, but most broods of "summer teals" (as Cinnamon and Blue-winged Teals might collectively be named) that have been identified to species have been Cinnamon. Given the subtlety of the differences between female and eclipse male Cinnamon and Blue-winged Teals (Cinnamons tend to be darker and more uniformly brown, with a slight "shoveler" shape to the bill), breeding Blue-winged Teals may easily escape detection.

By winter, the "summer teals" slip away, except for occasional stragglers. But duck diversity is increased by the addition of numbers of GREATER SCAUPS, COMMON GOLDENEYES, three species of SCOTERS, and RED-BREASTED MERGANSERS, mostly on saltwater. Scarce wintering species include EURASIAN WIGEON, REDHEAD, and LONG-TAILED DUCK.

The Eurasian form of Green-winged Teal, also known as "Common," or "Eurasian" Teal (*Anas crecca crecca*, including the "Aleutian Island" form, *A. c. nimia*), is reported annually in winter flocks of the common American form, the Green-winged Teal proper (*Anas crecca carolinensis,* or for splitters, *Anas carolinensis*), though at lower frequency than Eurasian Wigeons in our American Wigeon flocks. The Eurasian form—which may soon be elevated to full species status—sports a horizontal white line bordering the flanks, rather than the vertical white bar in front of the flanks of the American form. Intermediates are also noted, showing both types of white flank borders in some measure. The Eurasian form also shows somewhat coarser vermiculations on the flanks and more prominent buff margins to the green face patch. Females are essentially identical to the American form.

AMERICAN BLACK DUCKS are very rarely noted in King County anymore. It is difficult, if not impossible, to determine in such cases if they are escapes from some local waterfowl collection, stragglers south from a remnant of the now-defunct Snohomish County introduced population, or truly wild vagrants.

RARITIES

EMPEROR GOOSE. Four records.

1948 January 8 through February 24: A single subadult—judging by the flecking on the nape visible in the photograph—remained on Lake Union, Seattle, W. Tirre (*The Murrelet* 28(3):41); photograph published in Jewett et al. 1953:109).

1964 April 15: Seattle, V. Cannon, D. Jelliffe, B. and E. Boggs, photos (*AFN* 18.4).

1987 January 11: A subadult remained at Bitter Lake, Seattle (*AB* 41.2). Rumor had it that this individual was captured by a waterfowl breeder who had lost an Emperor from his collection, but on sexing the bird, realized it could not have been his. Though the wild origin of this individual has been questioned, given that it became quite tame, it should be noted that the 1948 individual also became tame and readily approachable after being fed (Jewett et al. 1953:110).

1988 August: Montlake Fill, K. Aanerud reported that one "remained for a short while," presumed to be the same individual of the previous year at Bitter Lake (*WB* 1:9).

ROSS'S GOOSE. Nine records.

1990 April 24: Montlake Fill, E. Norwood, multiple observers (*WOSNews* 47).

1990 April 29: North of Carnation, B. Pepper.

1992 April 30: Lake Killarney, Federal Way, V. Corley.

1995 January 13-29: Kent, M. Priebe, D. Beaudette, R. Sullivan, multiple observers (*FN* 49.2, *WOSNews* 37, *ECNW* 36(6):10).

1996 April 7: Kent, G. Revelas (*WOSNews* 45).

1997 January 24-31: Auburn, A. Freeland (*WOSNews* 50).

1998 September 8: Woodinville/Redmond, D. Beaudette (*WOSNews* 59).

1999 January 17: Kent, D. Beaudette, R. Orness (*WOSNews* 61).

2005 April 15-21: Kent, 2 birds, C. Wright (*WOSNews* 101).

AMERICAN BLACK DUCK. Status uncertain.
There are several well-documented records between 1972 and 1990. At that time, there was a small, introduced population north of Everett in Snohomish County, which was the most likely source for these birds. This population apparently died out by 2000 (WTM:364-365).

Late 1970s, late summer: Montlake Fill, two records, each of a molting bird that stayed several months, K. Aanerud (*WB* 1:10).

1979 December 29-June 10, 1980: Montlake Fill, male, E. Ratoosh (*WB* 4:10).

1981 October 18: Montlake Fill, female, E. Hunn.

1981 November 7: Montlake Fill, male, E. Ratoosh (*WB* 4:10).

The three most recently reported—a male at Marymoor Park, December 20, 2006; and females at Juanita Bay October 31, 2004 (*WOSNews* 98) and October 2007—could have been wild birds, though they might also have escaped from captivity.

BAIKAL TEAL. One record.

2004 December 12: A single male first noted at the Green River Natural Resources Area by C. Wright, subsequently observed off and on by many there and later five miles south in a flooded field in Auburn through April 19, 2005 (*WOSNews* 99, 101). The bird remained resolutely wild.

TUFTED DUCK. Thirteen records, including the first for Washington, and an indeterminate number of probable SCAUP X TUFTED DUCK hybrids.

1967   December 31 through February 12, 1968: Above Hiram M. Chittenden Locks, 2 males, Z. Schultz, E. Stopps (*The Murrelet* 51(2):25, *AFN* 22.3). One male, presumably the same individual, returned each winter through December 27, 1970 (*AFN* 24.3 and 25.2).

1981   October 13-22: Green Lake, male with a very short tuft but otherwise typical, D. Beaudette.

1982   November 20 to March 23, 1983: Green Lake, adult male with an immature male, E. Hunn, W. Fogelman, D. Beaudette, multiple observers (*AB* 37.3, 37.5).

1984   October 21 through November 7: Green Lake, immature male, E. Hunn, P. Mattocks, multiple observers (*AB* 39.1).

1985   October 19 through March 30, 1986: Green Lake, immature male, E. Hunn, M. Nixon, B. Meilleur, C. Wood, multiple observers (*AB* 40.2, 40.3).

1986   October 18 through November 2: Green Lake, 2 immature males, one of which stayed all winter, E. Hunn, B. Sundstrom (*AB* 41.1, 41.2).

1988   January 15 through April 2: Twin Ponds, Shoreline; and Green Lake, adult male, D. Beaudette, M. Muller, multiple observers (*AB* 42.2, 42.5).

1992   March 4: Green Lake, adult male, R. Taylor (*AB* 46.3, *ECNW* 33(9):10).

1996   May 3: Montlake Fill, J. Hebert (*WOSNews* 45).

2001   February 24: Issaquah, adult male, C.Haynie, E. Deal (*NAB* 55.2, *WOSNews* 75).

2002   December 31: Log Boom Park, adult male, M. Dossett.

2005   January 4-15: Phantom Lake, Bellevue, adult male, H. Jennings, multiple observers, O. Oliver, photo (*WOSNews* 99).

2006   January 8-22: Kent, adult male, S. Mlodinow, R. Merrill, multiple observers (*WOSNews* 105); likely the same individual reported March 20-April 1, Federal Way, G. McWethy, P. and R. Sullivan (*WOSNews* 107).

KING EIDER. Two records.

1948   October 23: An immature male remained off Lincoln Park, until it was collected October 30. The specimen is housed at the UW's Burke Museum. This was the first state record (Jewett et al. 1953:147).

2005   December 18: West Point, Discovery Park, female drifting south, E. and N. Hunn.

GROUSE, QUAIL, & THEIR RELATIONS

RUFFED GROUSE were a fixture on the University of Washington campus in Seattle before 1911 (Miller and Curtis 1940:42). As of 1980 they could still be found as close to Seattle as Bellefields Nature Park and St. Edward State Park on the east shore of Lake Washington. Since 2008 they are found regularly only as close to Seattle as the Snoqualmie River Valley, Tolt-MacDonald Park, and Carnation Marsh Sanctuary. In the montane zone, Ruffed Grouse give way to SOOTY GROUSE. Sooties may be heard hooting in April on cut-over land east of Duvall and in May on Alpine Lakes Wilderness trails. They may also be quite common at our Cascade passes, the tell-tale heartbeat booming of the males resounding there in June.

WHITE-TAILED PTARMIGANS may reward the persistent high-backcountry trekker. Nesting ptarmigans have been located recently near the summits of Granite Mountain, Snoqualmie Peak, and Big Snow Mountain above 5500 feet, and they probably occur above La Bohn Gap as well.

	status	Jan	Feb	Mar	Apr	May	Jun	Jul	Aug	Sep	Oct	Nov	Dec
Ring-necked Pheasant	pbi								▭				
Ruffed Grouse	pb				▭								
Spruce Grouse	<pb>												
White-tailed Ptarmigan	pb							▭					
Sooty Grouse	pb						▭						
Wild Turkey	vi					••							
Mountain Quail	xbi												
California Quail	pbi						▭						
Northern Bobwhite	xbi												

RING-NECKED PHEASANTS and CALIFORNIA QUAIL were quite common residents of farm fields and the larger city parks through the 1980s. Both species have become very scarce now. King County CBC counts have dwindled to near zero since 2005. The Washington Department of Fish & Wildlife releases pheasants for the benefit of bird hunters—as at Cherry Valley and Stillwater in the Snoqualmie River Valley—but few persist. Pheasant season runs from late September through November. Be alert if birding in these areas in season.

RARITIES

SPRUCE GROUSE, the "fool hen," has been reported by the Washington Department of Fish & Wildlife (D. Bellingham, personal communication) from north of the Tolt River on Weyerhaeuser property above 4000 feet. A vocalizing female in a Redmond backyard on October 1, 1994, defies belief. I include Spruce Grouse on the King County list on the assumption that a small breeding population likely exists, given nesting populations near the Cascade Crest to the south in Yakima and Skamania Counties.

WILD TURKEYS have been noted in rural King County in recent years, but such sightings are likely of barnyard strays. However, D. Schonewald has reported several sightings since 2005 of one to four birds along I-90 west of Snoqualmie Pass, which may well derive from a now well-established wild population of Merriam's Wild Turkeys (*Meleagris gallopavo merriami*) introduced about 2000 near Cle Elum, not far east of the Cascade Crest in Kittitas County.

NORTHERN BOBWHITE and MOUNTAIN QUAIL have been introduced and were briefly established; however, these game birds no longer persist and have not recently been released by the Washington Department of Fish & Wildlife. Bobwhites were last reported on Vashon Island in 1925 (Kitchin 1925:64). The Mountain Quail has not been noted since 1902, when Rathbun said it was "quite common" and breeding in the area (Rathbun 1902:133). Bobwhites and Mountain Quail are still found in some numbers southwest of Tacoma and on the Kitsap Peninsula and might be looked for between Auburn and Enumclaw.

LOONS

COMMON, PACIFIC, and RED-THROATED LOONS winter throughout Puget Sound in fair numbers; however, since the saltwater shoreline within the county is not particularly productive, our share of these wintering loon populations is limited. A survey of the West Seattle shoreline from Alki Beach south to the Fauntleroy Ferry Landing from November to January should produce a few Common and Red-throated Loons at least, and perhaps the more localized Pacific Loon as well. Discovery Park's West Point is also a good vantage point. A ferry ride to Vashon Island in winter provides an opportunity to study all three of these loon species in numbers, particularly in Quartermaster Harbor south of Burton, in Tramp Harbor, and off KVI Beach and Point Robinson. In addition, Common Loons winter on large freshwater lakes such as Lake Washington. At the turn of the century, they were recorded as breeding at lowland and foothill sites such as Pierce County's Kapowsin Lake, but when the first edition of this guide went to press in 1982, there had been no recent nesting records anywhere in the state. However, subsequent Breeding Bird Atlas efforts have documented regular nesting on the watershed reservoirs of the Tolt, Cedar, and Green Rivers.

RARITIES

YELLOW-BILLED LOON. At least eleven records. This loon may be recognized at a distance in winter plumage by its large size, pale brownish upper parts (the paleness particularly evident about the face, head, and neck), and large, pale, slightly upturned bill.

1956 December 23: Seward Park, one bird, well described, Z. Schultz (*The Murrelet* 51(2):23). First record for the state, and unusual in being on freshwater.

1979 December 29 through at least January 12, 1980: Lincoln Park, Seattle CBC. Subsequent reports from Vashon Island and Three Tree Point, Burien, to April 5, 1980 (*SAN* 20(8):5) probably refer to the same individual.

1987 May 17: Off South Beach, Discovery Park, first-summer bird, D. Beaudette.

1989 February 4: Seattle, K. Carpenter (*AB* 43.2).

1992 October 10-14: Seattle, M. Muller.

2001 March 13: Dash Point and Redondo Beach, a striking albino individual, first noted at Tacoma late in 2000. This same individual returned for three subsequent winters and was last reported in King County April 10, 2005, *fide* C. Wright, photo (*WOSNews* 97).

2005 March 5: Off Shilshole, Seattle.

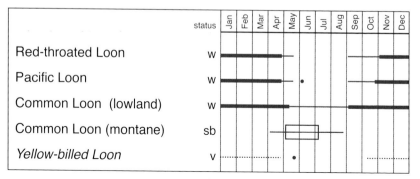

	status	Jan	Feb	Mar	Apr	May	Jun	Jul	Aug	Sep	Oct	Nov	Dec
Red-throated Loon	w												
Pacific Loon	w					•							
Common Loon (lowland)	w												
Common Loon (montane)	sb												
Yellow-billed Loon	v					•							

2008 January 24: Off Duwamish Head, Seattle, M. Hoekstra (*WOSNews* 117).

2008 January 25-27: In Tramp Harbor, Vashon Island, E. Hunn, C. Riddell, photo. Possibly the same bird as the one off Duwamish Head.

2010 March 27: Off Alki Beach, G. Smith.

2010 April 13: Off Madison Park, Lake Washington, Seattle, an alternate-plumaged individual, C. O'Reilly.

GREBES

The diminutive PIED-BILLED GREBE often breeds on the marshy margins of freshwater lakes. If you go to Montlake Fill or walk around Green Lake and scan the cattail and pond-lily margins, you should hear its bizarre breeding calls in spring. Perhaps you will spot its low, mud-and-stick nest, seemingly afloat, often with a grebe on top. In summer watch for the stripe-headed youngsters riding piggyback on their mothers. In winter, Green Lake supports 50 or more Pied-billeds. Martin Muller has carefully documented the lives of Green Lake's grebes, including their unusual carnivory (Muller, 2000:44-45). Pied-billed Grebes are uncommon on saltwater, in sharp contrast to their cousins, the WESTERN, RED-NECKED, and HORNED GREBES, which commonly winter on just about any substantial expanse of saltwater or freshwater. They are most abundant on Puget Sound, often in the company of loons and scoters. It is exciting to watch Horned Grebes metamorphose into breeding plumage in April.

Pied-billed Grebe with chick, Montlake Fill (© Tim Kuhn).

Look very carefully at our "Western Grebes," as two species are involved. The great majority of our birds are Western Grebes, which have a greenish-yellow bill and a black cap that extends down to include the eye. Perhaps one in a thousand "Western Grebes" is a CLARK'S GREBE, distinguished by its brighter, yellow-orange bill and by its more extensively white face (the white extending above the eye in breeding plumage, just grazing it in winter plumage). Clark's Grebes nest north to Moses Lake in eastern Washington but typically winter more to the south. Scattered among the Westerns, Clark's Grebes are recorded every year in the Seattle area. In August 2006 Western Grebes were seen building a nest at Juanita Bay Park on Lake Washington. Young had fledged by September. One of the adults involved appeared to be a hybrid WESTERN X CLARK'S GREBE (M. Mathis, to Tweeters). This remains the only western Washington nesting record for either species.

RED-NECKED GREBES are more local than Westerns and Horneds but are still common at favored sites, such as along Seattle's downtown waterfront. They nest on the larger northern Washington lakes east of the Cascades. EARED GREBES are just plain scarce. However, a few are found each winter off Seward Park in Lake Washington and in Quartermaster Harbor on Vashon Island. They are common in summer in eastern Washington.

TUBENOSES

Members of this order are birds of the open ocean. They come to shore only to nest, most often on oceanic islands or barren arctic cliffs, as in the case of the NORTHERN FULMAR. To see them, it is normally necessary to take a pelagic trip offshore to the vicinity of the continental shelf, as, for example, some 35 miles out of Westport, Grays Harbor County. Very occasionally, following severe storms or with strong westerly winds, stragglers or even major flights of these species may penetrate Puget Sound. Other stragglers may arrive with a "ship assist," which may explain the single LAYSAN ALBATROSS record. With contemporary, instantaneous electronic communications, one may quickly respond to the first reports of a pelagic incursion and catch a piece of the action from a Puget Sound vantage point or ferry run.

RARITIES

LAYSAN ALBATROSS. One record, plus a second, ship-assisted visitation.

1998 Early February: Arrived at Seattle as a captive on a barge and subsequently died (C. Sheridan, WTM:84).

2005 April 11: One "fell from the sky." It was captured in downtown Seattle by Seattle Animal Control officers and transported to PAWS for rehabilitation. It was then shipped to California for further treatment and released (J. Huckabee, personal communication). While this individual may well have hitched a ride on a container ship, it was not clearly brought here as a captive.

NORTHERN FULMAR. Five records.

1972 April 18: West Point, Discovery Park, M. Perrone (*AB* 26.4).

1981 June 17: North Seattle, M. Donahue (*AB* 35.6).

124

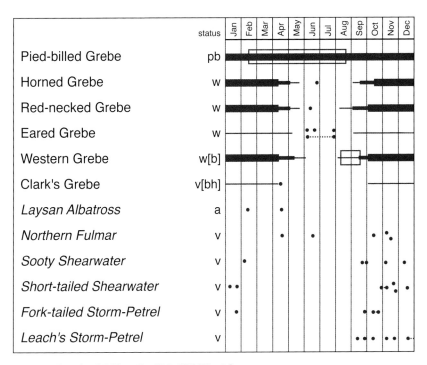

2002 November 4-5: Union Bay, K. Li (*WOSNews* 86).

2003 October 13-14: Dash Point, one seen October 13, H. Feddern; Lincoln Park and downtown Seattle, singles seen October 14, K. Li; Dash Point in Pierce County, at least a dozen on October 14, P. and R. Sullivan; Seattle (*WOSNews* 92, Swan 2005:121).

2003 November 11-13: West Point, at least 60 seen, mostly dark phase, J. Nance; one seen, Vashon Island, S. Caldwell, D. Beaudette, R. Sanders (*WOSNews* 92, Swan 2005:121).

SOOTY SHEARWATER. Five records.

1981 December 10: West Point, Discovery Park, D. Hutchinson (*AB* 36.3).

1983 September 19: West Point, D. Beaudette.

1992 September 29: Off Seattle, 300 birds, K. Aanerud (*AB* 47.1, *ECNW* 34(5):10).

1996 January 30: Vashon Island, S. Caldwell (Swan 2005:122).

2007 November 5: West Point, M. Bartels (*WOSNews* 116).

SHORT-TAILED SHEARWATER. Seven records.

1942 January 18: Vashon Island, J. Slipp (*The Murrelet* 23(2):54-59, Swan 2005:121).

1976 November 20: West Point, Discovery Park, D. Paulson (*AB* 31.2).

1977 November 17-18: Point Robinson, Maury Island, 1 to 4 birds seen, A. Richards (Swan 2005:121).

1984 January 1: Off Seattle, D. Paulson et al. (CBC).

1993 October 30-November 6: Off West Point, 1 to 2 birds seen, R. Rogers, E. Hunn et al. (*WOSNews* 29, *ECNW* 35(6):12).

1997 December 16: From Edmonds-Kingston ferry, D. Beaudette.

2005 December 28: Richmond Beach, D. Duffy; West Seattle, S. Terry (*WOSNews* 105).

FORK-TAILED STORM-PETREL. Three records.

1991 January 14: Off Seattle, M. Gracz (*AB* 45.2).

1997 October 13-17: Off Seattle, multiple birds sighted by multiple observers, up to 1900 birds on October 14 (*WOSNews* 54; D. Beaudette, in Swan 2005:122).

2005 September 24: In the waters of the Sound between Seattle and the Kitsap side, B. Waggoner, E. Hunn, G. Gerdts (reported in *WOSNews* 103 as off Point Jefferson in Kitsap County).

LEACH'S STORM-PETREL. Six records.

1993 November 4: West Point, Discovery Park, K. Aanerud (*WOSNews* 29, *ECNW* 35(6):12).

1994 October 8: Alki, M. Sears (*WOSNews* 35).

1995 December 20-25: Off Seattle, P. Sullivan, D. Beaudette, J. Tangren (*WOSNews* 43).

2006 November 20: Elliott Bay, B. Waggoner (*WOSNews* 110).

2007 September 25: Richmond Beach, M. Bartels (*WOSNews* 115).

2010 September 8: Off Alki Beach, E. Steffans.

CORMORANTS & RELATIVES

All three West Coast cormorants are regular winter residents. They may be seen in Puget Sound off West Point and Alki in Seattle, and from other vantage points. PELAGIC and BRANDT'S CORMORANTS are strictly saltwater species, with Brandt's less regularly noted, though a dozen Brandt's in full breeding plumage summered on Harbor Island in the Seattle harbor in 2007 but did not nest. DOUBLE-CRESTED CORMORANTS are ubiquitous on open water, occurring regularly on Green Lake, Lake Washington, Lake Sammamish, and Sikes Lake near Carnation, as well as on the Sound. Double-crested and Pelagic Cormorants breed in Puget Sound, but neither is presently known to breed in King County, perhaps due to the scarcity of appropriate nesting sites. (There is a single nesting record for the Double-crested Cormorant for Seattle in 2003, reported by F. Wood.) Seattle CBCs during the 1970s averaged 79 Double-crested, three Brandt's, and six Pelagic Cormorants. At a distance, Double-crested Cormorants may be easily identified in flight by their thick, crooked necks. Pelagic and Brandt's Cormorants fly with straight necks. Pelagic and Brandt's Cormorants are a bit harder to tell apart. The Pelagic has a pencil-thin neck, small head, and a tail nearly as long as the neck. Compared to Pelagic, Brandt's has a thicker neck, larger head, heavier bill, and shorter tail.

BROWN PELICANS were first recorded in King County in November 1983. Ten years later, reports became more regular as post-breeding flocks on the outer coast increased dramatically. Brown Pelicans are still rare stragglers in winter and early spring and are to be looked for in greater numbers in late summer and fall from Puget Sound vantage points.

RARITIES

BROWN BOOBY. One record.

2002 May 18: one reported to have been riding the mast of a sailboat from near Blake Island to Commencement Bay at Tacoma, passing through King County waters, John McMillan (*WOSNews* 82). The same bird may have been spotted the day before on the lower Duwamish River in Seattle by Kevin Li.

AMERICAN WHITE PELICAN. Eight records, three in late fall, four in late spring, and one in mid-winter.

1946 October 6: Redondo Beach, 2 seen, H. K. Nichols (*The Murrelet* 28(1):6).

	status	Jan	Feb	Mar	Apr	May	Jun	Jul	Aug	Sep	Oct	Nov	Dec
Brown Booby	a					•							
American White Pelican	v	•				•	••				••	•	
Brown Pelican	mf	•			••••	••••	••••			▬▬▬	▬▬▬		•
Brandt's Cormorant	w[s]	▬▬▬▬▬	▬▬▬						▬▬▬	▬▬▬	▬▬▬	▬▬▬	▬▬▬
Double-crested Cormorant	w[bs]	▬▬▬▬▬	▬▬▬	▬▬	▭				▬▬▬	▬▬▬	▬▬▬	▬▬▬	▬▬▬
Pelagic Cormorant	w	▬▬▬▬▬	▬▬▬	▬▬	──								
Magnificent Frigatebird	a										•		

1992   November 22: Union Bay, M. Smith, H. Stevens, R. Youel (*AB* 47.1, *ECNW* 34(5):10).

1994   October 4: Mercer Island, 5 seen (*WOSNews* 35).

1997   May 22: Renton, 6 seen, *fide* T. Bock (*WOSNews* 51).

1998   June 12: Seattle, 6 seen, *fide* P. Cozens (*WOSNews* 58).

2002   June 5: Seattle, 9 seen, D. Duffy (*WOSNews* 84).

2004   June 4: Seattle, 10 seen, C. Reinsch (*WOSNews* 96).

2005   January 10: Juanita Bay, *fide* M. Mathis (*WOSNews* 99).

MAGNIFICENT FRIGATEBIRD. One record.

1988   October 8: In flight north from Point Defiance Park, Tacoma, up Colvos Passage, J. Zimmerman and M. Miller. This individual was first noted at Tacoma October 7 and subsequently remained off Point No Point, Kitsap County, October 11-17 (Mattocks 1988:1-2).

HERONS, EGRETS, BITTERNS, IBISES, & VULTURES

The GREAT BLUE HERON, popularly but inaccurately called a "crane," is *the* heron for most Washingtonians and the official bird of Seattle. It is a familiar sight throughout much of the year in wetlands and on beaches of King County. In early spring Great Blue Herons retire to their heronries to nest, typically at large colonial roosts. One well-known heronry is located along the Black River Slough in Renton. Others are in Kiwanis Ravine adjacent to Discovery Park, behind the Kenmore park-and-ride lot, and at Lake Sammamish State Park. Heronries are in a constant state of flux, in part due to Bald Eagle predation or development schemes.

GREAT EGRETS have established substantial breeding populations in eastern Washington, now with a toehold west of the Cascades near Vancouver, Washington. In King County they are rare stragglers, with one or two turning up each year, mostly in the major river valleys. Great Egrets may turn up any month of the year, though May and September are the mostly likely.

Higman and Larrison's *Union Bay: The Life of a City Marsh* dramatically chronicles some of the first documented Washington records of the diminutive GREEN HERON and the first nesting records at Union Bay in Seattle in 1939 and

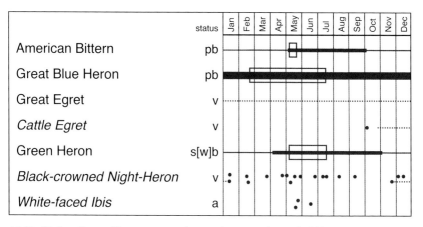

	status	Jan	Feb	Mar	Apr	May	Jun	Jul	Aug	Sep	Oct	Nov	Dec
American Bittern	pb												
Great Blue Heron	pb												
Great Egret	v												
Cattle Egret	v												
Green Heron	s[w]b												
Black-crowned Night-Heron	v												
White-faced Ibis	a												

1940. Today Green Herons are widespread spring through fall, most commonly encountered along woods-edged rivers such as the Duwamish and Snoqualmie. A pair nested at Union Bay in 1981, and this species has been noted there regularly since. Other Green Herons nest at Juanita Bay Park, Marymoor Park, and at various Kent and Auburn wetlands. A few now also stay the winter, having been recorded on Seattle's annual CBCs 14 times since 1970.

The AMERICAN BITTERN is secretive, thus poorly known. It frequented now defunct wetlands, such as once existed in Renton. Bitterns still regularly nest at the Green River Natural Resources Area and along the Snoqualmie River at Duvall and Stillwater. They are presumed to be permanent residents.

RARITIES

CATTLE EGRET. Nine records.

1980 November 22: Lake Union.

1989 November 22 through December 25: Montlake Fill and Ballard, R. Droker, K. Barton, F. Bird, found dead, specimen to the UW's Burke Museum (*AB* 44.2, *WOSNews* 5).

1992 October 23 through November 25: King County, 4 birds seen (*AB* 47.1), including 1 or more in Enumclaw November 1-14, G. Turalt, and 1 November 24-25 at Dockton on Vashon Island, J. Nelson (Swan 2005:126).

1994 November 15: Marymoor Park, B. Dolphin (*WOSNews* 35; *FN* 49.1)

1995 October 1: Enumclaw, *fide* R. Rogers.

1997 November 15: Green Lake, D. Beaudette, P. Sullivan, T. Aversa, multiple observers (*FN* 52.1, *WOSNews* 54).

2004 November 11 through 18: Montlake Fill, F. Bird, K. Andrich, E. Hunn (*WOSNews* 98).

2007 November 6 through 9: Montlake Fill, N. Larson, E. Hunn, multiple observers (*WOSNews* 116).

BLACK-CROWNED NIGHT-HERON. Fifteen records.

1940s, football season: Montlake Fill, adult (Higman and Larrison 1951:162, *WB* 4:32).

1974 December 5: Montlake Fill (Krause 1975, *WB* 4:32).

1975 December 10: Montlake Fill (*SAN*).

1976 February 8: Kellogg Island, Seattle (*SAN*).

1976 November 20 through January 8, 1977: Montlake Fill (*SAN*, *AB* 31.1).

1977 January 8: 2 birds, St. Thomas Seminary, north of Kirkland (*SAN*).

1979 February 11: Tolt-MacDonald Park, M. Egger (*SAN* 9(6):3).

1987 May 10: Kent, 2 birds, D. Beaudette.

1987 July 13, then August 15 through September 3: Montlake Fill, 1 immature, D. Beaudette, K. Aanerud (*WB* 1:8).

1988 July 4 through March 24, 1989: Seattle, 2 birds, R. Thorne (*AB* 43.1).

1992 August 5: Woodland Park, anon. (*ECNW*).

1993 April 22-29: Union Bay, *fide* D. Nyers (*ECNW* 35(1):10).

1994 May 22: Kent, 2 birds, D. Beaudette (*WOSNews* 67, 70).

1994 June 21-22: Mercer Slough, M. Breece (*WOSNews* 76).

2009 May 2: Boeing Ponds, 2 birds, A. and K. Slettebak (*WOSNews* 125).

WHITE-FACED IBIS. Four records, all late spring, with three in the Kent Valley.

2000 June 16: Kent, B. Feltner (*NAB* 54.4, *WOSNews* 67, 72).

2001 May 24-26: Kent, 1 to 2 individuals, R. Orness, D. Beaudette (*NAB* 55.3, *WOSNews* 76).

2007 May 20: Boeing Ponds, K. Kemper, multiple observers, photos (*WOSNews* 112, 113).

2008 May 17-19: Llama Lake, Sammamish, M. Saint Claire, multiple observers, photos (*WOSNews* 118, 119).

HAWKS, EAGLES, & FALCONS

The TURKEY VULTURE (sometimes judged more closely akin to storks and their relations than to hawks and eagles) is reported most frequently in fall migration, often in passage over Seattle. There is a very distinct fall movement of "TVs" through Victoria, B.C., which peaks the last week of September. They are presumed to nest in the foothills of the Cascades in King County, as they are regularly seen soaring over the Snoqualmie River Valley and near Enumclaw from April through October. An occasional individual lingers into winter, as did the one observed through January 22, 1977, on Mercer Island (*AB* 31.3).

BALD EAGLES are one of the great success stories of the past several decades. When the first edition of this guide was published in 1982, I was able to locate just three active Bald Eagle nests in King County. By 2007 that number had grown to 77 (Stinson, Watson, and McAllister 2007:2), a 2500 percent increase! Statewide, the number of known active nests increased 707 percent between 1981 and 2005, to 840 (Stinson, Watson, and McAllister 2007:22). It is generally assumed that Bald Eagle populations were pushed to the brink of extinction in the lower 48 states due to pesticide pollution, shooting, and loss of nesting habitat. The vigorous rebound of this species suggests that conservation efforts may be richly rewarded.

Our "sea-hawks," as OSPREYS are known in the local vernacular, arrive each year in late March or early April at their nest sites, which, in the great majority of cases, have been built with commanding views atop cell phone towers or other man-made structures. Ospreys also have staged a remarkable recovery since the 1980s, but, in this case, their increase might be due as much to the convenience of artificial towers for nesting as to the elimination of environmental toxins. There are a few mid-winter records, e.g., one noted during CBC count week in Bellevue in December 2003.

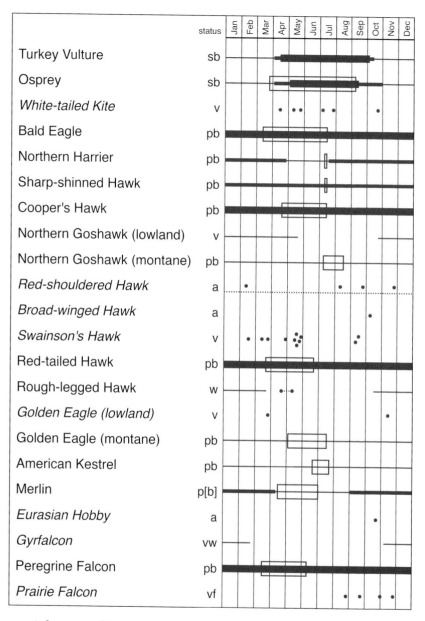

A few pairs of NORTHERN HARRIERS nest in King County each year. Favored locations include the fields along W Snoqualmie River Rd. northwest of Duvall, and at the Green River Natural Resources Area. In migration and winter they are more widely noted and may be seen in the city from time to time hunting at Montlake Fill or Magnuson Park.

COOPER'S and SHARP-SHINNED HAWKS are conspicuous in the Seattle vicinity in migration and winter. During the 1970s, 1980s, and 1990s, Seattle CBCs averaged 7.6, 9.9, and 18.0 Sharpies per year and 4.4, 6.4, and 10.9 Cooper's, respectively. In summer these accipiters are less often noted, although Cooper's Hawks nest quite frequently, for example in Discovery Park and in Wallace Swamp Creek Park. Sharp-shinned Hawks appear to be far less common than Cooper's in summer, though they have been noted all summer on the North Fork Snoqualmie River (D. Wechsler, personal communicaton), and there are confirmed Breeding Bird Atlas reports from near Auburn and Black Diamond.

NORTHERN GOSHAWKS are always hard to find, although they probably are year-round residents of our mountain forests and rare visitors to the lowlands. D. Wechsler found the remains of a fledgling Northern Goshawk on the North Fork Snoqualmie River in spring 1979. U.S. Forest Service files record pairs nesting in the Skykomish, Snoqualmie, Cedar, and Green River drainages. Seattle CBCs recorded single goshawks only four times during the 1970s, 1980s, and 1990s.

RED-TAILED HAWKS nest throughout King County and are particularly common at low elevations near open country. In winter they are nearly inescapable, scanning freeway margins in the middle of our cities and patrolling nearly every field and forest patch west of the dense montane forests. The distinctive, charcoal-gray race, *harlani*, is reported most winters, most often between Kent and Auburn or in the Snoqualmie River Valley. Look for a blackish or slate-gray (not dark reddish or brown) Red-tail-shaped hawk with a mostly white tail.

ROUGH-LEGGED HAWKS winter here infrequently or may be spotted in migration, favoring open areas of farmland. Their decided preference for short-grass habitat ensures their rarity in this county. Joyce Meyer has had particular success locating this raptor, finding one southwest of Duvall at the Snoqualmie River Bridge on NE 124th St. in January 2008 and another south of Woodinville near the Sammamish Slough off NE 124th St. (same street, different valley) in January 2009. Both stuck around for weeks.

Clear-cutting seems to have created opportunities for GOLDEN EAGLES in the mountains. A few are now year-round residents just west of the Cascade Crest in the headwaters of the Snoqualmie, Skykomish, and Green Rivers. I suspect they nest on Kelly Butte northwest of Naches Pass. They are noted infrequently in the lowlands (e.g., an immature in Shoreline on November 11, 2009, noted by L. Peter (photo) and one seen above Montlake Fill on March 21, 2010, by C. Sidles and J. Bopp (photo).

MERLINS and AMERICAN KESTRELS are found year-round, the Merlin actually the more common during much of the year, averaging 3.1, 5.3, and 8.3 to the kestrel's 1.3, 1.1, and 0.5 per Seattle CBC during the 1970s, 1980s, and 1990s. Note that Merlins appear to be increasing, while kestrels are decreasing. Both stay to nest, although Merlin nests are still rare in the county. American Kestrels typically nest in farm country, such as near Redmond, Duvall, and Kent, but also in the more open mountain areas, notably around clear-cuts. The single pair of Merlins known to have nested in King County as of 1979 was then just the fourth reported for the entire state. The pair used a Douglas Fir snag in the mountains east of North Bend and raised four young (P. Arcese). In 2008, however, a pair nested in north Seattle not far from the Seattle Audubon Society offices and repeated that feat nearby in 2009 and 2010, fledging five youngsters by late June each year. This pair usually sets up shop in mid-April, selecting an abandoned crow's nest in a tall conifer. The pair seems to seek trees with dense branches, either a Douglas Fir or Western White Pine (B. Deihl, *WOSNews* 123, and personal communication). So far, their nests have always been in residential yards.

Urban populations of PEREGRINES have exploded in parallel with those of Bald Eagles and Ospreys, with at least four nest sites regularly occupied in the city of Seattle: on a downtown skyscraper, and on the infrastructures of the I-5, Ballard, and West Seattle Bridges. CBC count totals have averaged 4.1 during the 1990s, though Peregrines were very rarely noted in earlier decades.

Outside the urban area, a Peregrine pair has nested on cliffs beside Snoqualmie Falls, where their parental chores may be monitored from vista points near the lodge. Another pair nests regularly on Rattlesnake Ledge just south of North Bend. A dedicated cadre of Peregrine watchers keeps a close eye on all our Peregrines.

RARITIES

WHITE-TAILED KITE. Six records.

1988   July 2-3: Kent, B. Chadwick, H. Fray, B. Odekirk (*AB* 43.1).

1990   October 18: Near Duvall, G. Adams (*AB* 45.2, *ECNW* 32(4):10).

1995   May 8: Magnuson Park, M. Smith (*FN* 49.3, *WOSNews* 39, *ECNW* 36(9):10).

1995   May 22: Kent, D. Burris (*FN* 49.3, *WOSNews* 39).

1999   April 13: Kent, R. Orness (*NAB* 53.3).

2010   July 24: Lake Forest Park, T. Haas.

RED-SHOULDERED HAWK. Five records, including one extended stay in Kent 2006-2009.

2002   September 20: Auburn, C. Wright (*WOSNews* 85).

2004   November 26: Juanita Bay Park, R. Howson, *fide* M. Mathis.

2006   August 7: Over Montlake Fill, C. Cox.

2006   August 27: An immature was first reported at the Green River Natural Resources Area by C. Wright et al. and appears to have remained in the area through 2009, molting into adult plumage by October 2007; photos (*WOSNews* 109, 111, 113, 114, 115, 116, 117, 122, 129).

2009   February 5-6: Montlake Fill, C. Sidles (*WOSNews* 129).

BROAD-WINGED HAWK. One record.

1990   October 6: Kent, 1 immature, E. Hunn (*WOSNews* 40).

SWAINSON'S HAWK. Eleven records, most late winter through spring.

1892   March 7: East shore Lake Washington, reported to be nesting (Rathbun 1902:133, Jewett et al. 1953:171).

1920   February 15: Renton, T. Burleigh (*The Auk* 46(4):511).

1975   April 28: South Seattle, B. Bernson.

1993 May 25: Seattle, R. Thorne (*AB* 47.3).

1997 March 21: Duvall, B. Helmboldt (*WOSNews* 50).

2000 May 14: Carnation Marsh, E. Hunn (*NAB* 54.3, *WOSNews* 70).

2007 May 11: Sikes Lake near Carnation, E. and N. Hunn (*WOSNews* 113).

2007 May 15: Marymoor Park, M. Hobbs (*WOSNews* 113).

2008 September 10: North Bend, 1 immature, J. Tubbs.

2008 September 18: Marymoor Park, 1 immature, H. Flores, photo (*WOSNews* 121).

2009 May 17: Three Forks Natural Area, M. Breece.

EURASIAN HOBBY. One record.

2001 October 20: Discovery Park, K. Aanerud, P. Cozens, videotaped (*WOSNews* 80; *WB* 9:43).

GYRFALCON. Eleven records.

1916 December 14: Near Seattle, *fide* D. Brown (Jewett et al. 1953:182).

1970s Kent: G. McDonald, photo.

1975 January 17: Kent, E. Hunn.

1981 November 7-27: Kent, E. Hunn, multiple observers (*AB* 36.2).

1991 December 20: Seatac, K. Brunner (*ECNW* 33(6):10).

1996 February 15: Seattle, R. Rogers (*FN* 50.2).

2000 November 7: Kent, gray phase immature, E. Hunn et al.

2000 December 10: Harbor Island, Seattle, brown immature, R. Taylor (*WOSNews* 75).

2005 January 11: Green River Natural Resources Area, E. Hunn, R. Rowlett (*WOSNews* 99).

2006 December 31: Auburn, E. Hunn (CBC).

2010 January 18-19: Near Carnation, gray phase immature, H. Queisser, E. Freedman, M. Hamilton, photo (*WOSNews* 129).

PRAIRIE FALCON. Four records.

1997 November 27: Kent, J. Flynn, R. Orness (*WOSNews* 54 with incorrect date, date is correct here).

1998 September 22: Near Red Mountain, D. Beaudette.

2000 October 30: Near Carnation, M. Wile (*WOSNews* 74).

2005 August 26: Kent, K. Armbruster (*WOSNews* 103).

RAILS, COOTS, & CRANES

The presence of rails is easily overlooked. These skulking marsh birds are rarely seen, and it is often necessary to excite them with tape-recorded calls to verify their presence vocally. In my experience, few cattail stands of any size lack rails, even in winter. VIRGINIA RAILS predominate, but their dominance is exaggerated due to their noisier nature. One may see or hear SORAS quite often, spring and fall, at such rail havens as the Union Bay marshes. The best viewing strategy is to arrive at a likely marsh early in the morning, find a comfortable hiding place near the marsh edge, then play a tape-recorded rail call softly once or twice. Your nerves may be shattered by a Virginia's raucous squawk practically underfoot. Sometime later you may catch a glimpse of the source of the sound, tip-toeing in and out of the reeds. Note that tape-recorded bird vocalizations must be employed with appropriate restraint to avoid unduly stressing the birds. There is no doubt that rails and most owls would go undetected without their use. Thus, when used with care, recordings are, in my judgment, a legitimate scientific tool of bird study. However, excessive reliance on recordings to get that close-in view of the rare or elusive individual bird is to be avoided.

AMERICAN COOTS are overgrown, extroverted rails. In summer they prowl the same marsh borders as do their rail cousins. They are uncommon nesters but are widely noted in late summer in wetlands along the Green River between Tukwila and Auburn. Young coots sport an improbable red head, then turn chalky white before assuming the adult's drab gray. In winter they abound along every freshwater shore. Some 10,000 may regularly winter on Lake Washington, concentrated at several favored locations, such as off Kenmore's Log Boom Park, in Union Bay, and off the Cedar River mouth in Renton.

As of 1980, there were just six records of SANDHILL CRANES. Since then, Sandhill Cranes have been recorded nearly every year, most often during fall migration between mid-September and mid-October. Historic records indicate that they nested in western Washington in some numbers. U. Hertz reported "large numbers of 'sandhill cranes' crossing White River Valley (near Kent) in a northerly direction in a continuous stream all the afternoon. Toward night they settled in a swampy pasture. . . . Hertz also saw a small band of cranes flying low at dusk on February 4, 1890." (Jewett et al. 1953:233) At this early date, such sights were apparently not unusual, since "on May 1, 1892, at Lake Washington, Rathbun saw a flock of 39 cranes going over at a great height, his attention being called to the flock by their rolling notes." (Jewett et al. 1953:233) A spate of sightings in 1980 may be related to the release of captive-bred Sandhills in British Columbia in an effort to augment the frail Pitt Meadows colony east of Vancouver (W. Weber, personal communication). M. Egger reported one in flight over Woodinville on May 10, 1980, while E. Ratoosh saw one over Magnuson Park on September 14, and two over Montlake Fill on October 12, 1980 (Ratoosh 1995). Cranes have been noted nearly annually since, but most often they are seen flying overhead. Rarely has one stayed put long enough to be relocated. The exception is a single bird that paused for several weeks in fields northwest of Fall City during the fall of 2006.

SHOREBIRDS

Three shorebirds nest here in King County. The KILLDEER is common and widespread in open terrain of the lowlands. The discovery of a Killdeer's four spotted eggs neatly arranged on a gravel scrape, with the adult piping frantically and wing-dragging in feigned injury, is a sure sign of spring's full measure. SPOTTED SANDPIPERS range as nesters from sea level up to timberline. They seem equally at home on a Montlake Fill scrap of cattail marsh, a Snoqualmie River gravel bar, or a talus-bordered alpine tarn. WILSON'S SNIPES are not common, but you may hear them winnowing along W Snoqualmie River Rd. northwest of Duvall, or at the nearby Cherry Valley Unit of the Snoqualmie Wildlife Area in June. They are presumed to nest.

	status	Jan	Feb	Mar	Apr	May	Jun	Jul	Aug	Sep	Oct	Nov	Dec
Virginia Rail	pb												
Sora	s[w]b												
American Coot	pb												
Sandhill Crane	v												

Migrant shorebirds are rather few in number and limited in variety. However, persistence will be rewarded from late April to mid-May and again from July to early October at Montlake Fill's ponds, Magnuson Park's ponds, at scattered wet spots in Kent and Auburn, or on Discovery Park and Alki beaches at low tide. Vashon Island's Fern Cove and KVI Beach are good spots for saltwater species.

SEMIPALMATED PLOVERS; both YELLOWLEGS; SOLITARY, WESTERN, and LEAST SANDPIPERS; LONG-BILLED DOWITCHERS; and RED-NECKED PHALAROPES may be counted on in spring and fall. SANDERLINGS, DUNLINS, BLACK TURNSTONES, and SURFBIRDS remain for the winter, Sanderlings being strictly confined to saltwater shores, and Black Turnstones and Surfbirds frequenting the breakwater at Duwamish Head. SEMIPALMATED, BAIRD'S, and PECTORAL SANDPIPERS are most likely as fall migrants (we rarely encounter any but juvenile birds), while WILSON'S PHALAROPES are regular in late spring. Perhaps they will remain to nest in the future.

Less regular but to be expected are BLACK-BELLIED PLOVERS, WHIMBRELS, and SHORT-BILLED DOWITCHERS. Short-billed Dowitchers are partial to saltwater mudflats, of which we have very few. Reports of adult Short-billed Dowitchers in late summer are suspect due to the difficulty of distinguishing them from Long-billed when both are in worn, alternate plumage. Juveniles are more readily distinguished on the basis of their tertial patterns. Absent definitive vocalizations or visual clues, local dowitchers are best presumed to be Long-billed.

Altogether, that adds up to 19 species that appear regularly in the county, and three more that are likely. Not bad, considering how little habitat is available. The other 19 species—for a grand total of 41 species recorded for the county—are casual at best.

RARITIES

AMERICAN GOLDEN-PLOVER. At least three records.
    1986 May 4: Auburn, adult, P. and R. Sullivan, R. Becker.
    1986 September 8: Discovery Park, juvenile, D. Beaudette.
    2008 October 8-10: Auburn, juvenile, G. McWethy, C. Pearson, multiple observers, photos (*WOSNews* 122).

PACIFIC GOLDEN-PLOVER. Four records, plus 10 of indeterminate golden-plovers, 2 of which were reported as Americans.

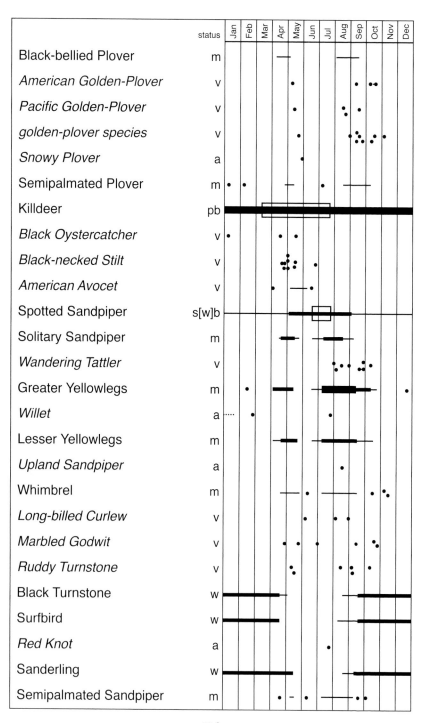

	status	Jan	Feb	Mar	Apr	May	Jun	Jul	Aug	Sep	Oct	Nov	Dec
Black-bellied Plover	m												
American Golden-Plover	v												
Pacific Golden-Plover	v												
golden-plover species	v												
Snowy Plover	a												
Semipalmated Plover	m												
Killdeer	pb												
Black Oystercatcher	v												
Black-necked Stilt	v												
American Avocet	v												
Spotted Sandpiper	s[w]b												
Solitary Sandpiper	m												
Wandering Tattler	v												
Greater Yellowlegs	m												
Willet	a												
Lesser Yellowlegs	m												
Upland Sandpiper	a												
Whimbrel	m												
Long-billed Curlew	v												
Marbled Godwit	v												
Ruddy Turnstone	v												
Black Turnstone	w												
Surfbird	w												
Red Knot	a												
Sanderling	w												
Semipalmated Sandpiper	m												

136

	status	Jan	Feb	Mar	Apr	May	Jun	Jul	Aug	Sep	Oct	Nov	Dec
Western Sandpiper	m[w]				━			━━	━━	━━			
Least Sandpiper	m[w]				━			━━	━━	━			
Baird's Sandpiper	mf				•	••		─					
Pectoral Sandpiper	m				─			─			•		
Sharp-tailed Sandpiper	v									•• •• •			
Rock Sandpiper	v	••	•									• •	• ···
Dunlin	w	━━━	━━	━━				─		━━	━━		
Stilt Sandpiper	v							• •• ••					
Buff-breasted Sandpiper	a								••	•			
Ruff	v								•	•			
Short-billed Dowitcher	mf				•	•		•	•• • •				
Long-billed Dowitcher	m				▭			━━	━━ ━━				
Wilson's Snipe	w[s][b]	━━	━	─	□			━━	━━ ━━				
Wilson's Phalarope	m				─		••	•					
Red-necked Phalarope	m				─			━━					
Red Phalarope	v								•	•• •	• ••		

1984 August 27: West Point, Discovery Park, juvenile, D. Beaudette.

1985 May 11-12: West Point, adult, E. Hunn, multiple observers (*AB* 39.3).

1998 August 21: Auburn, D. Beaudette (*WOSNews* 59).

2004 September 19: Kent, C. Wright (*WOSNews* 97).

Golden-plover species reported as American but uncertain:

1986 September 8: West Point, Discovery Park, D. Beaudette (description indeterminate).

1997 November 2: Auburn (late date suggestive of Pacific), P. and R. Sullivan (*WOSNews* 54).

Unidentified golden-plover species:

1965 October 9: Lake Washington (*AFN* 20:84).

1968 October 13: Montlake Fill, B. and P. Evans.

1970 September 9: Montlake Fill, B. and P. Evans.

1973 September 23: Montlake Fill, B. and P. Evans.

1979 May 6: Montlake Fill, E. Peaslee (*AB* 33.5, *WB* 4:16).

1981 August 29: Auburn, R. Carlson, T. Bock.

1981 September 14: Montlake Fill, juvenile, E. Ratoosh (*WB* 4:16).

2002 May 17: Kent, reported as golden-plover species, R. Orness, J. Flynn (*WOSNews* 82).

SNOWY PLOVER. One record.

2003 May 26: West Point, Discovery Park, M. Brittnacher (*NAB* 57.3, *WOSNews* 88, good details).

BLACK OYSTERCATCHER. Three records.

1981 January 3: West Point and Carkeek Park, Seattle, for the CBC.

1990 April 18: West Point, B. Winkler.

2002 May 18: Point Robinson, Maury Island, E. Swan (Swan 2005:158).

BLACK-NECKED STILT. Seven records.

1988 May 12: Montlake Fill, C. Evans, multiple observers (*AB* 42.5, *WB* 1:13).

1993 April 29: Montlake Fill, 3 birds flew overhead, M. Smith (*ECNW* 35(1):10).

2001 May 13: Redmond, D. DeSilvis (*NAB* 55.3, *WOSNews* 76).

2007 April 29: Kent, C. Wright (*WOSNews* 113).

2008 April 23-25: Auburn, M. Hobbs (*WOSNews* 119).

2009 April 25-29: Kent, G. Oliver, multiple observers (*WOSNews* 125).

2010 June 21-22: Auburn, J. Lemond, R. Bjorklund.

AMERICAN AVOCET. Eleven records.

1974 June 7: Kent, G. McDonald (*AB* 28.5).

1980 May 28: Montlake Fill, P. Mattocks, E. Ratoosh (*WB* 1:13, *WB* 4:16).

1986 May 3: Auburn, 10 birds, T. Bock et al. (*AB* 40.3).

1988 March 31: Seattle, K. Aanerud, D. Beaudette (*AB* 42.5, *WB* 1:13).

1993 May 7-9: Montlake Fill, anon. (*ECNW* 35(1):10).

1998 June 1: Montlake Fill, S. Hoskins (*WOSNews* 57).

2001 May 26: Lake Sammamish, 2 birds, P. Burr (*NAB* 55.3, *WOSNews* 76).

2003 June 17: Llama Lake, H. Flores (*NAB* 57.4, *WOSNews* 90).

2004 May 20: Kent, M. Bartels (*WOSNews* 95).

2007 May 8: Auburn, M. Breece, K. Kemper (*WOSNews* 113).

2008 June 3-8: Auburn, J. LeMons, G. and O. Oliver, photos (*WOSNews* 120).

WANDERING TATTLER. Seven records.

1981 July 28: Discovery Park, D. Hutchinson.

1982 August 1: Discovery Park, D. Beaudette.

1984 August 12: Discovery Park, D. Beaudette.

1984 September 26: Seattle, T. Schooley (*AB* 39.1).

1990 October 7: Lincoln Park, B. Reichert.

1992 September 26-29: West Point, Discovery Park, J. Winkler, B. Vandenbosch.

2002 August 30: KVI Beach, E. Swan (*WOSNews* 85, Swan 2005:161).

WILLET. Three records.

1922 July 23: Seattle, *fide* A. C. Bent, (*U.S. National Museum Bulletin* 146:41).

1950-1951 winter: Seattle, V. Cannon (*AFN* 5.3).

1954 February 22: Shilshole Bay, G. Eddy (*The Murrelet* 37(2):25).

UPLAND SANDPIPER. One record.

1998 August 18: Montlake Fill, T. Aversa (*NAB* 53.3, *WOSNews* 59).

LONG-BILLED CURLEW. Three records.

1856 August 1: Muckleshoot Prairie, G. Suckley (Suckley 1860:246).

1999 June 2: Kent, R. Orness (*WOSNews* 64).

1999 August 31: Cedar River Valley, 3 birds, S. Downes (*WOSNews* 65).

MARBLED GODWIT. Six records.

1972   October 22: West Point, Discovery Park, K. Brunner.

1974   October 15: Newport, Bellevue, J. Beaufort (*AB* 29.1).

1987   September 12: Discovery Park, D. Beaudette.

1993   June 25: Alki Beach, P. Cozens, photo.

1995   April 24: KVI Beach, J. Friar (Swan 2005:160).

2010   May 17: Discovery Park, J. Alexander.

RUDDY TURNSTONE. Six records.

1983   May 15: Discovery Park, E. Hunn (*AB* 37.5).

1983   September 4: Discovery Park, D. Beaudette, D. Paulson.

1984   October 11: Discovery Park, D. Beaudette.

1985   September 2: Discovery Park, D. Beaudette.

1990   May 7: Discovery Park, D. Beaudette.

1993   August 14-15: Discovery Park, 3 birds seen; 1 still there August 28, K. Aanerud, J. Bragg, (*WOSNews* 29).

RED KNOT. One record.

1988   July 26: Discovery Park, K. Aanerud, T. Haas.

SHARP-TAILED SANDPIPER. Six records.

1987   September 3-4: Kent, M. Scuderi, E. Hunn, G. Gerdts (*AB* 42.1).

1987   September 12: Seattle, M. Egger, S. Johnston (*AB* 42.1).

1996   September 29: Montlake Fill, K. Aanerud (*WOSNews* 47, *FN* 51.1), C. McInerny (*WB* 8:20-21).

1996   October 10: Montlake Fill, K. Aanerud (*FN* 51.1), C. McInerny (*WB* 8:20-21).

2004   October 15: Medina, K. Andrich (*WOSNews* 98).

2009   October 3-9: Auburn, 2 birds, C. and B. Pearson, multiple observers, photos (*WOSNews* 128).

ROCK SANDPIPER. Two or three records.

1996   December 13-January 6, 1997: West Seattle, D. Beaudette; at Des Moines February 2, 1997, M. Ellis (*WOSNews* 50).

2007   November 11: Alki Beach, E. Hunn, M. Bartels, M. Hobbs (*WOSNews* 116).

STILT SANDPIPER. Nine records.

1965   July 29: Union Bay, J. Chambless (Krause 21).

1981   August 30-September 8: Montlake Fill, first 1 bird, J. O'Connell, E. Ratoosh (*WB* 4:18), then 2, D. Beaudette.

1988   July 30: Auburn, adult, J. Gatchet, F. Bird (*AB* 43.1).

1989   August 29: Montlake Fill, juvenile, K. Aanerud (*WB* 1:14).

1991   July 22: Montlake Fill, juvenile, W. Thacker (*ECNW* 33(3):10).

1996   August 31-September 1: Montlake Fill, C. McInerny, C. Sidles (*WB* 8:24).

1997   August 17-18: Montlake Fill, C. McInerny, C. Sidles, P. Munno, photo (*WB* 8:24, *WOSNews* 48).

2003   September 4: Kent, M. Breece (*WOSNews* 91).

2010   August 13: Llama Lake, H. Flores, R. Hibpshman, photo, G. Thompson, photo.

BUFF-BREASTED SANDPIPER. Two records.

1940s: Union Bay marsh, stayed eight days (Higman and Larrison 1951:156, *WB* 4:33).

2005   August 31-September 2: Marymoor Park, B. Bell, multiple observers, photos (*WOSNews* 100, 103).

RUFF. Three records.

1995   July 27-28: Kent, adult female, D. Veit, D. Beaudette, multiple observers (*WOSNews* 40, *FN* 49.5).

1995   September 1-2: Seattle, R. Stogsdill, multiple observers (*FN* 50.1, *WOSNews* 41).

1997 September 28: Kent, juvenile female, E. Hunn (*WOSNews* 53).

RED PHALAROPE. Eight records, including a significant incursion of up to 10 birds in December 1995.

1987 August 26: Kent, adult, M. Scuderi (*AB* 42.1).

1995 December 4: Seattle, 4 birds, R. Rowlett, multiple observers (*FN* 50.2).

1995 December 16: Discovery Park, C. McInerny (*WOSNews* 43).

1995 December 19: Fauntleroy/Vashon Ferry, 10 birds, D. Beaudette (Swan 2005:167).

1995 December 20-22: Seattle, 3-5 birds, P. Sullivan, D. Buckley (*FN* 50.2, *WOSNews* 43).

1997 October 14: Vashon Island, 10 birds, D. Beaudette (Swan 2005:167).

1999 December 18: Vashon Island, B. LaBar, D. Beaudette (*NAB* 54.2, *WOSNews* 67, Swan 2005:167).

2002 October 4: Point Robinson, Maury Island, C. Wright (*WOSNews* 86, Swan 2005:167).

2005 December 24: Vashon Island, 2 birds, E. Swan (*WOSNews* 105).

2008 October 7: Discovery Park, E. Hunn.

2009 November 23: Dash Point, H. Feddern (*WOSNews* 128).

GULLS, TERNS, & JAEGERS

G. Eddy surveyed the GLAUCOUS-WINGED GULL breeding population on downtown Seattle rooftops for many years from his office window. He estimated that some 200 pairs nested in the downtown district (as of 1980). H. Gilbert and P. Rose noted 60 pairs nesting at a construction site in the Interbay District on June 16, 2007.

Other gull species are non-breeders, either migrants or winter residents. By late June, CALIFORNIA GULLS start to appear in the county, some in the finely patterned browns and grays of their first summer. By mid-July RING-BILLED, MEW, and BONAPARTE'S GULLS join the Glaucous-wingeds and Californias on the beaches of the Sound.

HEERMANN'S GULLS breed to the south in the Gulf of California then disperse northward in summer, sticking close to the outer beaches. As they drift back south in late summer, a few "take a wrong turn" at Admiralty Inlet and are seen regularly in King County from late July through mid-November. Presumably they regain the ocean by flying overland south of Olympia.

A close inspection of BONAPARTE'S GULL flocks may reveal a small, very dark-mantled gull with dark "goggles," a FRANKLIN'S GULL in juvenile plumage. This species was first recorded in King County by Higman and Larrison at Union Bay landfill in the 1940s (Higman and Larrison 1951:159-161). Bonaparte's flocks may also harbor the very rare LITTLE GULL and greater rarities still. Franklin's and Little Gulls have been very scarce in Puget Sound since the mid-1990s.

HERRING and THAYER'S GULLS return late from their northern breeding areas, and are rarely seen here before mid-October. Thereafter they may be studied most readily at Green Lake's north-end diving platforms, on the roof of the Foster Golf Links clubhouse in Tukwila, or at the Cedar River mouth in Renton. Thayer's was considered but a race of the Herring Gull until 1973, when the two were "split" by the American Ornithologists' Union. Thayer's may yet lose its identity as a species, but presumably as a race of the ICELAND GULL rather than the Herring. Thayer's represents the third step of a progression, from "true" Iceland Gulls through "Kumlien's" Iceland Gulls to Thayer's, each showing increasingly dark pigmentation of mantle, wing tip, leg, and iris, and slight lengthening of bill and leg. Thayer's and Herring Gulls are alike in their pearl-gray mantles and black wing tips, pink legs, and yellow bills with a daub of red under the tip. Herring Gulls are a shade paler than Thayer's, the same shade on the back as Ring-billed Gulls, paler even than Glaucous-winged. Thayer's adult mantle color is closer to Glaucous-winged. Thayer's also differs by its "gentle look," a function of a smaller, rounder head, slighter bill, and darker eye, normally rich yellow with varying amounts of brown flecking. Herring, by contrast, looks "mean," an impression accentuated by its baleful, almost-white yellow eye, like the eye of a coyote. Herring Gulls also have more extensive black on their wing tips, a triangle of black that shows both above and below. Thayer's has restricted black wing tips (dark gray on some individuals) that do not show through to the underside. The whitish underwing thus resembles that of the Glaucous-winged Gull. C. Wright photographed an immature Herring Gull at Renton December 27, 2006, judged to be of the Siberian *vegae* race, the only record of that form for the state (*NAB* 61.2).

Beware of GLAUCOUS-WINGED X WESTERN GULL hybrids. There are usually a few at Green Lake each winter, with perhaps one or two full-blooded WESTERN GULLS as well. These hybrids are frequently misidentified as Herring or Thayer's Gulls. Indeed, they may look just like the picture of the Herring Gull in the field guides, but they are always larger than Herring and heavier-billed, darker on the mantle (darker than Glaucous-winged, which in turn is darker than Herring), with dusky, not black, wing tips, and with dark irises. True Western Gulls are large and heavy-billed also, but darker gray above than California Gulls, with black wing tips. In winter their heads remain immaculately white (adults) while our other large gulls are dusky streaked at that season. Glaucous-winged X Herring Gull hybrids further complicate matters. An adult gull with a Herring Gull's head and Thayer's wing tips may be such a hybrid.

GLAUCOUS GULLS are rare winter visitors, found nearly annually since 1993. They have been noted from late November through March, most often with the large gull flocks at the south end of Lake Washington in Renton. Most are first-winter birds. The first county records include some in May. A subadult was collected by H. Hindshaw on May 12, 1896, at Seattle (Jewett et al. 1953:291), and a first-winter bird lingered at Green Lake from January 7 until mid-May 1982.

CASPIAN TERNS are common in summer and nested on a rooftop on Harbor Island in 2008, though most of the birds we see likely nest in Commencement Bay at Tacoma. At West Point in late summer and fall, the ranks of gulls are joined by COMMON TERNS—now rare—and cruising PARASITIC JAEGERS.

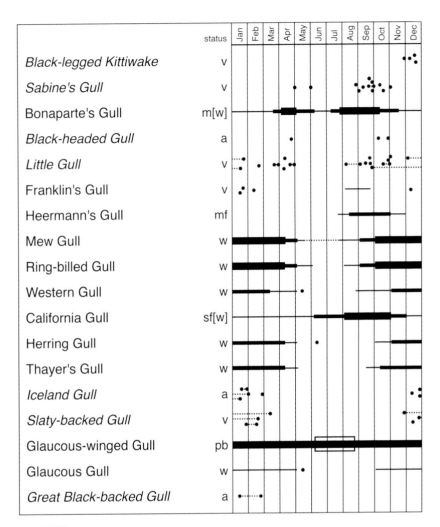

	status	Jan	Feb	Mar	Apr	May	Jun	Jul	Aug	Sep	Oct	Nov	Dec
Black-legged Kittiwake	v												
Sabine's Gull	v												
Bonaparte's Gull	m[w]												
Black-headed Gull	a												
Little Gull	v												
Franklin's Gull	v												
Heermann's Gull	mf												
Mew Gull	w												
Ring-billed Gull	w												
Western Gull	w												
California Gull	sf[w]												
Herring Gull	w												
Thayer's Gull	w												
Iceland Gull	a												
Slaty-backed Gull	v												
Glaucous-winged Gull	pb												
Glaucous Gull	w												
Great Black-backed Gull	a												

RARITIES

BLACK-LEGGED KITTIWAKE. Four records.

> 1981 December 13-14: West Point, Discovery Park, D. Hutchinson, D. Beaudette, multiple observers (*AB* 36.3).
>
> 2006 December 15: West Point, M. Bartels (*WOSNews* 111).
>
> 2007 December 3: Vashon Island, D. Willsie *fide* E. Swan (*WOSNews* 117).
>
> 2009 November 21: Off Dash Point State Park, immature, J. Bragg, T. Geernaert.

SABINE'S GULL. Twelve records.

> 1949 August 29: Seattle, Clark (*AFN* 4.1).
>
> 1966 September 25: Seward Park, Z. Schultz, E. Stopps (*The Murrelet* 48(1):19, *AFN* 21.1).
>
> 1981 October 31: West Point, Discovery Park, immature, D. Hutchinson.
>
> 1983 August 24: Seattle, adult, D. Hutchinson.

1991 September 7: Point Robinson, Maury Island, juvenile, R. Siegrist, D. Willsie (Swan 2005:173, *ECNW* 33(3):10).

1997 October 14: Fauntleroy/Vashon/Southworth Ferry, juvenile, D. Beaudette (Swan 2005:173).

1998 September 25: West Point, S. Atkinson (*WOSNews* 59).

2003 September 21-30: Dash Point, C. Wright, P. and R. Sullivan (*WOSNews* 91).

2004 September 21: North of Vashon Island, B. Waggoner.

2006 May 28: Off Richmond Beach, M. Dufort.

2008 October 7: Discovery Park, adult, E. Hunn (*WOSNews* 122).

2009 April 25: Bremerton Ferry, off Seattle, G. and O. Oliver.

BLACK-HEADED GULL. Three records.

1987 October 5: Green Lake, adult, E. and N. Hunn (*AB* 42.1, 42.2).

1994 October 27: Off Seattle, adult, R. Rogers, (*FN* 49.1, *WOSNews* 35, 61, *ECNW* 36(5):10).

1998 April 19: Montlake Fill, S. MacKay, C. Sidles (*WOSNews* 57).

LITTLE GULL. Fourteen records. Just two since 1991.

1975 November 15: Woodland Park, E. Hunn, multiple observers (*AB* 30.1).

1976 November 30: West Point, Discovery Park, D. Paulson, multiple observers (*AB* 31.2).

1981 March 18-24: Green Lake, E. Hunn, multiple observers (*AB* 35.5).

1981 October 16-30: Off Seattle, D. Hutchinson, T. Schooley, E. Peaslee (*AB* 36.2).

1982 February 14-19: West Point, D. Hutchinson, T. Schooley, multiple observers (*AB* 36.3).

1982 April 3: Green Lake, E. Hunn (*AB* 36.5).

1982 September 26 through at least January 10, 1983: Green Lake and West Point, adult, E. Hunn, D. Beaudette, B. Doe, multiple observers (*AB* 37.2, 37.3).

1985 December 3: Seattle, J. Zook, and 1986 January 19, B. Pendleton (*AB* 40.2).

1986 April 18-22: West Point, adult, D. Beaudette, M. Carmody (*AB* 40.3), perhaps the same bird noted above.

1986 August 3 to September 1: West Point, adult, R. Thorne, D. Beaudette (*AB* 40.5).

1987 October 31: West Point, adult, D. Beaudette, T. Bock (*AB* 42.1).

1988 September 10: Seattle, D. Herder (*AB* 43.1).

1990 April 5: Green Lake, adult, R. Muscat (*AB* 44.3).

	status	Jan	Feb	Mar	Apr	May	Jun	Jul	Aug	Sep	Oct	Nov	Dec
Caspian Tern	s[b]												
Black Tern	m												
Common Tern	mf												
Arctic Tern	a												
Forster's Tern	v												
Elegant Tern	a												
Pomarine Jaeger	v												
Parasitic Jaeger	mf												
Long-tailed Jaeger	v												

1990 September 22 and 25: Seattle, adult, E. Hunn, I. Ulsh (*AB* 45.2).

1991 September 21: West Point, subadult, R. Thorne (*AB* 46.2, *ECNW* 33(3):10).

1997 October 26: Off Seattle, adult, S. Downes (*FN* 52.1).

ICELAND GULL. One record, likely the same individual returning each winter 2004-2008.

2004 December 8: Renton, adult, D. Duffy, photo; J. Flynn, S. Pink (*NAB* 59.2, *WOSNews* 99).

2006 January 12: Kent and Renton, white-winged adult, possibly *L. g. glaucoides*; nicknamed "Bob," multiple observers, many photos but identity in dispute; also seen December 2006-January 2007, January 2008, and January 2009 (*WOSNews* 105, 117).

SLATY-BACKED GULL. Five records.

2004 January 20 to February 4: Renton, adult, M. and M.L. Denny, photo (*NAB* 58.2, *WOSNews* 93).

2004 December 11: Renton, first winter, K. Aanerud, S. Mlodinow, J. Barry, photo (*NAB* 59.2, *WOSNews* 99).

2005 November 24-March 1, 2006: Renton, adult, multiple observers, photos (*WOSNews* 105).

2006 December 25-February 8, 2007: Renton, multiple observers, photos (*WOSNews* 111).

2007 February 17: Renton, different bird, C. Wright (*WOSNews* 111).

GREAT BLACK-BACKED GULL. One record.

2004 January 12-February 16: Renton, first or second winter, E. Hunn, multiple observers, photos (*NAB* 58.2, *WOSNews* 93).

BLACK TERN. Sixteen records.

1975 May 28: Montlake Fill, 2 birds, Seattle, K. Aanerud (*WB* 1:15).

1976 late May: Montlake Fill, K. Aanerud (*WB* 1:15).

1977 early June: Montlake Fill, K. Aanerud (*WB* 1:15).

1979 September 16: Discovery Park, D. Paulson.

1982 May 24: Kent, P. Cozens (*AB* 36.5).

1983 August 23: Seattle, D. Hutchinson (*AB* 38.2).

1987 May 24-June 6: Auburn, adult, D. Beaudette (*AB* 41.3, 41.5).

1995 May 23: Kent, H. Jennings (*WOSNews* 39, *ECNW* 36(9):10).

1995 June 3: Sikes Lake, Carnation, S. Dang (*ECNW* 36(9):10).

1995 August 17-27: Cedar River, Renton, 3 birds, J. Flynn (*FN* 50.1, *WOSNews* 41).

1997 May 10: 1 seen at Kent, *fide* T. Bock; 3 at Sykes Lake, Carnation, *fide* T. Bock (*WOSNews* 51).

1998 May 18: Renton, C. Haynie (*FN* 52.3, *WOSNews* 57).

2000 May 14: Montlake Fill, C. Sidles.

2004 May 18-22: Kent, L. Schwitters, C. Wright (*NAB* 58.3, *WOSNews* 95).

2004 August 25-27: Lake Sammamish, M. Hobbs, multiple observers (*WOSNews* 97).

ARCTIC TERN. Three records.

1946 September 29: West Point, Discovery Park, G. Eddy (*The Murrelet* 27(1):53).

1991 September 8: West Point, second-summer bird, S. Atkinson (*ECNW* 33(3):10).

2008 August 27: KVI Beach, first-summer bird, E. Hunn (*WOSNews* 121).

FORSTER'S TERN. Five records.

1979 August 11 and September 18-23: Off Shilshole Bay, E. Hunn, B. Reichert, A. Richards, W. Beecher (*AB* 34:2).

1992 August 23: Off Magnuson Park, D. Paulson (*AB* 47.1).

1998 September 28: Fauntleroy, Seattle, D. Beaudette (*NAB* 53.1, *WOSNews* 59).

2006 August 29: South Beach, Discovery Park, M. Breece, photo (*WOSNews* 109).

2008 August 22: Log Boom Park, 2 adults, E. Hunn, multiple observers (*WOSNews* 121).

ELEGANT TERN. One record.

1992   September 11: Off West Point, Discovery Park, 2 birds, K. Aanerud; same 2 birds off Fauntleroy, anon. (*AB* 47.1, *WOSNews* 21).

POMARINE JAEGER. Four records.

1979   October 1: Off Shilshole Bay, B. Reichert.

1998   September 9: Off Vashon Island, D. Beaudette (*WOSNews* 59, Swan 2005:168).

2006   August 25: West Point, Discovery Park, 3 adults, M. Bartels; and 1 subadult, E. and N. Hunn (*WOSNews* 109).

LONG-TAILED JAEGER. Four records.

1977   October 7-8: West Point, Discovery Park, adult, D. Hutchinson, E. Spragg et al. (*AB* 32:2).

1990   August 25: West Point, immature, M. Mallas.

1990   August 28: Leschi, Seattle, D. Hutchinson.

2010   September 21: Mercer Island, juvenile, dropped by Bald Eagle, specimen to the Slater Museum, J. Roan.

ALCIDS

PIGEON GUILLEMOTS nest under the fringe of the Magnolia bluffs and are also reported to nest under downtown piers. A few MARBLED MURRELETS are present all year in the Sound off Seattle and no doubt nest somewhere in the county, as a just-fledged bird with egg tooth intact was found on July 24, 1971, in North Rosedale near Gig Harbor in Pierce County (Colby 1972:49). A nest found in a northern California forest was perched high in a tree, and Washington Department of Fish & Wildlife forest surveys report murrelets vocalizing in summer over patches of old growth in twelve sections west of the Cascade Crest, where they are presumed to nest. The species is recorded as a probable nester in three Breeding Bird Atlas quadrangles. RHINOCEROS AUKLETS are also year-round residents but breed no closer than Protection Island, west of Port Townsend in Jefferson County, where some 17,000 pairs nest. They range widely for food. Winter brings COMMON MURRES and, for a brief span from mid-October to early December, a variable number of ANCIENT MURRLETS. These little devils are hard to find, but you can see them with the aid of a boat or a good spotting scope during November, most readily off West Point. This species is likely to arrive as a flock flying in formation, while Marbled Murrelets characteristically associate in pairs.

RARITIES

CASSIN'S AUKLET. Six records. (Note that Seattle CBC reports of this species 1953-1973 are now thought to have been Rhinoceros Auklets.)

1978   October 10: Lincoln Park, K. Brunner (*SAN* 19(3):3).

1982   March 9: Shilshole Bay, found dead March 25, E. Smirnov, M. Egger.

1988   January 16: West Point, Discovery Park, D. DeSilvis (*AB* 42.2).

1990   August: Off KVI Beach, R. Sanders (Swan 2005:177).

1993   October 12: Off Alki Point, R. Rogers (*AB* 48.1, *WOSNews* 29, *ECNW* 35(6):12).

1998   September 19: Vashon Island, D. Beaudette (*NAB* 53.1, *WOSNews* 59, Swan 2005:177).

HORNED PUFFIN. Two records.

2001   May 29: West Point, Discovery Park, 6 adults, R. Hopper (*WB* 9:46).

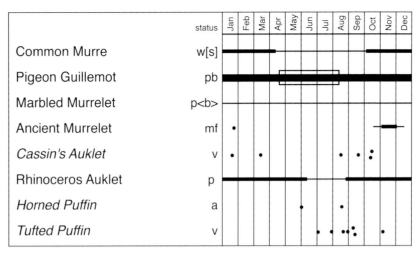

	status	Jan	Feb	Mar	Apr	May	Jun	Jul	Aug	Sep	Oct	Nov	Dec
Common Murre	w[s]	▬▬▬									▬▬▬		
Pigeon Guillemot	pb	▬▬▬			▭					▬▬▬			
Marbled Murrelet	p<b>												
Ancient Murrelet	mf	•									▬▬		
Cassin's Auklet	v	•		•			•	•	••				
Rhinoceros Auklet	p	▬▬▬							▬▬▬				
Horned Puffin	a					•	•						
Tufted Puffin	v						•	•••	•	•			

2006 August 12: West Point, adult, D. Hutchinson, P. Rose, et al. (*WOSNews* 109).

TUFTED PUFFIN. Seven records, just three since 1931.

- 1905 June 28: West Point, Discovery Park.
- 1918 September 6: Seattle, J. Munro, specimen to University of California at Berkeley.
- 1925 July 25: Quartermaster Harbor, E. Kitchin (*The Murrelet* 6(3):64).
- 1931 November 2: Seattle, F. Cook (Jewett et al. 1953:331).
- 1990 September 3: West Point, D. Beaudette, D. Buckley (*ECNW* 32(4):10).
- 2006 August 16: West Point, K. Dieffenbach (*WOSNews* 109).
- 2006 August 26: West Point, C. Cox (*WOSNews* 109).

PIGEONS, DOVES, & CUCKOOS

ROCK PIGEONS hang out at busy intersections, in the industrial underbelly of Seattle south of downtown, in farmlands, and even at such beaches as Alki. They show a variety of plumage patterns, though most birds appear to retain a plumage close to their "natural" colors.

Our native BAND-TAILED PIGEONS are somewhat larger and longer-tailed than the introduced Rock Pigeons and may be distinguished in flight overhead by their dark underwings and longer tails. In spring, watch for their odd fluttering display flight, and listen for their resonant, booming call notes. They nest widely throughout King County and winter locally in substantial numbers, as on the University of Washington upper campus and in the Arboretum, as well as in favored residential areas such as Lake Forest Park. Band-taileds shot around Puget Sound have been found with chinquapin nuts in their stomachs, indicative of a long and speedy flight north from Oregon. Might they likewise transport acorns? Our isolated Garry Oaks might thus be credited to the Band-tailed Freight Line.

MOURNING DOVES were quite common at one time (early 1940s), with numbers up to 100 and nests near Auburn (Slipp 1941:59-60). Now only occasional individuals or small groups are seen in more open country at scattered seasons. A flock of 50 reported near Carnation on the East Lake Washington CBC in 2006 was exceptional. One carrying food or nesting material over the Renton marshes on July 5, 1981, and a pair seen near Enumclaw seen on June 5, 1982, indicate a small nesting population. Breeding Bird Atlas surveys confirmed nesting in four quadrangles near Auburn.

RARITIES

EURASIAN COLLARED-DOVE. Fifteen records. This recent immigrant should be well established in the not-too-distant future.

2005 June 5-7: Sammamish, F. Trousdale, *fide* M. Lambert, photo (*WOSNews* 102).

2008 April 11: Marymoor Park, K. Kemper, multiple observers.

2008 April 18: Ballard, S. Hoskin.

2008 May 7: Shoreline, D. Norman.

2008 May 10: Montlake Fill, C. Sidles.

2009 April 18-20: Montlake Fill, G. and O. Oliver, C. Sidles

2009 June 19: North Bend, A. Richards.

2009 September 28: Near Seatac, R. Parsons.

2009 October 18-29: West of Enumclaw, up to 32 birds, M. Bartels, multiple observers (*WOSNews* 128).

2009 November 27: North Bend, 2 birds, P. Fahey.

2009 December 18 and thereafter: Pacific, up to 10 birds, B. Meilleur, multiple observers (*WOSNews* 129).

2010 April 1: Magnuson Park, B. Boyington.

2010 April 22: Vashon Island, E. Swan.

2010 July 7: Near Duvall, calling, E. Hunn.

2010 September 16: North Bend, 2 birds, K. Grant.

WHITE-WINGED DOVE. One record.

1999 May 19: Near Redmond, J. Meyer (*NAB* 53.3).

YELLOW-BILLED CUCKOO. This cuckoo once nested as far north as Vancouver, B.C. D. Brown recorded four nests in King County (Brown 1923:17): June 19 and 24, 1923; July 4, 1902; and July 18, 1909. T. Burleigh noted the cuckoo's arrival on Lake Washington on June 8, 1920, and observed that this species was "fairly plentiful in the scattered thick swampy woods about Lake Washington, but scarce elsewhere" (Burleigh 1929:512). There were no subsequent reports until

	status	Jan	Feb	Mar	Apr	May	Jun	Jul	Aug	Sep	Oct	Nov	Dec
Rock Pigeon	pbi												
Band-tailed Pigeon	pb												
Eurasian Collared-Dove	p[b]i												
White-winged Dove	a					•							
Mourning Dove	pb												
Yellow-billed Cuckoo	a/bx												

July 10, 1974, when G. Durr found one dead in Beaux Arts Village (specimen to the Burke Museum, *SAN* 15(1):6). We also have a bizarre report of a Peregrine Falcon feeding a Yellow-billed Cuckoo to its young in mid-June 1997. The images were caught by the remote video camera monitoring a downtown Seattle Peregrine Falcon's nest (D. Paulson)! The demise of this species in the Pacific Northwest seems most likely due to habitat destruction in the core of its range in California. A calling bird heard in July 1979 at Sultan in Snohomish County raised hopes that a few pairs may still be found nesting in similar habitats in King County, such as the riparian growth along the Snoqualmie River.

OWLS & NIGHTHAWKS

GREAT HORNED OWLS used to be rather common in the county but have recently become difficult to find. Walter English reported that they nested in Woodland Park in 1979. More recently, likely nesting Great Horneds have been reported at Marymoor Park, in Sammamish, at Eagle Landing Park in Burien, and along the Soos Creek Trail. Great Horned Owl pellets collected by Lambert in several Seattle city parks contained mainly remains of Norway and Black Rats plus a crow or two, proving the owls' highly beneficial role (Lambert 1981:2-5).

BARN OWLS commonly nest in lowland King County, including Seattle proper. W. English reported them nesting on Harbor Island in 1979. More recent Barn Owl breeding records come from nest boxes near the Green River Natural Resources Area, at Magnuson Park, and at Marymoor Park, where they are seen regularly. WESTERN SCREECH-OWLS were common permanent residents of Seward and Schmitz Parks until the 1980s but have disappeared from Seward Park and are just hanging on at a few favored West Seattle sites. SHORT-EARED OWLS, a species convergent on the harrier niche, have nested just twice in the county, at Sand Point. In 1977 the nest was vandalized. In 1978 the young were successfully fledged, but there have been no subsequent nesting attempts at Sand Point and none documented elsewhere in the county. A few Short-eared Owls winter at the Green River Natural Resources Area and may appear from time to time in winter at Montlake Fill and Marymoor Park. Western Washington's first BARRED OWL was a road kill picked up at Skykomish in December 1973 (Mattocks, Hunn, and Wahl 1976:15), another milepost in this species's dramatic westward expansion (Reichard 1974:138-140). A Barred Owl seen at Discovery Park on May 30, 1981, acted suspiciously like a juvenile (J. Wingfield and M. Ramenofsky), and an adult with downy young was reported there in late June 1982, the first confirmed breeding record for King County. Today Barred Owls are our most common owl, found throughout the county.

Often in late fall, local newspapers feature photos of a SNOWY OWL balanced on some suburban TV antenna, perched on a church steeple, or peering down from the roof of a public building. In flight years, such as 1973-1974 and 2005-2006, Snowy Owls may arrive as early as mid-November. During the winter of 1973-1974 one or two were fixtures at Montlake Fill, perched on the roof of the stadium or basketball pavilion or cruising the marsh for lame ducks.

Three owl species are denizens of the mountain forests: the NORTHERN PYG-MY-, SPOTTED, and NORTHERN SAW-WHET OWLS. Of these, only the Saw-whet is ever common in the low country. Vashon Island may support a substantial winter population; J. Van Os, a resident of Vashon, has had as many as eight Saw-whets calling at once in his backyard. However, they keep quiet much of the winter, breaking into "song"—a monotonous, night-long piping—in March and April, provoking dismayed inquiries from the public. In spring most depart for the north or the mountain forests, where they maintain a discrete silence until challenged by whistled imitations in fall. Adults with young were found in West Seattle in late July 1983 (*AB* 37.6) and on the lower slopes of Granite Mountain on July 12, 1986 (*AB* 40.5). In late September in recent years, one has responded at the meadow edge at the far end of FSR-70 below Naches Pass, and individuals have been discovered roosting in dense cedars in Discovery Park in winter.

Of all owls occurring in King County, the SPOTTED OWL has the greatest aura of mystery. During the 1970s, the U.S. Forest Service's Spotted Owl surveys reported calling birds at a number of King County locations. In 1980 there were reports of Spotted Owls a half-mile up Surprise Creek Trail east of Skykomish and up the Annette Lake trail below Snoqualmie Pass. A nest was reported in the Cedar River watershed in 1981. Two more recent reports are of one seen by K. Aanerud near the summit of McClellan Butte during a Breeding Bird Atlas survey in 1994, and a pair on territory east of Lake Hancock in 2004. Spotted Owls are hanging on by a thread in King County.

The COMMON NIGHTHAWK might well join the Spotted Owl on a King County endangered species list. Rathbun found it an "abundant summer resident" (Rathbun 1902:135). Nighthawks used to nest commonly on downtown Seattle roofs (*AFN* 11.4, 21.5). A bird on her nest at a downtown Seattle construction site in July 1981 made the TV news. However, they are now decidedly scarce in Seattle and not common anywhere else in the county. Recent reports of nesting Common Nighthawks are from clear-cuts in the foothills and the Cascades. Nighthawks are one of the last spring migrants to arrive, rarely putting in an appearance before early June. One seen and heard in Federal Way on February 15, 1974, by B. Bernson might have overwintered in a dormant state.

RARITIES

FLAMMULATED OWL. One record.
  1980 October 2: Mercer Island, D. Doe (*AB* 35.2).

BURROWING OWL. Four records.
  1978 February 19-26: Magnuson Park, P. Moore, E. Spragg (*AB* 32.3).
  1994 March 23: Downtown Seattle, *fide* G. Adams (*WOSNews* 31).
  2008 April 10: Marymoor Park, B. Bell, M. Hobbs, multiple observers (*WOSNews* 119).
  2010 March 17-21: Renton, B. and P. Webster, multiple observers, photos.

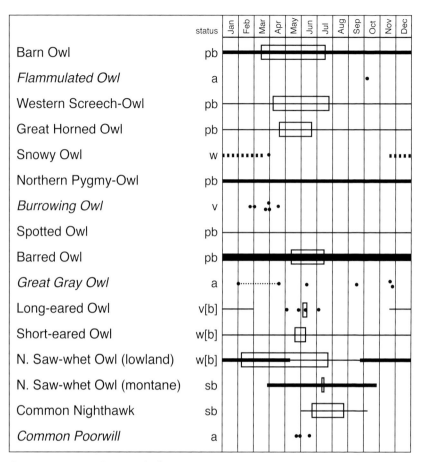

GREAT GRAY OWL. Five records, three since 1899.

    1897 November 19: Seattle, specimen (*fide* Washington Bird Records Committee in *WOSNews* 40, not 1899, as reported in Rathbun 1927:30).

    1899 November 21: Five miles south of Seattle (Rathbun 1927:30).

    1980 June 6: Near Chester Morse Lake, C. Arrendondo (WDFW).

    1987 September 13: Tacoma Pass, J. Ebel, heard calling (WDFW).

    1997 January 28-April 6: Bridle Trails State Park, D. and S. Stark, H. Opperman, multiple observers (*FN* 51.3, *WOSNews* 50, 51).

LONG-EARED OWL. Sixteen records, too many to list individually. Mostly mid-November through mid-February; three spring records. The following two records are of particular note:

    2000 November 24-November 18, 2001: Discovery Park, adults eventually seen with 3 young, P. Rose, K. Slettebak, multiple observers (*WOSNews* 74, 75, 76, 78, 80).

    2009 September 2: Green-Greenwater River divide, 7 seen at dusk foraging over subalpine meadows, E. Hunn (*WOSNews* 127), a seasonal movement noted elsewhere at higher elevations in Washington.

COMMON POORWILL. Two records.

    1964 June 19: Near Enumclaw, found dead, S. Johnson (*AFN* 18:5).

    2006 May 20, 25: Montlake Fill, A. Sedgley, L. Kittleson, photo (*WOSNews* 107).

Swifts & Hummingbirds

BLACK SWIFTS guard the secret of their nesting sites almost as well as do Marbled Murrelets. Rathbun suspected they nested on Mt. Si and probably also on Huckleberry Mountain in southeastern King County, but despite a lifelong search, he failed to find a nest (Jewett et al. 1953:381). Because Black Swifts return to the nest—most often placed in a crevice behind a waterfall—only at dusk, leaving at dawn to forage at great distances, the discovery of a nest would be a matter of great good fortune or exceptional dedication. L. Schwitters is our most devoted Black Swift searcher. During surveys of likely nest sites 2003-2007 he observed Black Swifts fly into Franklin and Keekwulee Falls just west of Snoqualmie Pass. VAUX'S SWIFTS typically nest in dead snags but have been known to use chimneys, as do their eastern cousins, the Chimney Swifts. A pair of Vaux's nested in a Seattle chimney July 8, 1924 (Jewett et al. 1953:382), and presumptive nesting birds have been reported recently in northeast Seattle chimneys. During fall migration at Selleck (northeast of Kangley) and in Monroe (just north of the King County line), thousands come to roost at dusk in tall chimneys. Peak numbers are noted in mid-September, with stragglers noted through mid-October.

ANNA'S HUMMINGBIRDS were first recorded in Washington on November 30, 1964, at a Seattle feeder (*AFN* 19.3). Their numbers have increased steadily since then, with nesting in King County first documented April 3, 1977, in G. Eddy's yard near Discovery Park (*AB* 32.5). This dramatic range extension is part of a larger expansion pattern of Anna's north and east from its California base (Zimmerman 1973: 827-835). This expansion seems heavily dependent on ornamental plantings and hummingbird feeding stations, as Anna's rarely have been noted outside of urban contexts in Washington. The first "wild" hummingbirds of spring here are the RUFOUS HUMMERS of March. They seek out the early blooming Salmonberry and get by flycatching in the absence of nectar. By mid-July, the adult males have departed and the less-than-definitively plumaged females and young are all you see. Rufous Hummingbirds are rare in winter. Males with green backs seen occasionally in spring are likely aberrant Rufous or Rufous x Allen's hybrids (Hunn and Gerdts 1994). CALLIOPE HUMMINGBIRDS turn up with some regularity in spring at urban and suburban feeders, and in summer at the Cascade Crest. They may breed rarely near Naches Pass.

RARITIES

BLACK-CHINNED HUMMINGBIRD. Four records.

1994 June 12: Cedar River watershed, female or immature, E. Hunn.
1998 July 27: Near Stampede Pass, female or immature, D. Beaudette.
2007 June 2: Kelly Butte, female or immature, E. Hunn (*WOSNews* 114).
2009 July 17: Near Windy Gap, E. Hunn, multiple observers.

COSTA'S HUMMINGBIRD. Three records.

2000 April 28 to at least May 10: Richmond Beach, adult male, D. Norman, multiple observers (*WOSNews* 70).

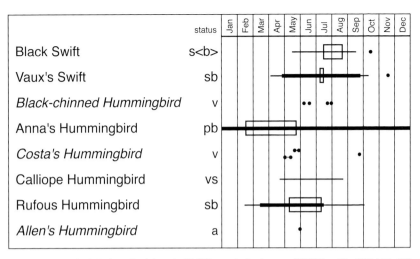

	status	Jan	Feb	Mar	Apr	May	Jun	Jul	Aug	Sep	Oct	Nov	Dec
Black Swift	s\<b\>												
Vaux's Swift	sb												
Black-chinned Hummingbird	v												
Anna's Hummingbird	pb												
Costa's Hummingbird	v												
Calliope Hummingbird	vs												
Rufous Hummingbird	sb												
Allen's Hummingbird	a												

2002   May 16-24: Redmond, adult male, M. Wile, multiple observers (*WOSNews* 82, *NAB* 56.3, *WB* 9:46).

2004   September 20: Fern Cove, Vashon Island, adult male, K. and R. Sanders (Swan 2005:188).

ALLEN'S HUMMINGBIRD. One old record.

1894   May 27: Seattle, male collected by S. Rathbun, specimen at the Burke Museum, verified by author (Rathbun 1927:31; Jewett et al. 1953: 388).

KINGFISHERS & WOODPECKERS

BELTED KINGFISHERS are common year-round in appropriate habitat, although they are somewhat more numerous in winter. Their rattling calls advertise their presence. They are most often spotted perched on a branch overlooking water, scanning for fish. For nesting, they require dirt banks on the shores of rivers, lakes, or Puget Sound.

It came as a surprise to me to learn that LEWIS'S WOODPECKERS were "a moderately common summer resident" in the Seattle area as of 1902, with a "partiality for the burned-over tracts where some dead timber remains standing...and appears to be quite generally...distributed" (Rathbun 1902:135). They were considered an uncommon breeder as late as the mid-1940s (Larrison 1947:65), but since 1956 have been recorded less than annually, with the majority of reports occurring between late August and mid-October. Apparently the burns and snags needed for nesting are much less in evidence now than 70 years ago. However, Lewis's Woodpeckers seem to be in decline over much of their range, so their demise in King County might be an early sign of more fundamental difficulties.

The intermontane form of the Yellow-bellied Sapsucker species complex, the RED-NAPED SAPSUCKER, is most often reported in the lowlands in May, coincident with its return to nesting areas east of the Cascades. Though the Red-naped Sapsucker is now considered a species distinct from the Red-breasted Sapsucker of the west side of the Cascade Crest, occasional hybridization occurs. A pair of sap-suckers I found nesting at a boggy meadow in the Commonwealth Creek Basin on June 13, 1981, included a male Red-naped and (presumably) a female Red-breast-ed. This location happens to be virtually on the crest, which is the usual boundary of the breeding ranges of these two forms. Recent field work near the Cascade Crest suggests that both pure Red-naped pairs and mixed pairs of Red-naped and Red-breasted are to be expected between Naches and Green Passes.

RED-BREASTED SAPSUCKERS are generally scarce in lowland Puget Sound in winter, as their spotty CBC record attests. However, following an unusually heavy winter snowfall in December 1978, 25 were counted on the Seattle CBC. They vanished soon after. Perhaps they normally winter in forested areas little fre-quented by birders, unless they are driven out by hard weather. In summer the Red-breasted Sapsucker is locally common, most often in foothill areas such as Flaming Geyser and Federation Forest State Parks and along the Snoqualmie Valley Trail between Duvall and Fall City.

HAIRY and DOWNY WOODPECKERS are common and widespread. Hairy Woodpeckers tend to favor coniferous forests and avoid urban habitats. Downy Woodpeckers prefer deciduous woodland, particularly willows and cottonwoods along riparian corridors. When seen side-by-side, the size contrast between these two woodpeckers is dramatic. Lone individuals are less easy to identify. It is best to focus on the bill, which is notably diminutive in the Downy, longer and heavier in the Hairy. The outer tail feathers are usually clean white in Hairies but have some black bars in Downies. Subspecies of both tend to be darker in west-side breeding populations. Occasional individuals show sharply contrasting black and white pat-terning; these may be strays from the east slope of the Cascades.

Our two "three-toed woodpeckers" have two toes pointing forward and one to the rear, unlike most woodpeckers, which have four toes—two forward, two back. The AMERICAN THREE-TOED and BLACK-BACKED WOODPECKERS are rare, high-mountain forest species. They favor dry, mature forests of pine, fir, and spruce largely absent from the wet side of the Cascades. In recent years, nesting pairs of both species have been located near Naches Pass, particularly in the old-growth Pa-cific Silver Fir forest that guards Government Meadow. I believe they are full-time residents here, but they can be so quiet as to avoid detection.

NORTHERN FLICKERS are common, vocal, and widespread in King County. Most Northern Flickers are "Red-shafted," though, particularly in winter, "Yellow-shafted" individuals and intergrades exhibiting a medley of features are not partic-ularly unusual. These intergrades may show virtually any combination of "Yellow-shafted" characteristics, such as red napes, black moustaches on one side or the other or both, and orange to yellow wing- and tail-feather shafts. Loose flocks of flickers may be noted in migration, and significant numbers occasionally forage together on wet lawns almost like robins, hardly what one expects of a woodpecker.

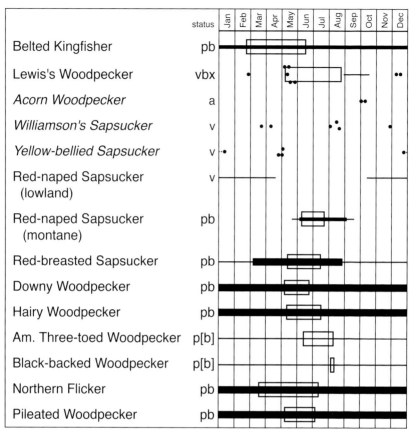

	status	Jan	Feb	Mar	Apr	May	Jun	Jul	Aug	Sep	Oct	Nov	Dec
Belted Kingfisher	pb												
Lewis's Woodpecker	vbx												
Acorn Woodpecker	a												
Williamson's Sapsucker	v												
Yellow-bellied Sapsucker	v												
Red-naped Sapsucker (lowland)	v												
Red-naped Sapsucker (montane)	pb												
Red-breasted Sapsucker	pb												
Downy Woodpecker	pb												
Hairy Woodpecker	pb												
Am. Three-toed Woodpecker	p[b]												
Black-backed Woodpecker	p[b]												
Northern Flicker	pb												
Pileated Woodpecker	pb												

PILEATED WOODPECKERS—the inspiration for the Woody Woodpecker of cartoon fame—are vocal, crow-sized birds that remain common and widespread, from city parks to high mountain forests. They can be almost shocking when encountered at close range, as they are often quite tame when engaged in stalking bark beetle larvae. Their cackles are vaguely flicker-like, but typically more halting and "crazed." Deep, rectangular excavations in rotten tree trunks are evidence of their presence.

RARITIES

ACORN WOODPECKER. One record.

2010 September 30-October 3: Magnuson Park, Seattle, K. Aanerud, multiple observers.

WILLIAMSON'S SAPSUCKER. Six records.

1981 March 15: Phinney Ridge, Seattle, male, found dead, specimen to the University of Washington, P. Negri.

1981 April 5: Bellevue, female, M. Janeke.

1985 July 31: Naches Pass, male, E. Hunn, P. Mattocks (*AB* 39.5).

2007 August 12: Near Naches Pass, immature female, M. Bartels, M. Mathis, T. Mansfield (*WOSNews* 115).

2008 August 17: Near Fall City, male, R. Conway.

2009 November 25: Northwest of Carnation, male, M. Wile (*WOSNews* 128).

YELLOW-BELLIED SAPSUCKER. Three records.

1993 April 30: Hamlin Park, Seattle, male, D. Beaudette (*ECNW* 35(1):10).

2001 December 30-January 5, 2002: Auburn, juvenile, D. Swayne, multiple observers (*NAB* 56.2, *WOSNews* 81, *WB* 9:47).

2007 April 22-29: Shoreline, C. and W. Turner, multiple observers, photos (*WOSNews* 112).

Tyrant Flycatchers

WESTERN WOOD-PEWEES and OLIVE-SIDED FLYCATCHERS normally arrive about the tenth of May. One wood-pewee reported on April 15, 1968, in Seattle (*AFN* 22.4) and a series of precocious Olive-sided Flycatchers, (February 24, 1977; March 1, 1980; March 5 to April 5,1976; and April 13, 1974) may have been birds inspired by some hot spells in early spring further south. However, reports based solely on the Olive-sided's "quick-three-beers" call are suspect, since starlings are capable of uncanny Olive-sided imitations. Olive-sided Flycatchers are occasionally noted in Seattle suburbs but generally keep to mountain forests. Western Wood-Pewees seem to favor tall riparian woodland. Look for them in spring and summer, especially along the Snoqualmie Valley Trail between Carnation and Duvall, at Marymoor Park, or along the Soos Creek Trail.

Our three breeding EMPIDONAX flycatchers normally arrive in order: first PACIFIC-SLOPE FLYCATCHERS in mid-April, then HAMMOND'S by late April, with WILLOW FLYCATCHERS following—after a respectable pause—after the middle of May. Tolt-MacDonald Park near Carnation hosts all three. Hammond's is found there in the company of Pacific-slope Flycatchers, under a towering cottonwood canopy on the Snoqualmie River floodplain. All three species also nest in Discovery Park, though Hammond's is more typically found—at times in abundance—in mountain forests above 2500 feet. The Pacific-slope Flycatcher accompanies Hammond's to above 4000 feet. The Willow Flycatcher is partial to low-elevation marsh and brushland, though individuals may be noted "fitz-bewing" from willow thickets in the meadows just below Naches Pass at nearly 5000 feet. A Pacific-slope Flycatcher reported on October 30, 1955, in Bellevue (*AFN* 10.1) is one of very few Empidonax records from the county after September, but see the bizarre January record of a LEAST FLYCATCHER from Kent in 2005 listed among the rarities below.

There are at least 23 King County records of DUSKY FLYCATCHERS. The great majority of them are during spring migration, with 14 May records, one in late April, and two in early June. I observed one on Foster Island on May 14, 1974, that gave a distinctive, mournful, rising "de-hic" call (McCaskie and De-Benedictus 1966:43). The June records, plus four in July and one in early August, are from foothill and montane sites and likely represent nesting birds. This species is common at the forest edge on the dry eastern slopes of the Cascades and Rocky

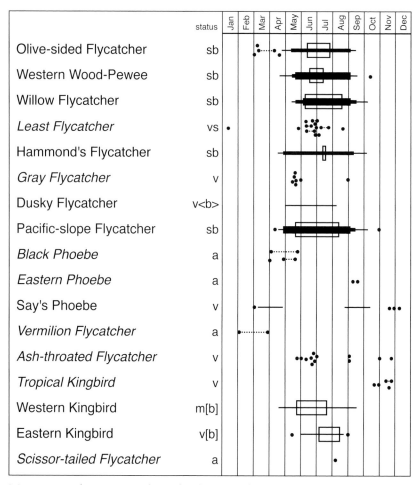

	status	Jan	Feb	Mar	Apr	May	Jun	Jul	Aug	Sep	Oct	Nov	Dec
Olive-sided Flycatcher	sb												
Western Wood-Pewee	sb												
Willow Flycatcher	sb												
Least Flycatcher	vs												
Hammond's Flycatcher	sb												
Gray Flycatcher	v												
Dusky Flycatcher	v<b>												
Pacific-slope Flycatcher	sb												
Black Phoebe	a												
Eastern Phoebe	a												
Say's Phoebe	v												
Vermilion Flycatcher	a												
Ash-throated Flycatcher	v												
Tropical Kingbird	v												
Western Kingbird	m[b]												
Eastern Kingbird	v[b]												
Scissor-tailed Flycatcher	a												

Mountain outliers ringing the Columbia River basin. It is not definitely known to nest in Washington west of the Cascade Crest, but might nest on Mt. Rainier's high, rain-shadowed northeast slopes.

Positive identification of the Dusky Flycatcher outside its normal range must be based on the observation of consistent multiple characteristics. Briefly, it is a largish, olive-grayish Empidonax with a smallish head and longish tail. It lacks the yellowish throat of the Pacific-slope Flycatcher, the brownish back of the Willow (and shows a more distinct eye ring than that species), and wags its tail upwards, not downwards like the more purely gray-plumaged Gray Flycatcher. Its characteristic location note is a soft "wit," quite unlike the Hammond's Black-headed-Grosbeak-like "bik." Also, its bill, when viewed from below, is quite broad in comparison with the narrow bill of Hammond's. When compared to the Least Flycatcher, a regular vagrant to Washington, the Dusky differs primarily in the subtleties of

156

size and shape noted above. In breeding, the Dusky prefers dry, broken forest or chaparral brush, or clear-cuts east of the Cascades, where it normally perches in the open. Its song is similar to Hammond's (and quite unlike that of any other Empidonax), but is less "tight" or harsh than Hammond's.

Three flycatchers characteristic of the arid desert and rangelands of eastern Washington regularly stray west to King County. These include SAY'S PHOEBE and two KINGBIRDS. Say's Phoebes are most often noted in early spring, coincident with their normal spring arrivals east of the Cascades. Of 52 records in my database, 42 occurred between February 28 and April 20, with the remaining 10 records between late August and early December. The kingbirds occasionally stay to nest. Two early EASTERN KINGBIRD nesting records were from Seattle in 1893 and 1906 (Jewett et al. 1953:418), with more recent reports at Lake Joy east of Duvall in 1978 and 1979 (B. and P. Evans) and at Duvall August 16, 2008 (E. Hunn). A pair of WESTERN KINGBIRDS nested along W Snoqualmie River Rd. northwest of Duvall in 2007, 2008, and 2009. Both Eastern and Western kingbirds are frequently recorded as spring vagrants, with several reported each year at favored locations such as Montlake Fill, Discovery Park, and Marymoor Park.

RARITIES

LEAST FLYCATCHER. Eleven records.

1983 June 5: Marymoor Park, singing male, R. Thorne (*AB* 37.6).

1991 June 22: South Seattle, singing male, M. Egger (*AB* 45.5, *ECNW* 33(3):10).

1993 May 23: Tolt-MacDonald Park, G. Ramsey (*AB* 47.3).

1998 August 17: Montlake Fill, K. Aanerud (*NAB* 53.1, *WOSNews* 59).

2005 January 5: Green River Natural Resources Area, K. Aanerud, multiple observers (*NAB* 59.2, *WOSNews* 99).

2007 July 5-19: Marymoor Park, singing male, M. Bartels, M. Hobbs, E. Hunn (voice recorded), multiple observers (*WOSNews* 114).

2009 June 10-15: Three Forks Natural Area, singing male, E. Hunn, multiple observers, song recorded by T. Brooks.

2009 June 21: Auburn, singing male, K. Andrich, multiple observers.

2009 June 6-21: North of Fall City, singing male, D. Norman.

2010 June 17-28: Marymoor Park, singing male, M. Bartels, multiple observers.

2010 June 24-27: Stillwater, singing male, C. Anderson, multiple observers.

GRAY FLYCATCHER. Seven records.

1975 May 11: Discovery Park, Seattle.

1984 May 28: Seattle, D. Beaudette (*AB* 38.5).

1993 May 9: Montlake Fill, K. Aanerud (*AB* 47.3, *ECNW* 35(1):10).

2003 May 15: Discovery Park, K. Aanerud (*NAB* 57.3, *WOSNews* 88).

2004 August 27: Montlake Fill, S. MacKay (*WOSNews* 97).

2007 May 15: Discovery Park, K. Dieffenbach (*WOSNews* 113).

2008 May 12: Lincoln Park, J. Flynn, multiple observers (*WOSNews* 119).

BLACK PHOEBE. Two records, including one extended record.

2005 April 26-May 16: Auburn, R. Baker, J. Simms, P. and R. Sullivan, multiple observers, photos (*WOSNews* 101).

2006 March 31-May 23: Auburn, bird returned to same location, M. Bartels, multiple observers (*WOS-News* 107).

2010 March 26: Mercer Island, J. Conforti, R. Hibpshman, photo.

EASTERN PHOEBE. Two records.

1994 September 4: Discovery Park, S. Atkinson (*FN* 49.1, *WOSNews* 35, *ECNW* 36(5):10).

1994 September 15: Kent, D. Beaudette (*WOSNews* 35, *ECNW* 36(5):10).

VERMILION FLYCATCHER. One record.

1988 January 25-March 17: Redmond, B. Overly, L. and R. Halpin, multiple observers, photos (*AB* 42.2, 42.5).

ASH-THROATED FLYCATCHER. Eleven records.

1956 November 24: West Seattle, E. Curtis, W. Hagenstein (*AFN* 11.1).

1975 August 31: Montlake Fill, C. Wentworth (*WB* 4:33).

1990 May 27-30: Auburn, B. Willison (*AB* 44.3).

1994 October 30: Seattle, R. Robinson, J. Hadley (*FN* 49.1, *WOSNews* 35).

2005 June 15-16: Marymoor Park, H. Flores, photos (*WOSNews* 102).

2005 June 19: Magnuson Park, J. Bragg (*WOSNews* 102).

2006 June 7-9: Marymoor Park, M. Hobbs, M. Mathis (*WOSNews* 108).

2009 August 31: Montlake Fill, C. Sidles, K. Lloyd, photo (*WOSNews* 127).

2010 June 17: Marymoor Park, M. Mathis, M. Hobbs, E. Hunn.

2010 June 20: Issaquah, L. Schwitters.

2010 June 26: Stillwater, P. Fahey.

TROPICAL KINGBIRD. Four records.

2006 November 16: Magnuson Park, P. Lynch, D. Paulson, multiple observers, photos, voice recorded.

2007 October 16: Marymoor Park, silent, could have been Couch's Kingbird, M. Bartels, M. Hobbs, photos (*WOSNews* 116).

2007 October 27: Montlake Fill, silent, could have been Couch's Kingbird, E. and N. Hunn (*WOSNews* 116).

This page: Ash-throated Flycatcher, Montlake Fill, August 31, 2009 (© Kathrine Lloyd).
Opposite page: Tropical Kingbird, Magnuson Park, November 17, 2006 (© Marv Breece).

2007 November 11-24: Auburn, 1 or 2 birds, calling, K. Andrich, D. Swayne, multiple observers, K. Hansen, photos (*WOSNews* 116).

SCISSOR-TAILED FLYCATCHER. One record.

2003 August 2: Montlake Fill, adult female, C. Miller, S. MacKay, photo (*NAB* 58.1, *WOSNews* 91).

SHRIKES & VIREOS

The NORTHERN SHRIKE is a regular winter visitor but in small numbers. It may be confidently expected at Montlake Fill, Marymoor Park, and in the Green River Valley by mid-October.

The vireos are being pinched between city and mountain and are also under heavy pressure from cowbird parasitism. Our resident HUTTON'S VIREOS nest

	status	Jan	Feb	Mar	Apr	May	Jun	Jul	Aug	Sep	Oct	Nov	Dec
Loggerhead Shrike	v		•• —		•		•				•		
Northern Shrike	w									...			
White-eyed Vireo	a						•						
Cassin's Vireo	sb				•	▬▭▬				•			
Blue-headed Vireo	a									•			
Hutton's Vireo	pb		▭▭										
Warbling Vireo	sb					▭▬▬							
Red-eyed Vireo	sb					▭▬▬							

regularly as early as March in Seattle, when their "song"—a monotonous "sreep"—is repeated across Discovery Park. WARBLING VIREOS have a wide tolerance for variable habitat, nesting everywhere from city parks to subalpine meadows, but most commonly along the riparian corridors such as the Snoqualmie Valley Trail. By the time our RED-EYED VIREOS arrive at the Snoqualmie Valley Trail at the tail end of May or early June, Warbling Vireos have fallen silent, busy with their young. CASSIN'S VIREOS are decidedly scarce, apparently absent from much seemingly appropriate habitat. Their halting, raspy songs may be heard in Discovery Park during spring migration, but Cassin's are not known to stay here long enough to nest. It is best to look for them in foothill and montane woodlands dominated by conifers. Carnation Marsh Sanctuary is well known as a haven for nesting Osprey, but it is also home to all four vireo species, as is nearby Tolt-MacDonald Park.

RARITIES

LOGGERHEAD SHRIKE. Thirteen records.

1915 April 11: North of Seattle, a specimen in S. Rathbun's collection "was secured by a boy about 7 miles north of Seattle. It was brought to Rathbun the next day, in the meantime having been partly eaten by a cat. Enough remained, however, for its identification by biologists of the Biological Survey..." (Jewett et al. 1953:544-545).

1955 April 2: Bellevue (*AFN* 9.4).

1972 April 21: Redmond, B. and P. Evans.

1975 May 25: Montlake Fill, D. Paulson (Krause 1975, *WB* 4:33, *AB* 29.4).

1975 July 3: Redmond, B. and P. Evans.

1988 October 23: Redmond, J. West (*AB* 43.1).

1989 April 10: Montlake Fill, T. Haas (*AB* 43.3, *WB* 1:18).

1995 March 12: Marymoor Park, A. Coles (*FN* 49.3, *WOSNews* 39).

1995 April 2: Magnuson Park, M. Smith (*FN* 49.3, *WOSNews* 39, *ECNW* 36(8):10).

1997 April 15-18: Magnuson Park, 1 to 2 birds, M. Hobbs, J. Blinn (*FN* 51.4, *WOSNews* 51).

2004 March 31: Montlake Fill, D. and S. McVay (*WOSNews* 95).

2008 April 12: Montlake Fill, C. Sidles, E. Hunn, multiple observers. (*WOSNews* 119).

2009 March 4-5: Montlake Fill, C. Sidles.

WHITE-EYED VIREO. One record.

1981 July 12 [July 11 *fide* WTM:256]: Vashon Island, P. Mattocks (*AB* 35.6).

BLUE-HEADED VIREO. One record.

1995 September 6 [September 8 *fide* WTM:257]: Montlake Fill, K. Aanerud (*FN* 50.1, *WOSNews* 41, 61).

CROWS & THEIR COUSINS

The CORVIDS are well adapted to rigorous northern climes. In winter in the mountains, the jays and ravens are the most conspicuous components of a small but hardy avifauna. It is an oversimplification to say that the GRAY JAY replaces the STELLER'S JAY at higher elevations, as the transition is gradual, with both species conspicuous between 1000 and 4000 feet. The Gray Jay is found typically in the densest coniferous stands. The Gray Jays that nested in Kirkland in 1920 (Burleigh 1929:516) and an individual in Discovery Park April 24 and again May 22, 1976

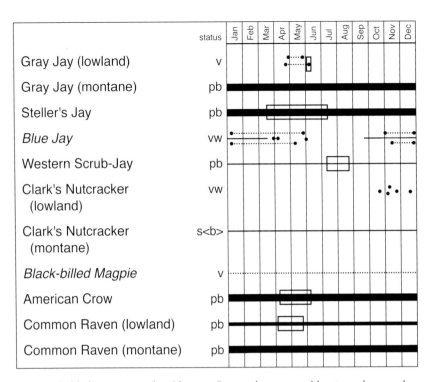

	status	Jan	Feb	Mar	Apr	May	Jun	Jul	Aug	Sep	Oct	Nov	Dec
Gray Jay (lowland)	v												
Gray Jay (montane)	pb												
Steller's Jay	pb												
Blue Jay	vw												
Western Scrub-Jay	pb												
Clark's Nutcracker (lowland)	vw												
Clark's Nutcracker (montane)	s\<b\>												
Black-billed Magpie	v												
American Crow	pb												
Common Raven (lowland)	pb												
Common Raven (montane)	pb												

(*AB* 30.4) likely represent the Olympic Peninsula races *rathbuni* or *obscurus* that nest at sea level.

Avid birders from all across the country are attracted to the Pacific Northwest in hopes of adding the NORTHWESTERN CROW to their life lists. They rarely leave disappointed, since they find that our crows indeed sound different from those back home, and some, at least, look smaller. According to many bird books, there are two crows here, the eclectic AMERICAN CROW and the beach-loving Northwestern Crow, analogous to the American and FISH CROWS of the Atlantic Coast. This I call the "Myth of Two Crows." After years of searching, I recognize but one local crow species, the "Puget Sound Crow." It is variable in size, vocal pattern, and habitat preference, and it bridges the gap between the western race of the American Crow and the smaller Northwestern Crow, a race best adapted to the narrow coastal strip that stretches from the Olympic Peninsula to southern Alaska (Johnston 1961). Euroamerican settlement cleared the land of forests west of the Cascades, removing the ecological barrier that had isolated Northwestern Crows since the last Ice Age. In the absence of this barrier, the two crow populations appear to have merged throughout western Washington (Marzluff and Angell 2005: 63-66).

Our crows thrive on human company. They follow I-90 up and over Snoqualmie Pass. The COMMON RAVEN, by contrast, keeps its own counsel, rarely descending to the edge of suburbia. The North American Indian sought preternatural advice from the Raven, not the Crow!

The BLUE JAY, the familiar eastern cousin of our Steller's Jay, now straggles each year to Washington, usually appearing after mid-September and often lingering well into spring. This is a recent pattern evident only since the late 1960s. The first county record was a bird at R. Amundsen's Seattle feeder in January and February 1971 (*AB* 25.3). The next individual frequented feeders in Des Moines from November 16, 1974, until late April 1975 (*AB* 29.1, 29.4).

WESTERN SCRUB-JAYS are quite sedentary, reaching their historical northern limits along the Columbia River from Skamania to Wahkiacum Counties, although they were known to occur regularly north to Lewis County. One appeared on a steep, alder-covered hillside in West Seattle overlooking scenic Harbor Island on December 24, 1977, where it remained for just over a year, being last reported January 6, 1979 (*AB* 32.3, 32.6, 33.3; *SAN* 19(6): 3). Since 1991, families of the Western Scrub-Jay have become established, nesting and remaining year-round in Enumclaw, Kent, and Renton; and in Seattle in West Seattle, Queen Anne, Ballard, Beacon Hill, Capitol Hill, and Montlake. These county records are part of a wider pattern of expansion northward, both west and east of the Cascades.

CLARK'S NUTCRACKER is rarely noted in King County, though small flocks have been found regularly along the Cascade Crest near Naches and Windy Passes in recent summers. Nesting was suspected on a ridge above the Tolt Reservoir on one Breeding Bird Atlas survey on July 10, 1999 (*WOSNews* 64). Away from the mountains, there are a few late fall records.

We think of magpies as birds of the semi-arid plains, brushy thickets, and scattered farm towns east of the Cascades. However, that is not always the case. For

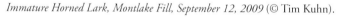

Immature Horned Lark, Montlake Fill, September 12, 2009 (© Tim Kuhn).

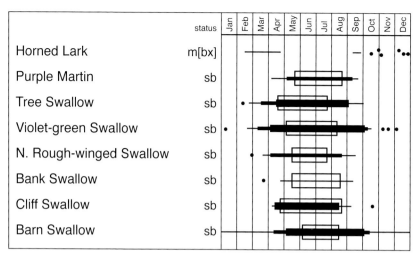

	status	Jan	Feb	Mar	Apr	May	Jun	Jul	Aug	Sep	Oct	Nov	Dec
Horned Lark	m[bx]												
Purple Martin	sb												
Tree Swallow	sb												
Violet-green Swallow	sb												
N. Rough-winged Swallow	sb												
Bank Swallow	sb												
Cliff Swallow	sb												
Barn Swallow	sb												

example, BLACK-BILLED MAGPIES nest in south-central Alaska in spruce forests bordering saltwater. In Washington they sometimes straggle west of the Cascades. The odd individual may turn up in lowland King County at any season, and some have remained from one year to the next. The winter of 1959-1960 saw an invasion, with 11 individuals reported (*AFN* 14.3). More recently, a magpie entertained observers in Seattle from January 6 to 18, 2010, wandering from Alki Beach to Discovery Park and points between (*WOSNews* 129).

Horned Larks & Swallows

HORNED LARKS are scarce migrants in open country, such as at Montlake Fill and in the Kent Valley. Larks once may have nested on the Duwamish River delta, now dredged for Seattle's port. If so, they would have represented the race *strigata*, which nests on southwestern Washington prairies, flats, and beaches, such as those at Ocean Shores. There is no evidence that the race *alpina* of Washington's high peaks nests here, though it does nearby, above Sunrise on Mt. Rainier.

Swallows have been recorded in King County every month of the year, with the latest laggard BARN SWALLOWS overlapping the most enterprising TREE and VIOLET-GREEN SWALLOWS. However, not before the end of February can you count on finding coursing flocks of Trees and Violet-greens over Montlake Fill or the Kent and Auburn marshes. By mid-April the whole suite of swallows has returned in force. Violet-green, Barn, and CLIFF SWALLOWS prefer to nest on structures such as houses, barns, and bridges, respectively. NORTHERN ROUGH-WINGED and BANK SWALLOWS excavate burrows in sand banks. Study their calls as an essential aid to their identification. In my mind they form a series from Purple Martin through Tree, Violet-Green, Barn, Cliff, Northern Rough-Winged, and Bank Swallow, the calls become progressively "drier." The martin's notes are "juicy," while the calls of Rough-winged and Bank are "dry" trills or rattles. Adjacent species in this series may sometimes be confused. After July it seems as if all but Violet-green and Barn Swallows have vanished. This is in part an illusion; the others' first broods have fledged and dispersed, but Violet-green and Barn Swallows are conspicuously busy raising additional broods.

PURPLE MARTINS now are locally common in King County. Fall migratory concentrations of 30 to100 birds have been noted over Seattle in recent years from late August to early September. These numbers should be compared to the estimated 12,500 at a migratory roost on Green Lake on August 2,1945 (Larrison 1945:45-46). Colonies of just a few nesting pairs hung on into the 1980s, but thanks to vigorous efforts—by such martin lovers as the late Kevin Li—to woo them back with specially designed and carefully placed nesting boxes and gourds, they have made a striking comeback. Clusters of nesting gourds attached to pilings on tidal flats, as at Tramp Harbor and in Shilshole Bay, attracted nesting pairs as early as 1993. By 2008, small colonies were established at Jack Block Park on Harbor Island, as well as on Lake Washington in Kenmore and Juanita. I know of no contemporary nesting anywhere in King County at a natural site, such as the mountain snags exploited elsewhere on the west coast. Our resurgent martin populations peaked in 2007 at 125 pairs at 18 sites, then declined to just 30 pairs in 2008 and 2009 (S. Kostka, personal communication).

Until 1980, BANK SWALLOWS were not known to nest west of the Cascades, but since 1994 three substantial colonies have been discovered in King County alone. The first, active since 1999, is along the Green River above Auburn at O'Grady Park; the second at Stillwater on the Snoqualmie River since at least 2005; and most recently, the third on the White River southeast of Auburn.

	status	Jan	Feb	Mar	Apr	May	Jun	Jul	Aug	Sep	Oct	Nov	Dec
Black-capped Chickadee	pb												
Mountain Chickadee (lowland)	vw												
Mountain Chickadee (montane)	pb												
Chestnut-backed Chickadee	pb												
Bushtit	pb												
Red-breasted Nuthatch	pb												
White-breasted Nuthatch	v												
Brown Creeper	pb												

Chickadees, Nuthatches, etc.

The CHESTNUT-BACKED CHICKADEE is the original inhabitant of our coniferous forests. Its back and flanks match the bark of red cedar perfectly. It ranges peerless above 1000 feet but is not seen as often—or at least not seen as well—as the BLACK-CAPPED CHICKADEE of deciduous and mixed woods, shrubby thickets, and suburban yards. The Black-capped is an intruder from the east. It was unknown until recently on Vancouver Island and in the San Juan Islands, where the Chestnut-backed alone occurred. It is noteworthy that the Black-capped is also relatively scarce on Vashon Island, apparently only recently establishing a beachhead there. Two miles of water is sufficient to slow the Black-capped's march appreciably. MOUNTAIN CHICKADEES occasionally straggle to Seattle and other lowland points in winter, typically in years of heavy northern or montane finch invasions, perhaps indicative of a dearth of food available in their normal winter haunts. The Mountain Chickadee appears to be absent over large tracts of subalpine forest in King County, preferring drier, pine-dominated, east-slope forests. It has recently been documented as a regular nesting species at the Cascade Crest between Naches and Green Passes.

BUSHTITS are responsible for the elegant, woven-bag nests often hanging in suburban shrubbery. After nesting, they troop about in flocks that "trickle" from tree to tree. Resident RED-BREASTED NUTHATCHES reveal their presence in the forest canopy by their persistent "yank, yank" call. BROWN CREEPERS are close associates but only occasionally emit their characteristic double "tsee-tsee" call, which is pitched at the upper limit of human hearing. Bushtits scarcely penetrate the Cascade foothills at all, but the nuthatch and creeper nest commonly up to the upper timberline.

RARITIES

WHITE-BREASTED NUTHATCH. Six recent records. S. Rathbun "noted this species a number of times" about Seattle around the turn of the 20th century (Rathbun 1902:139). Five early Seattle CBCs recorded it: four in 1935; one each in 1938, 1939, and 1952; and two in 1969 (WTM:281). One was also reported in Seattle on August 11, 1969 (*AFN* 24.1, WTM:281).

1990 September 23: Auburn, J. Gatchet.

1997 March 6: Carnation, H. Jennings (personal communication, WTM:281).

1998 August 9: Near Naches Pass, D. Beaudette.

1998 August 25: Enumclaw, F. Boeshe (*NAB* 53.1).

2004 November 7: Vashon Island, 2 birds through the winter, C. Elder, A. and A. Huggins, P. Murray, photos (*WOSNews* 98, Swan 2005:213).

2008 October 30 to November 9: Snoqualmie, A. Cockman, H. Flores, multiple observers, photos (*WOSNews* 122).

Wrens, Kinglets, Gnatcatchers, & Dippers

ROCK WRENS sporadically nest high in the Cascades—for example, on Kelly Butte in 2006. Singing males were noted there in previous summers, such as 1986

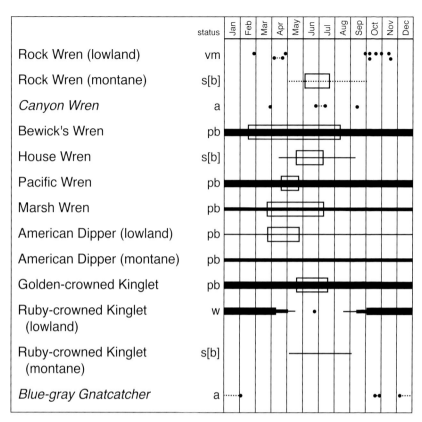

and 1995, and on Mt. Si in 1985 and 2007. However, in 2008 none could be found at these locations. On rare occasions, Rock Wrens straggle west to the shores of Lake Washington and Puget Sound, with records in February, April, September, October, and November.

The HOUSE WREN was characterized by Rathbun as a "common summer resident" and breeder (Rathbun 1902:139). A few may still nest in foothill clear-cuts; singing House Wrens were heard near Lake Joy in June 1979 near the nest of an Eastern Kingbird pair. House Wrens are still common south of Tacoma and in the Olympic rain shadow between Sequim, Victoria, and the San Juans, where the sun is a bit more liberal. The fate of the House Wren parallels that of Western Blue-bird, Lewis's Woodpecker, and Lazuli Bunting. Occasional migrants are reported, but care is essential to avoid confusion with migrant, out-of-habitat Marsh Wrens.

BEWICK'S, PACIFIC, and MARSH WRENS are common residents in appropriate habitat, often singing at odd seasons and waxing vociferous in spring. Bewick's Wrens are partial to brushy patches in urban, suburban, and bucolic settings. Pacific Wrens (formerly known as Winter Wrens but recently renamed when they were split from their eastern U.S. counterparts) haunt our deep coniferous forests and are particularly at home in sword fern tangles. Marsh Wrens—as their name suggests—hang out in cattails and other freshwater and/or saltwater marsh vegetation. Dull immature Marsh Wrens may wander in winter to wet grassy fields, where they could be mistaken for House Wrens, which are very rare for us in winter.

AMERICAN DIPPERS nest along rushing mountain streams and may forage at nearby lakes. A few also nest at low elevations, such as below Snoqualmie Falls and on Tokul Creek near Fall City. A pair with young was studied on April 20, 2007, in Wallace Swamp Creek Park in Kenmore just upstream from Lake Washington, where one had stayed the previous winter. Other winter records from the lowlands include one that frequented the Seward Park trout hatchery outlet for the Seattle CBC for twelve years, 1978-1989. It presumably died of old age.

GOLDEN-CROWNED KINGLETS are inconspicuous but common permanent residents of our forests at all elevations. The RUBY-CROWNED is conspicuous in winter, bursting into its improbable song as an early sign of spring (heard mostly late February through April). It is just as conspicuously absent in summer, shunning our wet, westside forests, though it nests only a few miles east in the Cle Elum River Valley and rarely at the Cascade Crest near Naches Pass.

RARITIES

CANYON WREN. Three records.

> 1993 June 21 and July 7: Mt. Index, B. Boyes, K. Knittle (personal communication, *AB* 47.5, WTM:284).
>
> 1998 September 12: Kelly Butte, D. Beaudette (*NAB* 53.1, *WOSNews* 59).
>
> 2010 March 23: Mt. Si, near summit, singing male, L. Boyle.

BLUE-GRAY GNATCATCHER. Two records.

> 1986 December 6-January 30, 1987: Foster Island, Seattle, Dennis Paulson, N. Smith, multiple observers (*AB* 41.2, *WOSNews* 40).
>
> 1999 October 21-26: Marymoor Park, Michael Hobbs, multiple observers. (*NAB* 54.1, *WOSNews* 66, WTM:290).

Thrushes, Thrashers, & Near Relations

I would first like to pay tribute to the AMERICAN ROBIN. Its Latin moniker should be changed from *Turdus migratorius* to *Turdus ubiquitous*. It is indeed migratory, although the replacement of summer populations by migrants from farther north gives the illusion that local robins are permanent residents. But more characteristic of the bird is its catholic success. It breeds everywhere—in city and wilderness, from beaches to alpine meadows, and from deserts to dense forests, where it rubs shoulders with its specialized cousin, the VARIED THRUSH. How does it manage such adaptability?

Though adapted to deep forest, the Varied Thrush still has an impressive range. You may hear its eerie hum in spring from the Federation Forest in the White River Canyon, scarcely 1000 feet above sea level, to the upper margins of timber, where it

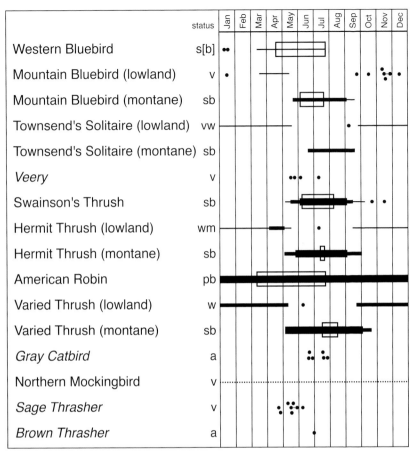

	status	Jan	Feb	Mar	Apr	May	Jun	Jul	Aug	Sep	Oct	Nov	Dec
Western Bluebird	s[b]												
Mountain Bluebird (lowland)	v												
Mountain Bluebird (montane)	sb												
Townsend's Solitaire (lowland)	vw												
Townsend's Solitaire (montane)	sb												
Veery	v												
Swainson's Thrush	sb												
Hermit Thrush (lowland)	wm												
Hermit Thrush (montane)	sb												
American Robin	pb												
Varied Thrush (lowland)	w												
Varied Thrush (montane)	sb												
Gray Catbird	a												
Northern Mockingbird	v												
Sage Thrasher	v												
Brown Thrasher	a												

sings bass to the HERMIT THRUSH'S intricate fluting. Only in winter, mostly after late September, is it conspicuous in the broken woods of our city parks.

Our spot-breasted thrushes, the Hermit and SWAINSON'S, prefer very different elevations. Swainson's ranges up to about 3000 feet, while Hermits rarely nest below that line. Both may be heard at Snoqualmie Pass and on the summit of Tiger Mountain. The Hermit Thrush's greater tolerance for cold is reflected in its status as uncommon (but regularly seen) in winter. In contrast, valid winter reports of Swainson's Thrushes north of Mexico are exceedingly few. Identification is not as straightforward as the field guides suggest. The Hermit Thrush's "red" tail is a subtle reddish brown, not always readily inspected, as the bird skulks in deep shade, though the Hermit Thrush's habit of nervously flicking its tail and wings may give it away. The Swainson's Thrushes in our area are a rich russet brown, quite unlike the olive-backed Swainson's Thrushes of the eastern United States. Look as well for the Swainson's broader, buffy eye ring, longer tail, and larger size, and the Hermit's blacker and more distinct breast spotting and dove-gray flanks. Call notes also are valuable aids to identification. Hermits sometimes "chuck" like a Fox Sparrow or scold like a Spotted Towhee. Swainson's Thrushes typically give a soft "heep" note or an odd chortle.

The WESTERN BLUEBIRD has been nearly eliminated as a breeding bird in King County. This is likely due to habitat changes, as the EUROPEAN STARLING (often blamed for its demise) did not become common until two decades after the bluebirds' decline, as documented by Seattle CBC records. Western Bluebirds bred "abundantly about the city in any suitable locality" at the turn of the 20th century (Rathbun 1902:140), but there have been few nesting records for King County in recent years. Two young were raised near Issaquah in 1966 (*AFN* 20.5), and a pair were seen investigating a nest hole in a clear-cut in the foothills on June 3, 1995 (D. Beaudette). Recent reports include a pair that attempted to nest at Stillwater in 2006 and a pair that fledged two young from a snag on the Cascade Crest north of Windy Gap on July 28, 2007. J. Tubbs installed two nest boxes at the Chinook Bend Natural Area northwest of Carnation, hoping to attract a nesting pair from a small flock that foraged there in March and April 2008, but as yet has not had success. MOUNTAIN BLUEBIRDS have nested each summer since at least 1986 (D. Beaudette) in an old burn on the Cascade Crest north of Windy Gap and at the edges of clear-cuts near Naches Pass. Scattered nesting in foothill clear-cuts was noted during Breeding Bird Atlas surveys, e.g., on May 28, 1995 (H. Opperman, *WOSNews* 39). Mountain Bluebirds also straggle to the lowlands of western King County, most from mid-March through mid-May, but rarely also in fall.

TOWNSEND'S SOLITAIRES are to be found at forest edges up to timberline in summer. Listen for their complex song, likened to that of a thrasher or finch. They are decidedly rare winter stragglers to the lowlands, but a few descend to the lowlands September through early May.

NORTHERN MOCKINGBIRDS have been recorded in the county in every month of the year. Like Anna's Hummingbird—but not yet so forcefully— the mocker is pressing beyond its California confines. When present, it is typically encountered in urban neighborhoods, where it is yet another beneficiary of human habitat alteration.

RARITIES

VEERY. Four records.
> 1978 May 21: Lake Joy, singing, P. Evans (*AB* 32.5).
> 1980 June 1: Tolt-MacDonald Park, singing, E. Hunn.
> 1980 July 5: Deception Creek, seen, S. Hills.
> 1985 May 11: Carnation, seen well, D. Paulson (*AB* 39.3).

GRAY CATBIRD. Two old records and two more recent sightings.
> 1925 July 18-20: Near Snoqualmie, 2 birds, adult female collected, L. Bishop (*The Murrelet* 8(2):34).
> 1931 July 12: Seattle, F. Cook (Jewett et al. 1953:506).
> 1992 June 14: Wallingford neighborhood, Seattle, D. Victor.
> 2009 June 14-17: Three Forks Natural Area, T. Brooks, multiple observers; photos and sound recordings.

SAGE THRASHER. Seven records.

1976 April 21: North of Redmond, B. Evans (*AB* 30.4).

1989 May 11: Seattle, P. Murtaugh (*AB* 43.3,*WOSNews* 47).

2001 May 13 [May 1, *fide* WTM:300]: Bothell, H. Opperman, J. Edwards (*NAB* 55.3, *WOSNews* 76).

2002 April 17: Marymoor Park, B. Bell (*NAB* 56.3, *WOSNews* 82).

2002 May 11-24: Montlake Fill, D. Paulson, C. Sidles (*WOSNews* 82).

2007 May 3: Marymoor Park, 2 birds, M. Hobbs (*WOSNews* 113).

2010 June 4: Renton, T. Rohrer, photo.

BROWN THRASHER. One record.

1966 June 26: Federal Way, E. Peaslee.

Pipits, Waxwings, Wagtails, Phainopeplas, & Starlings

AMERICAN PIPITS lead a double life here, nesting at alpine heights in summer in the company of ROSY-FINCHES and PTARMIGANS, then becoming conspicuous in migration and appearing occasionally in winter in appropriate lowland habitats.

Were it not for a small wintering population, the CEDAR WAXWINGS' arrival might be seen as a sign of spring. They are not numerous until late in May, when the greater proportion of the breeding population arrives. They linger through October, most departing when the berries are depleted. The boreal "great gray" BO-HEMIAN WAXWING, or "Bo" for short, is typically rare, staging occasional winter invasions, presumably in response to food shortages northward. Most recently, a single bird was reported at Magnuson Park on November 18, 2007, and was seen off and on until at least January 12, 2008. A separate flock of seven was reported at Magnuson on November 25, 2007, then quickly disappeared. Three Bohemians were reported near Issaquah on January 6, 2008, and a single bird joined Cedar Waxwings in Duvall on February 17, 2008.

Can you imagine a world without EUROPEAN STARLINGS? Their snarling swarms and mocking chatter are so familiar to us that it is hard to appreciate that the first county record was of a bird at Fort Lawton (now Discovery Park) in De-

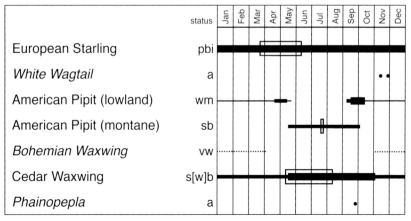

cember 1945 (Larrison, *The Murrelet* 28(1):12). A flock of ten east of Bellevue on January 16, 1949 (Bennett and Eddy 1949:18) reflects an early pattern of winter incursions. By the winter of 1955-56, the flocks east of Lake Washington were estimated at 5000 (*AFN* 10.3), with similar winter roosts on the University of Washington campus and beneath the Ballard Bridge by 1960. Locally reared young were first noted in 1962 in Des Moines (*AFN* 16.5). The rest is history.

RARITIES

WHITE WAGTAIL. Two records.

1981 November 8-9: West Point, Discovery Park, subspecies undetermined, B. and J. McMurtrie, D. Hutchinson (*AB* 36.2, *WOSNews* 47).

2000 November 26: Lake Sammamish, identified as a "Black-backed Wagtail," M. Bailey (*NAB* 55.3).

PHAINOPEPLA. One record.

1994 September 24: West Seattle, female, D. Buckley (*WOSNews* 35, 40, WTM:305).

WOOD WARBLERS

COMMON YELLOWTHROATS and ORANGE-CROWNED WARBLERS are the first wood warblers to arrive each spring, welcome splashes of yellow to brighten a dull day in early April. Yellowthroats soon occupy virtually every patch of cattails and Reed Canary Grass in the lowlands, while Orange-crowneds trill from brushy thickets and shrubby alders. Our YELLOW WARBLERS arrive in early May, favoring riparian forest and edge habitat. Our other common nesting warblers favor foothill and montane habitats.

BLACK-THROATED GRAY and TOWNSEND'S WARBLERS show a geographic pattern similar to that of Swainson's and Hermit Thrushes, with Townsend's largely replacing Black-throated Gray Warblers at elevations above approximately 2000 feet. They both also occur in the Federation Forest southeast of Enumclaw at an elevation of 1650 feet, where Black-throated Grays seem

Above: Sage Thrasher, Marymoor Park, May 3, 2007. Right: Palm Warbler, Renton, January 12, 2009 (both photographs © Ollie Oliver).

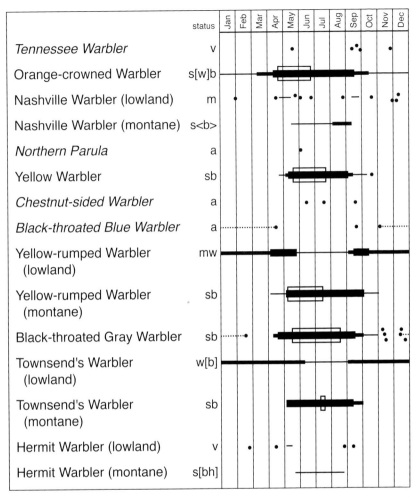

	status	Jan	Feb	Mar	Apr	May	Jun	Jul	Aug	Sep	Oct	Nov	Dec
Tennessee Warbler	v					•				••		•	
Orange-crowned Warbler	s[w]b												
Nashville Warbler (lowland)	m	•		•	•	•		•		•	—	•	••
Nashville Warbler (montane)	s<b>												
Northern Parula	a					•							
Yellow Warbler	sb										•		
Chestnut-sided Warbler	a						•	•		•			
Black-throated Blue Warbler	a					•				•			
Yellow-rumped Warbler (lowland)	mw												
Yellow-rumped Warbler (montane)	sb												
Black-throated Gray Warbler	sb	•									••	••	
Townsend's Warbler (lowland)	w[b]												
Townsend's Warbler (montane)	sb												
Hermit Warbler (lowland)	v	•		•	—				•	•			
Hermit Warbler (montane)	s[bh]												

to favor deciduous, riverside gallery forest, while Townsend's sing from the tips of tall Douglas Firs. HERMIT WARBLERS have also been reported here (M. Egger, June 1980) but may not be present every year. Hermit Warblers are not regular anywhere north of Mt. Rainier in the Cascades. Identification of these three close relatives is complicated by their treetop foraging habits. Each species is also capable of a bewildering array of song variants. I believe no two individuals sing alike. Furthermore, recent studies indicate hybrid TOWNSEND'S X HERMITS outnumber "pure" Hermits in the southern Cascades. Hybrids may sound like Hermits, but a close look may reveal hybrid features, such as a Hermit face with greenish back and black-streaked yellow flanks characteristic of Townsend's. I have observed such individuals several times, for example, on June 9, 1990, at Cedar Falls; June 12, 2006, below Naches Pass; and July 14, 2007, south of Snoqualmie Pass.

Orange-Crowned, "AUDUBON'S" YELLOW-RUMPED, MACGILLIVRAY'S, and WILSON'S WARBLERS are variably common and widespread in season. Orange-crowned, MacGillivray's, and Wilson's Warblers favor brushy avalanche tracks, bog edges, or cut-over forest in the lower foothills and at middle elevations. "Audubon's" Warblers (the western form of the Yellow-rumped) prefer subalpine timber, though they may nest sporadically in the lowlands and are abundant migrants throughout the lowlands in spring and fall. They are also regular winter visitors. Migrant and winter flocks often include a minority of "MYRTLE WARBLERS," the eastern form of the Yellow-rumped, joined by the occasional overwintering Orange-crowned.

NASHVILLE WARBLERS are rare but regular spring migrants in the lowlands and late summer migrants along the Cascade Crest, nesting sparingly west of the Cascades, for example, near Concrete in the Skagit Valley. A singing male on Tiger Mountain in June 1982 (E. Hunn), another near Stevens Pass in 1996 (D. Beaudette), and several Washington Breeding Bird Atlas records suggest the possibility of nesting in our region. The YELLOW-BREASTED CHAT is likewise an eastside breeder, occasionally straggling west. Territorial males returned each summer from 2006 to 2008 to the Green River Natural Resources Area in Kent—where one was also present in 1995—and to Stillwater each summer since 2007, though we have no positive evidence of successful nesting in King County since 1935.

Since 1981, PALM WARBLERS have been recorded 17 times in the King County lowlands—12 sightings between October 20 and January 16, plus two

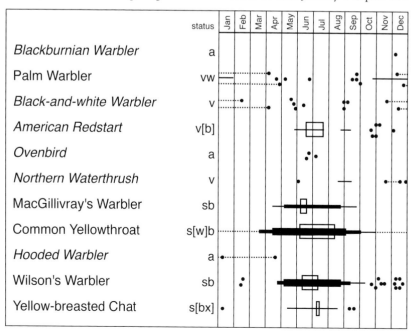

	status	Jan	Feb	Mar	Apr	May	Jun	Jul	Aug	Sep	Oct	Nov	Dec
Blackburnian Warbler	a											•	
Palm Warbler	vw												
Black-and-white Warbler	v												
American Redstart	v[b]												
Ovenbird	a												
Northern Waterthrush	v												
MacGillivray's Warbler	sb												
Common Yellowthroat	s[w]b												
Hooded Warbler	a												
Wilson's Warbler	sb												
Yellow-breasted Chat	s[bx]												

September records, and three in spring. Palm Warblers show a decided preference for lake and river shoreline brush, with most records from the shoreline of Lake Washington or the lower reaches of the Cedar and Green Rivers. A singing male was found near Naches Pass on June 17, 1988 (D. Beaudette).

In winter, roving bands of chickadees should be carefully inventoried for wintering Townsend's Warblers, joined by Red-breasted Nuthatches, Golden-crowned and Ruby-crowned Kinglets, Brown Creepers, and Hutton's Vireos.

RARITIES

TENNESSEE WARBLER. Five records.

1973　September 25: University of Washington campus, Seattle, M. Perrone (*AB* 28.1).

1991　September 17: Seattle, K. Aanerud (*AB* 46.2, *ECNW* 33(3):11).

1995　September 8-9: Montlake Fill, K. Aanerud, G. Toffic (*FN* 50.1, *WOSNews* 41).

1998　November 25: Seattle, B. Feltner (*NAB* 53.2).

2007　May 13: West Seattle, D. Heiden (*WOSNews* 113).

NORTHERN PARULA. One record.

1992　May 30: Queen Anne, Seattle, singing male, J. Elder (*AB* 46.3, *WOSNews* 21).

CHESTNUT-SIDED WARBLER. Three records.

1983　June 13-14: Tolt-MacDonald Park, E. Hunn, D. Finch, P. Mattocks, multiple observers, M. Egger, T. Schooley, photos (*AB* 37.6).

1985　July 18: Naches Pass, M. Donahue, multiple observers (*AB* 39.5).

2001　September 19: Arboretum, Seattle, K. Aanerud (*NAB* 56.1, *WOSNews* 79).

BLACK-THROATED BLUE WARBLER. Two records.

1994　November 2-April 5, 1995: Mercer Island, male, M. Hatheway, multiple observers, photos (*FN* 49.2, 49.3; *WOSNews* 34, 35; *ECNW* 36(5):10, 36(6):10, 36(8):10, 36(9):10).

2006　September 17: Juanita Bay Park, female, M. Mathis (*WOSNews* 109).

BLACKBURNIAN WARBLER. One record.

1987　December 4: Discovery Park, immature, K. Aanerud, T. Haas (*AB* 42.2).

BLACK-AND-WHITE WARBLER. Eight records.

1965　December 10-March 27, 1966: Arboretum, Seattle, D. Jelliffe, P. Mattocks, R. Boggs.

1966　August 29: Dumas Bay, E. Peaslee.

1978　May 13: Foster Island, singing male, D. Galvin.

1983　June 5: Beckler River near Skykomish, singing male, D. and L. McLeod (*AB* 38.6).

1996　November 21-February 2, 1997: Seattle, K. Aanerud et al. (*FN* 51.1, 51.3, *WOSNews* 48, 50).

1997　August 31-September 1: Foster Island, photo (*WOSNews* 53).

2003　May 22: Carnation, M. Wile, M. Mann (*NAB* 57.3, *WOSNews* 88, *WB* 9:48).

2009　May 24: Kent, G. and O. Oliver, photos.

AMERICAN REDSTART. Eighteen records, all since 1988, including one nesting record, 2009.

1988　August 26-28: Montlake Fill, adult male, K. Aanerud, T. Haas, B. Sundstrom (*AB* 43.1).

1988　October 25-26: female, Foster Island, K. Aanerud, R. Thorne (*AB* 43.1, *WB* 1:19, *WTM*:316).

1990　May 20: Arboretum, Seattle, two birds, M. Salano (*ECNW* 33(4):10).

1990　August 19 to September 3: Montlake Fill, K. Aanerud, H. Opperman, E. Hunn.

1991　September 8: Seattle, S. Atkinson (*AB* 46.2, *ECNW* 33(3):11).

1992　May 25: Discovery Park, K. Slettebak (*AB* 46.3, *ECNW* 33(9):10).

1996　September 12: Seattle, S. Atkinson (*FN* 51.1, *WOSNews* 47).

2000 September 4: Montlake Fill, 1 bird in basic plumage, M. Breuninger, *fide* J. McCoy.

2000 October 21: Seattle, D. Oliver (*NAB* 55.1, WTM:316).

2002 August 22: Marymoor Park, M. Hobbs (*NAB* 56.4, *WOSNews* 85).

2004 June 30: Vashon Island, singing male, E. Swan (*NAB* 58.4, *WOSNews* 96, Swan 2005:233).

2005 November 27-December 2: Auburn, C. Wright, R. Shaw, multiple observers (*WOSNews* 104, 105).

2006 June 23-July 13: Federal Way, T. Bock (*WOSNews* 108).

2007 May 30-June 7: Stillwater, singing male, R. Lawson, M. Hoffman, M. Breece, photos (*WOSNews* 112, 113, 114).

2008 July 6-8: Juanita Bay Park, R. Merrill, multiple observers (*WOSNews* 120).

2008 August 22: Juanita Bay Park, R. Merrill (*WOSNews* 121).

2009 June 11-July 19: Stillwater Unit of Snoqualmie Wildlife Area, 2 singing males and 1 female, C. Anderson; nest built; young fledged by July 19.

2010 May 27-June 20: Stillwater Unit of Snoqualmie Wildlife Area, at least 1 male, C. Anderson, multiple observers, photo.

OVENBIRD. Three records.

1980 June 26: West Seattle, specimen to Burke Museum, S. Sweeney (*WOSNews* 40).

1991 July 2: South of the Arboretum, singing male, R. Robinson, J. Hadley.

2001 June 17: Rainier Beach, killed by flying into window, specimen to Slater Museum, University of Puget Sound, D. Paulson (*NAB* 56.1, *WOSNews* 78).

NORTHERN WATERTHRUSH. Fourteen records, including four from August 14 to September 11, 2010.

1968 November 17-December 15: University of Washington, E. Willis (*AFN* 23.3) .

1978 December 30: Redmond, killed at window, specimen to Burke Museum, C. and C. Fanders (*AB* 33.3).

1986 September 8: Seattle, R. Thorne (*AB* 41.1).

1989 August 17: Montlake Fill, K. Aanerud (*AB* 44.1, *WB* 1:19).

1998 August 30: Montlake Fill, B. Vandenbosch, multiple observers (*NAB* 53.1, *WOSNews* 59).

2003 August 21: Montlake Fill, T. Aversa (*NAB* 58.1, *WOSNews* 91).

2004 September 2: Golden Gardens Park, D. McVay (*WOSNews* 97).

2006 August 21: Maple Leaf, Seattle, D. Paulson (*WOSNews* 109).

2006 August 21: Yarrow Bay, G. Luhm, photo (*WOSNews* 109).

2007 May 30: Rattlesnake Lake, C. and B. Pearson (*WOSNews* 113).

2010 August 14-16: Twin Ponds Park, Shoreline, M. Breuninger, multiple observers.

2010 August 16: Spring Lake near Maple Valley, T. Rohrer.

2010 September 10: Boeing Ponds, M. Breuninger.

2010 September 11: Treasure Island Park, Federal Way, H. Feddern.

HOODED WARBLER. One record.

1975 December 31-April 8, 1976 [April 4, *fide* WTM:319]: Discovery Park, adult male, L. Campbell, W. and E. Simpson-Stanton, multiple observers, E. Spragg, photo (*AB* 30.3:759).

TOWHEES, SPARROWS, LONGSPURS, BUNTINGS, TANAGERS, & GROSBEAKS

SPOTTED TOWHEES, the western species now split from the old Rufous-sided Towhee, are common permanent residents of shrubby thickets throughout the county, often in the company of our ubiquitous and conspicuous SONG SPARROWS. Other sparrows that are present in King County year-round exhibit season-

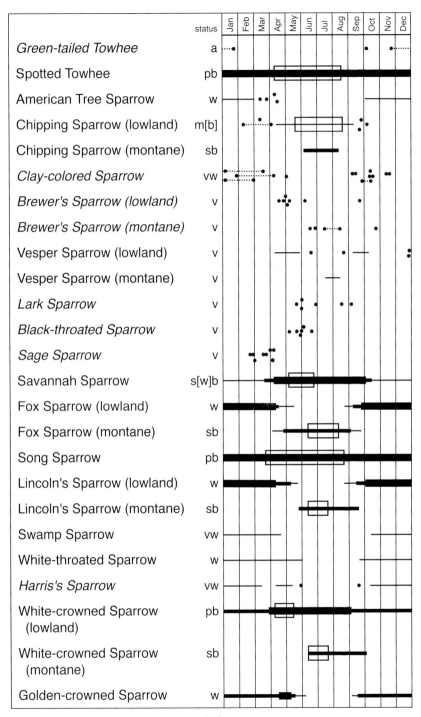

	status	Jan	Feb	Mar	Apr	May	Jun	Jul	Aug	Sep	Oct	Nov	Dec
Green-tailed Towhee	a												
Spotted Towhee	pb												
American Tree Sparrow	w												
Chipping Sparrow (lowland)	m[b]												
Chipping Sparrow (montane)	sb												
Clay-colored Sparrow	vw												
Brewer's Sparrow (lowland)	v												
Brewer's Sparrow (montane)	v												
Vesper Sparrow (lowland)	v												
Vesper Sparrow (montane)	v												
Lark Sparrow	v												
Black-throated Sparrow	v												
Sage Sparrow	v												
Savannah Sparrow	s[w]b												
Fox Sparrow (lowland)	w												
Fox Sparrow (montane)	sb												
Song Sparrow	pb												
Lincoln's Sparrow (lowland)	w												
Lincoln's Sparrow (montane)	sb												
Swamp Sparrow	vw												
White-throated Sparrow	w												
Harris's Sparrow	vw												
White-crowned Sparrow (lowland)	pb												
White-crowned Sparrow (montane)	sb												
Golden-crowned Sparrow	w												

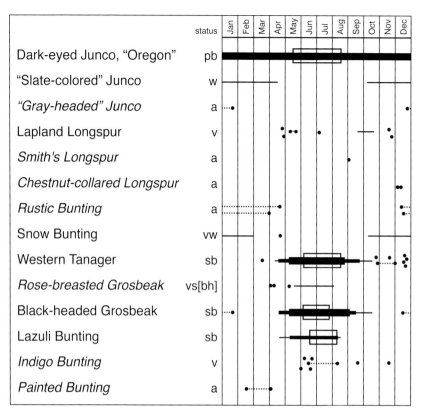

	status	Jan	Feb	Mar	Apr	May	Jun	Jul	Aug	Sep	Oct	Nov	Dec
Dark-eyed Junco, "Oregon"	pb												
"Slate-colored" Junco	w												
"Gray-headed" Junco	a												
Lapland Longspur	v												
Smith's Longspur	a												
Chestnut-collared Longspur	a												
Rustic Bunting	a												
Snow Bunting	vw												
Western Tanager	sb												
Rose-breasted Grosbeak	vs[bh]												
Black-headed Grosbeak	sb												
Lazuli Bunting	sb												
Indigo Bunting	v												
Painted Bunting	a												

al movements. WHITE-CROWNED SPARROWS are represented by two subspecies that may be distinguished by song and, with care, by plumage. They may prove to represent distinct species, as both have been found nesting in close proximity near Naches Pass, apparently without mixing (D. Beaudette, personal communication). In spring (from late March) and summer, the *pugetensis* race is predominant, nesting from urban shrub borders to subalpine clearings. There, they may share habitat with a few "Gambel's" White-crowneds *(gambelii),* at the southern limit of their more boreal breeding range. In winter, "Gambel's" White-crowneds mix with *pugetensis* White-crowneds across the King County lowlands, most commonly in brushy edges of farm fields and pastures, particularly in the Green River and Snoqualmie River Valleys.

FOX and LINCOLN'S SPARROWS exhibit a similar pattern, wintering in the lowlands, nesting in the mountains. Dark, brown-backed "Sooty" Fox Sparrows are fairly common in winter in mixed sparrow flocks, while "Slate-colored" Fox Sparrows nest in summer in brushy, subalpine habitats. Reports in winter of "Slate-colored" and/or "Red" Fox Sparrows (e.g., on November 18, 2009, "Red" Fox Sparrow north of Fall City, T. Aversa, *WOSNews* 128)—the latter from eastern and far northern populations—are rare and should be carefully documented.

DARK-EYED ("OREGON") JUNCOS are abundant in the lowlands in winter, favoring coniferous woodland patches and edges. A few remain to nest, even in Seattle city parks and adjacent suburbs. However, most depart for montane forests to nest, where they are common up to the timberline. Winter junco flocks predictably contain a small percentage of eastern "Slate-colored" Dark-eyed Juncos and, very rarely, perhaps a "Pink-sided" or even a "Gray-headed" Junco. One "Gray-headed" was well documented at a feeder east of Auburn in 2007. "Pink-sided" Juncos have been reported but not officially verified. They look a lot like female "Oregon" Juncos.

SAVANNAH SPARROWS are common from early spring through summer and are abundant during fall migration on lawns and in pastures and fallow fields. By October they have thinned out and are quite scarce until the following April.

GOLDEN-CROWNED SPARROWS are strictly winter visitors in King County, nesting rarely only as far south as Hart's Pass in the North Cascades. With SONG, WHITE-CROWNED, FOX, and LINCOLN'S SPARROWS, they constitute the "usual suspects" in shrubby thickets and field edges in winter. Such flocks deserve careful scrutiny, however, as they may hide one or more of our less regularly occurring winter sparrows, most often a WHITE-THROATED, less often a HARRIS'S, AMERICAN TREE, or CLAY-COLORED SPARROW. The Clay-colored remains sufficiently rare to have each record detailed among the rarities noted below.

The CHIPPING SPARROW is now a rare migrant and scarce nesting species along the Cascade Crest. By contrast, at the turn of the 20th century, Rathbun considered it a "rather common summer resident" and breeder (Rathbun 1902:137). As late as 1940, Miller and Curtis rated it a "common resident" on the University of Washington campus. It has declined to the vanishing point as a nester in the lowlands, in synch with the decline of the HOUSE WREN and WESTERN BLUE-BIRD, most likely due to the evolution of habitat from rough, clear-cut clearings to the more tidy suburban woodlands of today.

VESPER SPARROWS may have nested sparingly in the county in past decades, as at Marymoor Park in the 1960s, but now they are no more than annual vagrants, primarily during spring migration. In recent years (2006-2008), occasional Vesper or BREWER'S SPARROWS have been noted in late summer in clear-cuts and old burns on the Cascade Crest between Naches and Green Passes. They are not known to nest there and are more likely to be post-breeding wanderers from lower eastern Washington habitat.

Since the first state record at Lake Sammamish State Park in February 1972, SWAMP SPARROWS have come to be annual winter visitors. Given their skulking habits, they are often difficult to find, revealing their presence only by a sharp, metallic note from a cattail or Reed Canary Grass tract, and occasionally creeping into view at the base of a shrubby willow in mid-swamp. AMERICAN TREE SPARROWS are likewise rare winter visitors. They are reported regularly at the Marymoor Park compost piles and at the GRNRA in Kent but might turn up wherever there are winter sparrow concentrations.

LAPLAND LONGSPURS are rare but somewhat regular migrants at Montlake Fill and Sand Point. A single record, on July 1, 1975, at Montlake Fill is precisely between the end of spring and the beginning of the regular period of fall migration and must represent a very confused individual. SNOW BUNTINGS are irregular visitors, recorded in most but not all winters. A small flock foraged for a time in November 2005 at West Point Lighthouse in Discovery Park. Another flock was at Point Robinson on Maury Island from December 2005 through January 2006.

Rathbun considered the LAZULI BUNTING a "not uncommon summer resident" and breeder. He noted further that it seemed to be "more common than formerly" (Rathbun 1902:138), a fact he had noted as well for the Western Bluebird. These species, along with Northern Bobwhite, Mountain Quail, House Wren, and Chipping Sparrow, have all but vanished from King County lowlands since Rathbun's era. These species all still nest in loose association on cut-over land south of Tacoma. Perhaps the initial logging of the lowlands created favorable habitat that now has been converted to suburban residential use. In the past few years, only the Lazuli Bunting has staged a significant comeback in King County. Several singing males are now noted each spring along the Snoqualmie River Trail between Duvall and Carnation and at GRNRA in Kent. The summer of 2008 saw pairs likely nesting also at Marymoor Park and Montlake Fill. Lazuli Buntings are a colorful addition to our urban scenery, joining forces with our other summer spectaculars, the BLACK-HEADED GROSBEAK, WESTERN TANAGER, and BULLOCK'S ORIOLE.

Western Tanagers add a tropical flavor to our summers. They arrive at the end of April; rarely, one may stay the winter at an urban bird feeder. You might meet them anywhere from a Seattle park to a high Cascade forest. Their "kerreck" calls and scratchy, robin-like songs are heard more often than the birds are seen.

RARITIES

GREEN-TAILED TOWHEE. Two records.

1965 November 28-January 24, 1966: Newport Beach, D. Jelliffe, V. Cannon, E. Larrison, photos (*AFN* 20.3).

2006 October 2: Boeing Ponds, E. Hunn, M. Bartels, P. Rose, multiple observers (*WOSNews* 110).

CLAY-COLORED SPARROW. Nine records.

1992 January 25-March 28 [February 4, *fide* WTM:325]: Kent, E. Hunn, D. Beaudette, multiple observers (*AB* 46.3).

1998 January 2 until at least March 3: Duvall, E. Hunn, M. Hobbs, multiple observers (*FN* 52.2; *WOSNews* 55, 56; WTM:325).

1999 November 7-10: Montlake Fill, C. Sidles, M. Hobbs (*NAB* 54.1, *WOSNews* 66,WTM:325).

2003 October 7-10: Magnuson Park, K. Aanerud (*WOSNews* 92).

2005 September 28-October 9: Marymoor Park, M. Hobbs, B. Bell, E. Hunn (*WOSNews* 103, 104).

2006 January 1-February 16: Auburn, D. Swayne, T. Aversa, photo (*WOSNews* 105).

2006 October 7-8: Marymoor Park, M. Breece, multiple observers (*WOSNews* 110).

2008 April 28: Montlake Fill, M. Bartels (*WOSNews* 119).

2008 September 5-6: Montlake Fill, J. Bryant, C. Sidles (*WOSNews* 121).

BREWER'S SPARROW. Twelve records.

1995 April 27: Montlake Fill, C. Hill (*FN* 49.3, *WOSNews* 39, *ECNW* 36(9):11).

1995 May 3: Northeast Seattle P-patch, D. Beaudette (*FN* 49.3, *WOSNews* 39, *ECNW* 36(9):11, WTM:326).

1998 June 2: Green River Natural Resources Area, D. Beaudette.

1998 September 22: Marymoor Park, T. Aversa, K. Aanerud (*NAB* 53.1, *WOSNews* 59).

2000 April 29-30: Marymoor Park, singing male, E. Hunn, multiple observers (*NAB* 54.3, *WOSNews* 70).

2001 June 12: Rattlesnake Ridge, B. Boyes (*NAB* 56.4, addendum).

2007 April 10: Redmond, J. Tubbs (*WOSNews* 113).

2007 July 12 through August 9: North of Windy Gap, E. Hunn, multiple observers: first 1; then 20 on July 8, R. Merrill; 2 plus a juvenile July 28, M. Bartels; with 1 still there August 9, M. Breece, photos. Most likely a post-breeding, up-slope movement (*WOSNews* 114, 115).

2008 June 22: North of Windy Gap, silent bird, E. Hunn (*WOSNews* 120).

2010 April 23: Stillwater, singing male, S. Cormier-Aagaard.

Including "Timberline" Sparrow. One record.

2006 September 24: Windy Gap, E. Hunn, M. Bartels (*WOSNews* 109).

LARK SPARROW. Six records.

1965 June 23: Seattle, E. Stopps (*AFN* 19.5).

1990 May 28: Skykomish, D. Batchelder, S. Givan (*AB* 44.3).

1990 September 1: Discovery Park, D. Harville, G. Litwer.

1993 May 14: Montlake Fill, T. Hahn (*ECNW* 35(1):10).

2006 May 28: Lake McDonald, Renton, B. and B. Meyer, photos (*WOSNews* 107).

2007 August 12: Montlake Fill, C. Sidles, multiple observers, photo (*WOSNews* 115).

BLACK-THROATED SPARROW. Six records.

1981 June 14: Issaquah, A. and N. Lang (*AB* 35.6, *WOSNews* 47).

1989 May 19-20: Seattle, male, T. Haas, R. Thorne, K. Aanerud (*AB* 43.3, *WOSNews* 47, *WB* 1:20).

1994 May 1: Carnation, B. Chubb (*FN* 48.5, *WOSNews* 33, *ECNW* 36(1):10).

1994 May 30: Shoreview Park, Shoreline, D. Beaudette, E. Hunn, multiple observers (*FN* 48.5, *WOSNews* 33, *ECNW* 36(1):10).

1999 May 29: Carnation, S. Pink (*NAB* 53.3, *WOSNews* 63).

2007 May 27: Carnation, J. Cooper (*WOSNews* 113).

SAGE SPARROW. Five records.

1980 February 17-19: Montlake Fill, B. and P. Evans, E. Ratoosh, E. Hunn, multiple observers (*AB* 34.3, *WB* 4:27).

1987 March 14-15: Montlake Fill, D. Beaudette, S. Schaefer et al. (*AB* 41.3).

1990 March 31: Seattle, K. Aanerud (*AB* 44.3).

1999 February 23: Lake Sammamish State Park, M. Hobbs (*NAB* 53.2, *WOSNews* 62).

2007 March 29 to April 2: Marymoor Park, M. Bartels, M. Hobbs, multiple observers, photos (*WOSNews* 113).

SMITH'S LONGSPUR. One record.

2006 August 30: Marymoor Park, M. Bartels, multiple observers, O. Oliver, photos (*WOSNews* 109).

CHESTNUT-COLLARED LONGSPUR. One record.

1995 December 3-12: Montlake Fill, adult male, C. McInerny, multiple observers, photos (*FN* 50.2, *WOSNews* 42, 43, 47).

RUSTIC BUNTING. Two records.

 1986 December 15-March 22, 1987: Kent, D. Beaudette, multiple observers, D. Paulson, photos (*AB* 41.2, 41.3, *WOSNews* 40).

 1988 December 11-April 9, 1989: Kent, E. Hunn, J. Gatchet (*AB* 43.2, 43.3, *WOSNews* 40).

ROSE-BREASTED GROSBEAK. Thirteen records.

 1979 June 22: Dash Point, singing male, T. Bock (*WOSNews* 40).

 1982 June 30: Near Green Lake, adult male, M. Keplinger (*AB* 36.6, *WOSNews* 40).

 1991 June 20-July 30: South of Issaquah, male, S. Mottaz, D. Paulson, M. Hatheway, photos (*AB* 45.5, *ECNW* 33(3):11), may have mated with a female Black-headed Grosbeak.

 1994 May 22: Seattle, W. Iverson (*FN* 48.3, *WOSNews* 33, 40, *ECNW* 36(1):11).

 1998 May 3: Seattle, male, G. Eddy (*FN* 52.4).

 1999 July 22-23: Seattle, C. Cretin (*NAB* 53.4).

 2001 June 8-12: East Lake Sammamish, A. Weinmann, E. Hunn, photos (*WOSNews* 78).

 2002 April 1-4: Seattle, immature male, R. Lawson, M. Hobbs, I. Samowitz, photos (*NAB* 56.3, *WOSNews* 82, *WB* 9:48).

 2003 June 1-3: Montlake Fill, male, J. Engel, M. Dossett (*NAB* 57.4, *WOSNews* 90).

 2005 July 22: Lake Forest Park, male, M. Bolender (*WOSNews* 102).

 2006 May 29: Discovery Park, singing male, N. Bogue (*WOSNews* 107).

 2008 July 5: Near Kent, male, D. Streiffert, photo (*WOSNews* 118, 120).

 2010 June 4: Bellevue, adult male, R. Rowlett.

INDIGO BUNTING. Seven records.

 1988 September 13: Seattle, immature, K. Aanerud (*WOSNews* 40, WTM:343, *WB* 1:20).

 1993 June 12-13: North Bend, anonymous (*ECNW* 35(1):10).

 1996 June 1: Montlake Fill, Seattle [Redmond, *fide* WTM:343], male, photo (*FN* 50.5, *WOSNews* 46, 47).

 2004 May 25: Soos Creek, male, J. Greene (*WOSNews* 95).

 2008 June 11: Auburn, male, S. Daniels, K. Steiner, K. Andrich (*WOSNews* 120) .

 2008 November 15: Juanita Bay Park, female, R. Merrill, photos (*WOSNews* 122).

 2009 June 10-August 9: Three Forks Natural Area, North Bend, adult male, K. and T. Grant, E. Hunn, multiple observers, photos (*WOSNews* 126, 127).

PAINTED BUNTING. One record.

 2002 February 10-13: South Seattle, then February 25 to March 31, Capitol Hill, male, R. Lawson, multiple observers, photos (*NAB* 56.3; *WOSNews* 81, 82; *WB* 9:48).

ICTERIDS

WESTERN MEADOWLARKS find little appropriate habitat in our largely wooded county. In winter they regularly frequent the open grasslands of Montlake Fill and Magnuson Park, and there may be modest flocks in Kent, Sammamish, and Snoqualmie Valley fields. However, there was but a single reference to nesting prior to 1982, and that referred vaguely to the "Seattle-Tacoma area" (Jewett et al. 1953:583). An adult feeding young south of Renton on July 4, 1982, provided confirmation (E. Hunn). RED-WINGED BLACKBIRDS are full-time residents, flocking with their near-relations in farm fields in winter. In late winter, males in full "song" and with crimson epaulets flaring, stake out territories in virtually every cattail marsh. YELLOW-HEADED BLACKBIRDS are stragglers primarily in spring, but they also turn up now and then in summer, late fall, and early winter. BREWER'S BLACKBIRDS are most abundant about farmland, especially in Kent and Auburn and the Snoqualmie River Valley, but they also favor civilized oases well into the montane zone, such as the Snoqualmie Pass ski resorts. In winter a few scattered flocks frequent shopping center parking lots. BULLOCK'S ORIOLES have increased in recent years; sightings prior to 1970 were cause for considerable excited commentary by local birders. There is only one record for the county prior to 1950, that of a nest in July 1924 "north of Seattle" (*The Murrelet* 5(3):11). The Bullock's Oriole is now a regular nester in streamside cottonwoods throughout the lowlands. The BROWN-HEADED COWBIRD is likewise on the increase. It was unknown before May 15, 1954 (*AFN* 8.4). Young were noted on July 4, 1955, on the University of Washington campus (*AFN* 9.4), the first breeding record for western Washington. The cowbird is now all too common in a variety of lowland habitats, and it nests up to Snoqualmie Pass. A few join blackbird and starling congregations in winter, most often near Kent. Cowbirds are nest parasites that lay eggs in the nests of other birds. The cowbird egg hatches before those of the host, and the baby cowbird then proceeds to expropriate all food intended for the cowbird's nest-mates. Cowbird parasitism is implicated in population declines of Willow Flycatchers, vireos, and the Yellow Warbler (U.S. Fish and Wildlife Service, Sensitive Bird Species, Region One, 1982).

RARITIES

BOBOLINK. Ten records.

1979   May 25: Montlake Fill, male, B. Meilleur (*WOSNews* 47, *WB* 4:28).

1980   June 2-3: Montlake Fill, female, E. Ratoosh (*WOSNews* 47, *WB* 4:28).

1981   May 26-28: Montlake Fill, male, M. Robertson, E. Ratoosh (*AB* 35.5, *WB* 4:28).

1981   September 3-14: Montlake Fill, D. Paulson, multiple observers (*AB* 36.2, *WOSNews* 47, *WB* 4:28).

1982   August 15: Montlake Fill, male, M. Robertson (*AB* 37.2, *WB* 4:28).

1983   October 10: Montlake Fill, J. Flynn, D. Beaudette (personal communication, *AB* 38.2 , *WB* 4:28).

1995   September 5: Magnuson Park, J. Flynn (*FN* 50.1, *WOSNews* 41).

1995   October 1-2: Seattle, B. Sundstrom (*FN* 50.1, *WOSNews* 42).

2001   June 1: Genesee Park, Seattle, S. Terry (*NAB* 55.3, *WOSNews* 78).

2006   June 5: Duvall, M. Harenda (*WOSNews* 108).

RUSTY BLACKBIRD. Seven records.

1980s: Maury Island, J. Van Os (Swan 2005:249).

1993   October 5-8: Montlake Fill, E. Norwood, K. Aanerud, D. Beaudette (*AB* 48.1, *ECNW* 35(3):11, *WOSNews* 29, 42, 47).

1994   September 24: Montlake Fill, E. Norwood (*WOSNews* 35, *ECNW* 36(5):11).

1995   October 31: Montlake Fill, K. Aanerud, E. Norwood (*FN* 50.1, *WOSNews* 42, 47).

2003   October 24-28: Kent, female, M. Breece (*NAB* 58.1, *WOSNews* 92).

2007   January 4-31: Carnation, 1 to 3 individuals, males and female, E. Hunn, M. Breece, multiple observers, photos (*WOSNews* 111).

2009   November 21: North of Fall City, female, B. Meilleur, multiple observers (*WOSNews* 128).

COMMON GRACKLE. Two records.

1965   June 26-27: South Seattle, E. Stopps, photo (*The Murrelet* 47(1): 19-20).

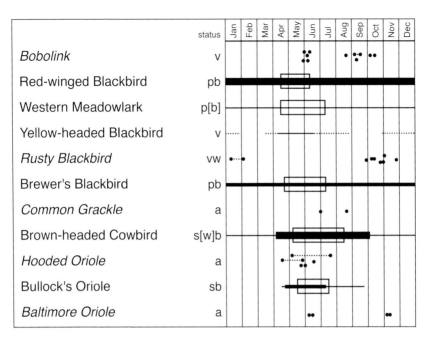

	status	Jan	Feb	Mar	Apr	May	Jun	Jul	Aug	Sep	Oct	Nov	Dec
Bobolink	v												
Red-winged Blackbird	pb												
Western Meadowlark	p[b]												
Yellow-headed Blackbird	v												
Rusty Blackbird	vw												
Brewer's Blackbird	pb												
Common Grackle	a												
Brown-headed Cowbird	s[w]b												
Hooded Oriole	a												
Bullock's Oriole	sb												
Baltimore Oriole	a												

2003 August 15: Auburn, A. Roedell (*NAB* 58.1, *WOSNews* 91).

An odd bird frequenting a parking lot in Auburn from October 19 to 24, 2002, was thought to be a Brewer's Blackbird x Great-tailed Grackle hybrid (M. Willison, J. Higbee, R. Sullivan, photos, *WOSNews* 86).

HOODED ORIOLE. Two records, one represented by the same adult male that returned for three successive summers.

2005 June 12: Magnolia, Seattle, adult, C. Conelly and R. Brown (*WOSNews* 102).

2006 May 2 until at least July 14: Magnolia, Seattle, multiple observers, photos (*WOSNews* 107, 108).

2006 May 20-29: Enumclaw, M. Rosenberger, *fide* G. Gillson, photo (*WOSNews* 107).

2007 April 12 until at least May 23: Magnolia, C. Conelly and M. Bartels (*WOSNews* 113).

BALTIMORE ORIOLE. Two records.

1975 November 5-8: Seattle, adult male, D. Pengelley, P. Duxler (*WB* 5:21).

2006 June 4-11: Marymoor Park, young male, D. White, multiple observers, photos, sound recordings (*WOSNews* 108).

Finches, Crossbills, Siskins, & Allies, & the House Sparrow

The PINE GROSBEAK is known only as an erratic winter visitor in the lowlands. It was widely reported during the winter of 1973-1974, which was also a great Snowy Owl invasion winter. In recent years Pine Grosbeaks have proved to be regular in summer—probably nesting—near Naches Pass at the Cascade Crest. GRAY-CROWNED ROSY-FINCHES (of the race *littoralis*, the Hepburn's form) nest in rocky alpine areas. I have found them in summer near the summits of Red Mountain and Snoqualmie, Kendall, and Malachite Peaks, all above 5500 feet. Rosy-Finches descend erratically to the lowlands (or come south from Alaska) some winters, where they favor open sandy or gravelly ground, such as along the shores of Puget Sound. RED CROSSBILLS may at times be common in lowland King County and are regular in the mountains. However, several "call types" may be represented, each adapted to forage on a different species of conifer. To the unaided ear, the calls of these various Red Crossbill varieties are virtually indistinguishable, but played back at half- or quarter-speed (thus more accurately representing how the crossbills themselves might perceive these calls) they are quite distinct. The call types most likely to be found in King County are types 3 and 4, which are partial to Douglas Fir and Western Hemlock, respectively (Groth 1993). In some years, crossbills of any kind are nearly impossible to find, as they move in search of ripe cone crops. In other winters, they may be abundant and readily approached at ski resorts, such as at Stevens Pass. January and February 2008 were fantastic months for crossbills and other winter finches at Stevens Pass and along the Skyline Trail on the ridge just north of the highway. Snowshoe hikers were rewarded here with dozens of both Red and WHITE-WINGED CROSSBILLS—the latter always a rare treat for us—which were joined by CASSIN'S FINCHES, EVENING GROSBEAKS, and COMMON REDPOLLS. Even a flock of Gray-crowned Rosy-Finches and a pair of Pine Grosbeaks put in an appearance. Some of the White-winged Crossbills were in juvenal plumage, suggestive of breeding nearby, stimulated by the abundant conifer seed crop. Such "winter finch" congregations are not to be expected every winter. In some winters, even PINE SISKINS are hard to find, though more often they are common—and in some years abundant—throughout the county.

HOUSE FINCHES are a relatively recent addition to the local bird scene. The species was first recorded in the county on April 22, 1953, in West Seattle. Two pairs were feeding young there June 18 of the same year (*AFN* 7.5). It is a species "on the move," having expanded its range to occupy much of the eastern United States since being released in New York in 1940. Curiously, the species may have spread to Seattle initially from introductions in Victoria, B.C. (Edwards and Stirling 1961:38-42). House Finches are now continuously distributed nearly from coast to coast. They are characteristic of more "humanized environments" than is the PURPLE FINCH, which has been in retreat from our suburban margins for the past several decades. Neither species is found in the montane zone.

The AMERICAN GOLDFINCH—our official Washington State Bird—may be found foraging in brushy fields or in alder and birch tops at every season, though in fall, winter, and early spring, the males are far less conspicuously brilliant than in their breeding glory.

CASSIN'S FINCHES nest regularly in small numbers at the Cascade Crest and may infrequently join winter finch flocks when seed crops are abundant. Lowland records come from four Seattle CBCs. Single birds were counted in 1927, 1928, and 1934, and four birds were counted in 1953. E. Larrison identified another

Species	status	Jan	Feb	Mar	Apr	May	Jun	Jul	Aug	Sep	Oct	Nov	Dec
Brambling	a												
Gray-crowned Rosy-Finch (lowland)	v												
Gray-crowned Rosy-Finch (montane)	s[w]b												
Pine Grosbeak (lowland)	vw												
Pine Grosbeak (montane)	s[w]b												
Purple Finch	pb												
Cassin's Finch (lowland)	v												
Cassin's Finch (montane)	s[w]b												
House Finch	pb												
Red Crossbill	p[b]												
White-winged Crossbill (lowland)	v												
White-winged Crossbill (montane)	vw[b]												
Common Redpoll	w												
Hoary Redpoll	a												
Pine Siskin	pb												
Lesser Goldfinch	a												
American Goldfinch	pb												
Evening Grosbeak	pb												
House Sparrow	pbi												

on the University of Washington campus on March 16, 1939 (Miller and Curtis 1940:46), but his identification has been questioned (Slipp 1947:86-87). These extralimital records of Cassin's Finch require careful scrutiny. Specimens recently collected at what was believed to be a low-elevation colony in western Washington proved to be Purple Finches. The songs of Cassin's and Purple Finches are distinguishable with practice, but each species exhibits great individual variation.

The Purple's song is more "vague," less sharply and forcefully presented, and less thrasher-like compared to the Cassin's. Call notes also differ. Purple Finches give a soft "kip" reminiscent of distant Red Crossbills. Cassin's Finches often repeat a querulous, slurred, two-syllable "kerr-ip." Females are at least as easy to separate by plumage characters as males. Female Cassin's show fine, sharp breast-streaking and lack the Purple's olive tones on the back. Male and female Cassin's Finches have clearly streaked under-tail coverts, while those of the Purple Finch are unmarked or only lightly and indistinctly streaked. This characteristic, however, is not readily seen in the field. The culmen ridge of Cassin's Finch is less curved than that of either Purple or House Finches.

EVENING GROSBEAKS used to arrive in lowland King County in numbers each spring with great regularity about the first of May, when several hundred could be seen feeding in the maples and dropping to the lawns on the University of Washington upper campus. They would remain for several weeks, then repair to the forests of the east slopes of the Cascades to nest. (They were the most abundant species on the Cle Elum Breeding Bird Survey when that was my route in the 1970s.) These spring lowland flocks come no longer. In recent years, Evening Grosbeaks occur only irregularly and in small numbers in King County, though some may remain to nest, as suggested by an adult feeding young on July 25, 1952, at Maple Valley (*AFN* 6.5). Others probably nest in the county near the Cascade Crest. Winter abundance varies from locally common to nonexistent.

HOUSE SPARROWS have been with us since June 1897, the date of Rathbun's first record. In 1898 he saw 14; in 1899, 70; and by 1901 House Sparrows were "scattered about the business portion of the city" (Rathbun 1902:140-141). While the starling is pernicious, the House Sparrow is simply unattractive and a scourge at urban bird feeding stations.

RARITIES

BRAMBLING. One record.
> 1982   January 16 [January 6, *fide* WTM:351] to March 22: Issaquah, A. and N. Lang, multiple observers, photos (*AB* 36.3, 36.5, *WOSNews* 40).

HOARY REDPOLL. One record.
> 2001   December 29: Foster Island, Seattle, 2 birds, E. Hunn, multiple observers (CBC).

LESSER GOLDFINCH. Three records.
> 1997   July 1: Duvall, B. Helmboldt (*FN* 51.5, [June 28 *fide* WOSNews* 52]).
> 2008   May 18: Redmond, male, R. and L. Reis.
> 2009   May 25: Stillwater Unit, SnoqualmieWildlife Area, female, E. Hunn.

5. OTHER LIVING THINGS

To see only birds—no matter how conspicuous, diverse, and endearing they may be—without a growing awareness of the other living things whose fates are entwined with those of the birds, is to applaud nature's drama with one hand only. I have neither the expertise nor the space here to treat the natural history of King County as a whole, on a par with Storer and Usinger's magnificent *Sierra Nevada Natural History.* I can only offer the following preliminary lists of mammals, herps (that is, reptiles and amphibians), dragonflies and damselflies, butterflies, and trees, with some sketchy remarks to stimulate more detailed research in the future.

Mammals

The nomenclature and distribution for terrestrial species are based largely on Johnson and Cassidy 1997, with help from the Burke Museum. In addition, Taylor and Shaw 1929 cite many local records compiled in surveys conducted at intervals dating from 1889, and from concentrated field work done in 1897 and again from 1917 through 1921.

MARSUPIALS

Common Opossum *(Didelphis marsupialis).* Introduced ca. 1941. Widespread in the lowlands, though apparently still absent from Vashon Island.

INSECTIVORES

Marsh Shrew/Pacific Water Shrew/Bendire's Shrew *(Sorex bendirii).* Widespread in wetlands mostly below 4000 feet.

Cinereus Shrew/Masked Shrew *(Sorex cinereus).* Rare in King County; a record from near Snoqualmie Pass.

Dusky Shrew/Montane Shrew *(Sorex monticolus).* Widespread in coniferous forests.

American Water Shrew/Northern Water Shrew *(Sorex palustris).* Favors mountain streams with cold, clear water.

Trowbridge's Shrew *(Sorex trowbridgii).* In forests mostly below 3000 feet; also on Vashon Island.

Vagrant Shrew *(Sorex vagrans).* Our most common and widely distributed shrew.

Shrew-mole *(Neurotrichus gibbsii).* Nearly universal, from Seattle to Stevens Pass.

Coast Mole/Pacific Mole *(Scapanus orarius).* Widespread into the lower mountains; also on Vashon Island.

Townsend's Mole *(Scapanus townsendii).* In open areas below 2000 feet.

BATS

Californian Myotis *(Myotis californicus).*

Long-eared Myotis *(Myotis evotis).* Presumed to be widespread though uncommon.

Little Brown Myotis/Little Brown Bat *(Myotis lucifugus).* Common in forests and urban areas.

Long-legged Myotis *(Myotis volans).* Presumably widespread in forests.

Yuma Myotis *(Myotis yumanensis).* A bat of low elevation forests.

Hoary Bat *(Lasiurus cinereus).* Common in coniferous timber near Seattle; flies fast and straight.

Silver-haired Bat *(Lasionycteris noctivagans).* A forest bat.

Big Brown Bat *(Eptesicus fuscus).* Ubiquitous.

Townsend's Big-eared Bat/Western Big-eared Bat *(Corynorhinus (formerly Plecotus) townsendii).* In forests at lower elevations.

LAGOMORPHS

American Pika *(Ochotona princeps).* Common in talus slides in the high Cascades; occasionally at lower elevations.

Snowshoe Hare *(Lepus americanus).* May occur throughout the county in forests but most often seen at higher elevations, as near Naches Pass; no pure white phase here.

Eastern Cottontail *(Sylvilagus floridanus).* Introduced in Washington since 1926; our only "cottontail"; also on Vashon Island.

RODENTS

Mountain Beaver *(Aplodontia rufa).* Sentimental favorite to become our state mammal. Mountain Beavers' burrows are everywhere underfoot in Discovery Park. A key food item for Golden Eagles in high mountain clear-cuts.

Hoary Marmot *(Marmota caligata).* Listen for their sharp whistles above timberline, as on Kelly Butte.

Cascade Golden-mantled Ground Squirrel *(Spermophilus saturatus).* Common at or near timberline, as near Naches Pass.

Yellow-pine Chipmunk *(Tamias amoenus).* Replaces Townsend's Chipmunk above the treeline.

Townsend's Chipmunk *(Tamias townsendii).* Common chipmunk from the Sound to the highest forests.

Eastern Gray Squirrel *(Sciurus carolinensis).* Introduced about 1920 at Woodland Park; now common about the city and in the suburbs.

Fox Squirrel *(Sciurus niger).* Introduced; scarce; coexisted with the Eastern Gray Squirrel in the Arboretum in the 1970s but apparently no longer.

Douglas Squirrel/Chickaree *(Tamiasciurus douglasii)*. Familiar scolds of deep woods throughout; active all winter.

Northern Flying Squirrel *(Glaucomys sabrinus)*. Favorite food of the Spotted Owl. Most abundant in old-growth forest.

American Beaver *(Castor canadensis)*. Still at work in Union Bay. One (or more) recently felled a large cottonwood at the southeast corner of Montlake Fill.

Mazama Pocket Gopher *(Thomomys mazama)*. No positive record, but an isolated prairie population is known from Pierce County near Dash Point.

Northern Pocket Gopher *(Thomomys talpoides)*. One record from the upper Green River for this eastside species.

Bushy-tailed Woodrat *(Neotoma cinerea)*. Uncommon to rare; one recent record east of Lake Washington.

Northwestern Deermouse/Forest Deermouse/Keen's Mouse *(Peromyscus keeni)*. Widespread in forests; backpack thieves of the high country.

North American Deermouse *(Peromyscus maniculatus)*. Lower elevation forests; may outnumber Forest Deer Mice in clear-cuts.

Southern Red-backed Vole *(Myodes [Clethrionomys] gapperi)*. Widespread in forests; also on Vashon Island.

Long-tailed Vole *(Microtus longicaudus)*. Common throughout the county, especially near water.

Creeping Vole/Oregon Vole *(Microtus oregoni)*. Common throughout the county; abundant in clear-cuts.

Richardson's Vole *(Microtus richardsoni)*. Beside clear, cold mountain streams.

Townsend's Vole *(Microtus townsendii)*. Common below 1000 feet.

American Beaver at Montlake Fill (© Tim Kuhn).

Common Muskrat *(Ondatra zibethicus)*. Can be found, for example, at Union Bay and in the Green River Valley marshes.

Western Heather Vole *(Phenacomys intermedius)*. In mountain forests and meadows above 2400 feet.

Pacific Jumping Mouse *(Zapus trinotatus)*. Common throughout the county in forests; if you see a "kangaroo rat" in the mountains, this is it.

North American Porcupine *(Erethizon dorsatum)*. Recent invader from eastern Washington, now widespread though not common in King County.

Nutria *(Myocastor coypus)*. Introduced from South America; escaped in the Green River Valley during a flood in 1935; established along the Snoqualmie River by 1948; now conspicuous at Montlake Fill.

House Mouse *(Mus musculus)*. Introduced and common in cities and adjacent farmlands.

Norway Rat *(Rattus norvegicus)*. Appears to dominate the Black Rat; common alien in urban areas, spreading beyond and along streams.

Black Rat *(Rattus rattus)*. Both *Rattus* species are introduced; both are important prey items for urban Great Horned Owls; Black Rats appear to prefer beach habitats and ports.

CETACEANS

(Scheffer and Slipp 1948 is a key reference.)

Orca/Killer Whale *(Orcinus orca)*. Rated second most common local cetacean by the American Cetacean Society.

False Killer Whale *(Pseudorca crassidens)*. Recorded up-Sound from Seattle.

Harbor Porpoise *(Phocoena phocoena)*. Occasionally enters freshwater via the Ship Canal.

Dall's Porpoise *(Phocoenoides dalli)*. Looks like a miniature Orca. Our most common local cetacean, often escorting ships.

Gray Whale *(Eschrichtius robustus)*. Recorded up-Sound from Seattle.

Fin Whale *(Balaenoptera physalus)*. Recorded up-Sound from Seattle.

Common Minke Whale/Piked Whale *(Balaenoptera acutorostrata)*. One was found stranded 15 miles up the Snohomish River (Scattergood 1949).

Humpback Whale *(Megaptera novaeangliae)*. One sighted about once a year in Puget Sound.

CARNIVORES

Coyote *(Canis latrans)*. Common in the suburbs and not scarce in Seattle either, as at Carkeek and Seward Parks; said to prey regularly on house cats and small dogs; not yet known from Vashon Island. Present at Montlake Fill.

Gray Wolf *(Canis lupus)*. King County high country is within the historic range; current status uncertain; recent reports likely of large dogs or feral hybrids.

Red Fox *(Vulpes vulpes)*. Lowland populations introduced; native at timberline; the two populations separated by wet mid-elevation forest they both avoid.

Black Bear *(Ursus americanus)*. Still resident on Cougar Mountain; a young bear was spotted on fraternity row in the University District in 2007. It was killed inadvertently in the effort to capture it.

Grizzly Bear *(Ursus arctos horribilis)*. King County high country north of Snoqualmie Pass is within the historic range; some recent sightings just east and south of us.

Raccoon *(Procyon lotor)*. Prowls city backyards and fishes in Union Bay; mostly below 3000 feet.

American Marten *(Martes americana)*. One cooperative individual entertained a Seattle Audubon Society field trip at Naches Pass in 2007.

Fisher *(Martes pennanti)*. Present status uncertain; may be locally extirpated; one specimen from just west of Snoqualmie Pass.

Short-tailed Weasel/Ermine *(Mustela erminea)*. Widespread at all elevations; also on Vashon Island.

Long-tailed Weasel *(Mustela frenata)*. Widespread and common, but absent from Vashon; most sightings in and near Seattle are probably this species.

American Mink *(Mustela vison)*. Widespread at low to middle elevations near water.

Wolverine *(Gulo gulo)*. The Wolverine's local status was summarized by Johnson 1977. Two recent sightings on Mt. Adams and on the Yakima Indian Reservation suggest that the occasional Wolverine might stray along the Cascade Crest of King County; however, the best current estimate for the population of Wolverines in the entire state is just 25.

Striped Skunk *(Mephitis mephitis)*. Widespread in open areas below 2000 feet; absent from Vashon Island.

Western Spotted Skunk *(Spilogale gracilis)*. I found one dead at 3250 feet elevation on the road to Naches Pass in 2006; occurs on Vashon.

North American River Otter/Northern River Otter *(Lontra [Lutra] canadensis)*. Frequently observed frolicking in saltwater off Carkeek Park and Alki.

Cougar/Mountain Lion *(Puma concolor)*. A young male—dubbed D. B. Cougar by the local press—was captured in Discovery Park in 1981 then released in the mountains; another young male was trapped in Discovery Park over Labor Day 2009 and also released in the Cascade foothills. How these big cats managed to get to Discovery Park remains something of a mystery. Dozens of bounties were paid during the 1950s for Mountain Lions killed in King County.

Bobcat *(Lynx rufus)*. Reported infrequently as close in as Woodinville; common in the foothills.

Steller's Sea Lion *(Eumetopias jubatus)*. Visits King County waters on occasion, as off West Point.

California Sea Lion *(Zalophus californianus)*. Common; a group lounges on the yellow channel buoy off West Point. May be heard bellowing at Shilshole Bay.

Harbor Seal *(Phoca vitulina)*. Fairly common about Vashon Island. Breeds at McNeil Island in Pierce County.

Northern Elephant Seal *(Mirounga angustirostris)*. An adult male was photographed one-half mile off Edmonds in 1963 (Scheffer and Kenyon).

Coyote hunting (© Gregg Thompson).

UNGULATES

Elk/Wapiti *(Cervus canadensis)*. May once have been a native, but present populations are introduced; common at Government Meadow near Naches Pass.

Mule Deer *(Odocoileus hemionus)*. Ours are "Black-tailed Deer" *(Odocoileus hemionus columbianus)*.

Mountain Goat *(Oreamnos americanus)*. Look for them on Kelly Butte and Mt. Si's
northwest face; said to host the large ticks one may encounter on Kelly Butte.

HERPS

SALAMANDERS

Northwestern Salamander *(Ambystoma gracile)*. Prefers lakes, marshes, and riparian
zones at lower elevations (Dvornich, McAllister, and Aubry 1997:36). Breeds
in mid-February at Camp Long in Seattle and is common in bogs east of Lake
Sammamish.

Long-toed Salamander *(Ambystoma macrodactylum)*. Said to depend on drier open-
ings or remnant prairies in forests (Dvornich, McAllister, and Aubry 1997:38).
I have found this one at Duvall and on Vashon Island, under logs.

Coastal Giant Salamander *(Dicamptodon tenebrosus)*. Likes swift streams. Said to
live in Thornton Creek and in Carkeek Park, Seattle.

Rough-skinned Newt *(Taricha granulosa)*. Prefers lakes and riparian habitats
(Dvornich, McAllister, and Aubry 1997:50). Known for migrating across roads
after heavy rains. It doesn't always make it. Common, as at Carnation Marsh.

Western Red-backed Salamander *(Plethodon vehiculum)*. Conifer-lined riparian areas are good habitats for this species (Dvornich, McAllister, and Aubry
1997:58). I found one once high on Cougar Mountain, under bark.

Ensatina *(Ensatina eschscholtzii)*. Our most common salamander. Occurs at Discovery Park, the Arboretum, and Seward Park. Occasionally found in piles of debris in suburban yards.

FROGS & TOADS

Coastal Tailed Frog *(Ascaphus truei)*. Favors high mountain streams. Tadpole has a sucker mouth to cling to rocks in fast water.

Western Toad *(Bufo boreas)*. Needs no introduction. May occur high in the mountains. Not known from Vashon or Maury Islands (Dvornich, McAllister, and Aubry 1997:66).

Pacific Treefrog *(Pseudacris regilla)*. Croaks, "Rainier," on summer nights. Heard in midwinter, the croak slowing to a groan in cold weather. Ubiquitous.

Northern Red-legged Frog *(Rana aurora)*. "… breeds in floodplain pools in the open areas of riparian hardwood forests" (Dvornich, McAllister, and Aubry 1997:72). Our most common lowland "true frog," the introduced Bullfrog excepted. Bullfrogs may eat Red-legged Frogs and pose a threat to their survival.

Cascades Frog *(Rana cascadae)*. Common above 4,000 feet in mountain ponds and streams.

Oregon Spotted Frog *(Rana pretiosa)*. Recorded long ago from Seattle but now known only from Pierce and Klickitat Counties.

Bullfrog *(Rana catesbeiana)*. Introduced and common in lower elevation ponds. Says, "Jug-o-rum." Drives out native frogs. Common at Montlake Fill.

TURTLES

Painted Turtle *(Chrysemys picta)*. Prefers lake margins at low elevations. Common in Union Bay. May be losing out to the introduced Red-eared Slider (Dvornich, McAllister, and Aubry 1997:86).

Western Pond Turtle *(Clemmys marmorata)*. Most likely extirpated from King County by the 1950s.

Red-eared Slider *(Trachemys scripta)*. Introduced. A common pet-store turtle; has also escaped or been released and is now established.

LIZARDS

Northern Alligator Lizard *(Elgaria coerulea)*. Rather common at low to middle elevations. Occurs at Discovery Park.

Western Fence Lizard *(Sceloporus occidentalis)*. Western Washington records limited to Puget Sound beaches. Known from Vashon Island and Lincoln Park, Seattle, though may not persist.

SNAKES

Rubber Boa *(Charina bottae)*. Historic records from Seattle but now apparently rare, though its nocturnal habits make it difficult to find.

Western Terrestrial Garter Snake *(Thamnophis elegans)*. Wide ranging and variable.

Our subspecies is the Puget Sound Garter Snake *(T. e. pickeringii)*. It tends to be blackish, sometimes sporting a row of red spots along the sides (Storm and Leonard 1995:148-153).

Northwestern Garter Snake *(Thamnophis ordinoides)*. Common at low to middle elevations, even in cities.

Common Garter Snake *(Thamnophis sirtalis)*. Common and widespread at low to middle elevations, including developed areas. Highly variable. Our subspecies is the Wandering Garter Snake *(T. s. elegans)* (Storm and Leonard 1995:138-143).

DRAGONFLIES & DAMSELFLIES (ODONATA)

With 57 species (of 25 genera of 9 families), King has the highest county list for the state. Okanogan is second with 56. Washington's list of 80 species is half that of most eastern states, and Sussex County, New Jersey, has the all-American single-county record of 142 species. (The nomenclature and distribution of King County species are based largely on Paulson 2009.)

DAMSELFLIES (Zygoptera)

Broad-winged Damsels (Calopterygidae)

River Jewelwing *(Calopteryx aequabilis)*. So far known only from Stossel Creek, east of Duvall. Habitat: small rivers and slow streams. June 1-September 3 (known flight seasons refer to entire state).

Spreadwings (Lestidae)

Spotted Spreadwing *(Lestes congener)*. Common throughout lowlands and to 5800 feet in mountains (elevation ranges refer to entire state). Habitat: ponds and lakes, often larger water bodies than those inhabited by others of this genus. The last damselfly species to fly in autumn. June 23-November 15.

Northern Spreadwing *(Lestes disjunctus)*. Common throughout lowlands and to 5800 feet in mountains. Habitat: ponds and lakes. June 23-October 21.

Emerald Spreadwing *(Lestes dryas)*. Locally distributed throughout lowlands but more common in mountains to 5800 feet. Habitat: ponds, often temporary, with dense marsh vegetation. June 1-September 29.

Sweetflag Spreadwing *(Lestes forcipatus)*. Apparently widespread but locally common, known from a marshy bog pond near Issaquah. Habitat: marshy ponds and lakes. July 12-September 3.

Lyre-tipped Spreadwing *(Lestes unguiculatus)*. Known only from Swans Mill Pond, east of Duvall. Habitat: ponds, often temporary, with dense marsh vegetation. June 7-September 14.

Pond Damsels (Coenagrionidae)

Western Red Damsel *(Amphiagrion abbreviatum)*. Locally common, usually in small numbers throughout lowlands and to 3700 feet in mountains. Habitat: marshy ponds, sloughs and edges of slow streams, typically in dense sedges.

April 27-September 22.

Vivid Dancer *(Argia vivida).* Very local on west side of Cascades (2700 to 4600 feet). Habitat: springs, seeps, and streams. March 17-October 22.

Northern Bluet *(Enallagma annexum).* Common throughout lowlands and in mountains to 4550 feet. Habitat: ponds, lakes, and slow streams. May 5-October 14.

Boreal Bluet *(Enallagma boreale).* Widespread from lowlands well into mountains but usually less common than Northern Bluet (may be more so in mountain lakes). Habitat: ponds and lakes, usually with marsh vegetation. April 11-October 22.

Tule Bluet *(Enallagma carunculatum).* Common throughout lowlands to 2300 feet. Habitat: ponds and lakes, usually with marsh vegetation; often abundant at large lakes with beds of cattails and tules. April 17-November 6.

Pacific Forktail *(Ischnura cervula).* Common throughout lowlands and in mountains to 5800 feet; most ubiquitous odonate in county. Habitat: marshy edges of lakes, ponds and slow streams. Only species typically found in middle of dense cattail and bulrush beds. Easily established in small urban ponds. First odonate to appear in spring. March 20-October 30.

Swift Forktail *(Ischnura erratica).* Locally common in lowlands. Habitat: ponds, especially beaver ponds. Primarily a spring species, with very few records after July. April 4-September 15.

Western Forktail *(Ischnura perparva).* Common throughout lowlands and in mountains to 5800 feet, usually less so than Pacific Forktail. Habitat: marshy edges of lakes, ponds, and slow streams. April 25-October 26.

Sedge Sprite *(Nehalennia irene).* Normally in mountains, one record at Langendorfer Lake, east of Duvall. Habitat: dense sedge marshes. June 17-September 20.

DRAGONFLIES (Anisoptera)

Petaltails (Petaluridae)

Black Petaltail *(Tanypteryx hageni).* Local in Cascades (2500 to 5200 feet). Habitat: seeps on hillsides, larvae in burrows. June 15-September 19.

Darners (Aeshnidae)

Canada Darner *(Aeshna canadensis).* Local throughout lowlands and to 4300 feet in mountains. Habitat: ponds and lakes. July 19-October 13.

Lake Darner *(Aeshna eremita).* Local throughout lowlands and to 4200 feet in mountains. Habitat: lakes. July 8-October 13.

Variable Darner *(Aeshna interrupta).* Locally common in lowlands and to 6000 feet in mountains. Habitat: ponds and lakes. Also common away from water. July 3-October 26.

Sedge Darner *(Aeshna juncea).* Local in Cascades (2200 to 5800 feet). Habitat: ponds and small lakes. July 12-October 8.

Paddle-tailed Darner *(Aeshna palmata).* Common throughout lowlands and to 5800 feet in mountains. Habitat: ponds and lakes. Also common away from

Paddle-tailed Darner (© Dennis Paulson).

water. June 16-November 10.

Shadow Darner *(Aeshna umbrosa)*. Common throughout lowlands and to 5700 feet in mountains. Habitat: ponds, lakes, and slow streams. Along with Autumn Meadowhawk, last dragonfly of autumn. June 17-November 19.

Common Green Darner *(Anax junius)*. Fairly common throughout lowlands and to 3500 feet in mountains. Habitat: ponds, lakes, and slow streams. Most are spring immigrants from the south, their offspring migrating back south in fall. April 22-October 26.

California Darner *(Rhionaeschna californica)*. Common throughout lowlands and to 5800 feet in mountains. Habitat: ponds and lakes. Typically first dragonfly to fly in spring. April 1-August 22.

Blue-eyed Darner *(Rhionaeschna multicolor)*. Common throughout lowlands and to 4200 feet in mountains. Habitat: ponds and lakes. Also common away from water. May 15-November 5.

Clubtails (Gomphidae)

Pacific Clubtail *(Gomphus kurilis)*. Historical records from Lake Washington in early 20th century; generally rare in state. Habitat: lakes, possibly streams. June 4-August 12.

Grappletail *(Octogomphus specularis)*. Known only from Stossel Creek, east of Duvall. Habitat: wooded streams and small rivers. May 22-August 7.

Sinuous Snaketail *(Ophiogomphus occidentis)*. Historical record from Seattle in early 20th century. Habitat: streams and rivers. May 24-August 28.

Spiketails (Cordulegastridae)

Pacific Spiketail *(Cordulegaster dorsalis)*. Known only from Stossel Creek, east of

Duvall; probably more widespread. Habitat: small streams. June 15-August 29.

Emeralds (Corduliidae)

American Emerald *(Cordulia shurtleffii).* Locally common throughout wooded lowlands and to 5800 feet in mountains. Habitat: ponds and lakes. May 10-September 12.

Beaverpond Baskettail *(Epitheca canis).* Few known sites in lowlands of county. Larvae in ponds in stream drainages; males seen in patrol flight over long pools in slow-flowing streams. May 5-July 21.

Spiny Baskettail *(Epitheca spinigera).* Locally common in forested lowlands and to 4200 feet in mountains. Habitat: ponds and lakes. Mostly seen away from water. April 29-August 29.

Ringed Emerald *(Somatochlora albicincta).* Cascades (2200 to 6000 feet). Habitat: ponds and lakes. July 18-October 15.

Ocellated Emerald *(Somatochlora minor).* Known only from Stossel Creek, east of Duvall. Habitat: small, slow-flowing streams through sedge meadows, in or away from forest. July 8-August 17.

Mountain Emerald *(Somatochlora semicircularis).* Known from Cedar River watershed down to 1700 feet; one record from Bellevue. Habitat: bogs and fens. June 2-October 15.

Brush-tipped Emerald *(Somatochlora walshii).* Known only from Langendorfer Lake, east of Duvall. Habitat: sedge meadows, typically with small streams flowing through them. July 8-September 3.

Skimmers (Libellulidae)

Western Pondhawk *(Erythemis collocata).* Locally common in lowlands to 2200 feet. Habitat: ponds and marshy lake borders. May 10-September 19.

Chalk-fronted Corporal *(Ladona julia).* Locally common throughout and to 3400 feet in mountains. Habitat: lakes, ponds, and bogs. May 14-August 27.

Crimson-ringed Whiteface *(Leucorrhinia glacialis).* Known only from Langendorfer Lake, east of Duvall. Habitat: ponds and lake borders with dense emergent vegetation. June 3-August 12.

Hudsonian Whiteface *(Leucorrhinia hudsonica).* Locally common in wooded lowlands and to 6600 feet in mountains. Habitat: ponds and bogs with dense emergent vegetation. April 21-October 8.

Dot-tailed Whiteface *(Leucorrhinia intacta).* Common throughout lowlands and to 4200 feet in mountains. Habitat: ponds and lake edges. May 10-September 6.

Belted Whiteface *(Leucorrhinia proxima).* Known only from Langendorfer Lake, east of Duvall. Habitat: ponds and lake borders with abundant emergent vegetation. June 14-September 9.

Eight-spotted Skimmer *(Libellula forensis).* Common throughout lowlands to 3300 feet. Habitat: ponds and lakes of most kinds. April 28-October 2.

Four-spotted Skimmer *(Libellula quadrimaculata).* Common throughout lowlands and to 4200 feet in mountains. Habitat: ponds and lakes, typically with abundant emergent vegetation. April 16-September 29.

Blue Dasher *(Pachydiplax longipennis)*. Locally common in lowlands to 2200 feet. Habitat: ponds and lakes with abundant emergent vegetation. June 7-October 5.

Common Whitetail *(Plathemis lydia)*. Common throughout lowlands and to 3400 feet in mountains. Habitat: lakes and ponds. May 6-October 2.

Variegated Meadowhawk *(Sympetrum corruptum)*. Common throughout lowlands to 2200 feet. Breeds in open ponds and lakes, typically rather eutrophic ones. May be seen anywhere, especially along coast but also to 5800 feet in mountains, during infrequently observed mass movements in August and September. April 10-November 21.

Saffron-winged Meadowhawk *(Sympetrum costiferum)*. Common throughout lowlands and to 5800 feet in mountains. Habitat: open ponds and lakes. June 21-November 8.

Black Meadowhawk *(Sympetrum danae)*. Above 1700 feet in Cascades; records from Cedar River watershed. Habitat: ponds and lakes with emergent vegetation. July 11-October 26.

Cardinal Meadowhawk *(Sympetrum illotum)*. Common throughout lowlands. Habitat: ponds and lakes. May 8-October 2.

Red-veined Meadowhawk *(Sympetrum madidum)*. Only record so far from Beaver Lake, near Issaquah. Habitat: small ponds and slow streams. June 5-September 21.

White-faced Meadowhawk *(Sympetrum obtrusum)*. Locally common throughout lowlands and to 4200 feet in mountains. Habitat: ponds and lakes with associated meadows. June 24-October 8.

Striped Meadowhawk *(Sympetrum pallipes)*. Common throughout lowlands and to 4000 feet in mountains. Habitat: ponds and lakes with associated meadows. June 20-November 4.

Autumn Meadowhawk *(Sympetrum vicinum)*. Locally common in forested lowlands. Habitat: ponds and lakes with dense emergent vegetation. Latest-flying dragonfly in Washington. July 16-November 24.

Black Saddlebags *(Tramea lacerata)*. A few observed recently at Kent Ponds. They favor ponds and lakes up to 2000 feet but might be seen wandering anywhere. June 21-September 19.

BUTTERFLIES

This list with annotations is abstracted from John Hinchliff's *An Atlas of Washington Butterflies* (Evergreen Aurelians, 1996) and Robert Michael Pyle's *The Butterflies of Cascadia: A Field Guide to All the Species of Washington, Oregon, and Surrounding Territories.* (Seattle Audubon Society, 2002). I list here 67 species of 37 genera of seven families.

Skippers *(Hesperioidea, Hesperiidae)*

Silver-spotted Skipper *(Epargyreus clarus)*. Recorded at Seattle; only known host plant here is *Lotus crassifolius*.

Northern Cloudy-wing *(Thorybes pylades)*. Recorded at Seattle but "very sparing about southern Puget Sound" (Pyle 2002); larvae feed on a variety of legumes.

Dreamy Dusky-wing *(Erynnis icelus).* "From sea level to mid-elevations in the Cascades" (Pyle 2002); larvae feed on willows, aspens, and poplars.

Propertius Dusky-Wing *(Erynnis propertius).* Closely associated with Garry Oak *(Quercus garryana).*

Persius Dusky-wing *(Erynnis persius).* Recorded throughout the county; favors meadows, glades, and mountain tops (Pyle 2002); larvae feed on lupines and *Lotus.*

Two-banded Checkered Skipper *(Pyrgus ruralis).* Widespread in King County; larvae feed on strawberry, cinquefoil, and avens.

Juba Skipper *(Hesperia juba).* Widespread but not common near Seattle; larvae feed on various native grasses.

Western Branded Skipper *(Hesperia colorado).* Recorded at Seattle; favors prairies; larvae feed on various grasses.

Sonora Skipper *(Polites sonora).* Widespread in King County; in forest clearings; larvae feed on grasses.

Woodland Skipper *(Ochlodes sylvanoides).* Nearly universal; larvae feed on various grasses; most abundant in late summer.

Dun Skipper *(Euphyes vestris).* In and west of the Cascades; favors "sedgy edges" (Pyle 2002); larvae feed on sedges.

Swallowtails and Parnassians (Papilionidae)

Clodius Parnassian *(Parnassius clodius).* Cascades and west at all elevations; larvae feed on Bleeding Heart *(Dicentra formosa).*

Anise Swallowtail *(Papilio zelicaon).* "Potentially everywhere … but deep woods" (Pyle 2002); larvae feed on native and introduced plants of the carrot family (Apiaceae).

Western Tiger Swallowtail *(Papilio rutulus).* Widespread; "one of the best all-round urban butterflies" (Pyle 2002); the big green bug-eyed larvae feed on a variety of broad-leaved trees.

Pale Tiger Swallowtail *(Papilio eurymedon).* Widespread at all elevations; larvae favor Red Alder *(Alnus rubra)* among other native shrubs.

Whites and Sulphurs (Pieridae)

Pine White *(Neophasia menapia).* Widespread near conifers; larvae feed on pine and Douglas Fir needles.

Western White *(Pieris occidentalis).* In the Cascades; larvae favor peppergrasses *(Lepidium).*

Margined White *(Pieris marginalis).* Well adapted to "maritime Northwest forests" (Pyle 2002); larvae favor various native herbs of the mustard family (Brassicaceae).

Cabbage White *(Pieris rapae).* In every open habitat but most abundant in disturbed places; larvae prefer *Brassica oleracea* (cabbage and related cultivars); an introduced species accused of displacing native relatives, but more likely occupies disturbed sites unfavorable to native species (Pyle 2002).

Sara's Orange-tip *(Anthocharis sara).* "Nearly every open habitat" (Pyle 2002); larvae feed on various Brassicaceae.

Clouded Sulphur *(Colias philodice).* "… invading weedy and urban habitats" (Pyle 2002); larvae favor plants of the pea family (Fabaceae).

Orange Sulphur *(Colias eurytheme).* Widespread; larvae favor alfalfa and related Fabaceae.

Western Sulphur *(Colias occidentalis).* Known from southeastern King County; larval hosts include wild peas *(Lathyrus)* and lupines.

Gossamer Wings (Lycaenidae)

Purplish Copper *(Lycaena helloides).* "Every habitat from vacant lot to wildland…" (Pyle 2002); larvae feed on docks *(Rumex)* and knotweeds *(Polygonum).*

Mariposa Copper *(Lycaena mariposa).* Cascades; larvae may feed on huckleberries and their relatives *(Vaccinium).*

Sylvan Hairstreak *(Satyrium sylvinum).* Near the Cascade Crest, e.g., north of Kelly Butte; larvae feed on certain willows *(Salix).*

Johnson's Hairstreak *(Mitoura johnsoni).* Recorded from Seattle only three times, in 1891, 1941, and 1969; larvae prefer dwarf mistletoe growing on Western Hemlock and Douglas Fir.

Thicket Hairstreak *(Mitoura spinetorum).* Reported from near Greenwater; larvae prefer dwarf mistletoe on pines.

Cedar Hairstreak *(Mitoura grynea).* Mapped only for northwestern King County (Pyle 2002); larvae require Western Red Cedar *(Thuja plicata).*

Gray Hairstreak (Strymon melinus) (© Idie Ulsh).

Brown Elfin *(Incisalia augustinus).* Widespread, including Seattle; diverse hosts.

Gray Hairstreak *(Strymon melinus).* Widespread, though not common; "in virtually all habitats" (Pyle 2002).

Western Tailed-blue *(Everes amyntula).* In "largely natural moist habitats…" (Pyle 2002); larvae feed on various plants of the pea family (Fabaceae).

Spring Azure *(Celastrina argiolus).* Throughout, "especially osier-lined streams…" (Pyle 2002); many hosts.

Silvery Blue *(Glaucopsyche lygdamus).* Throughout; larvae hosted by lupines and various other Fabaceae.

Anna's Blue *(Plebejus anna).* Along the Cascade Crest; hosts are various legumes.

Greenish Blue *(Plebejus saepiolus).* "Lush wet meadows" (Pyle 2002) at the Cascade Crest; larvae favor clovers *(Trifolium).*

Boisduval's Blue *(Plebejus icarioides).* Disjunct near Puget Sound, where now threatened, and at the Cascade Crest; larvae specialize in lupines.

Brush-footed Butterflies (Nymphalidae)

Great Spangled Fritillary *(Speyeria cybele).* Low to middle elevations; larvae on violets.

Coronis Fritillary *(Speyeria coronis).* High Cascades; larvae on violets.

Zerene Fritillary *(Speyeria zerene).* Puget Trough subspecies "species of concern"; Cascade Crest; larvae on violets.

Hydaspe Fritillary *(Speyeria hydaspe).* Widespread, though more common at higher elevations; larvae on violets.

Mormon Fritillary *(Speyeria mormonia).* Above 3,500 feet; host is Marsh Violet *(Viola palstris).*

Western Meadow Fritillary *(Boloria epithore).* Widespread; larvae on violets.

Arctic Fritillary *(Boloria chariclea).* Above 3,000 feet; larvae on violets, willows, and other species.

Hoffmann's Checkerspot *(Chlosyne hoffmanni).* Cascade Crest, as at Skykomish; larvae on certain asters.

Field Crescent *(Phyciodes pulchellus).* Mostly high in the Cascades; larvae on certain asters.

Mylitta Crescent *(Phyciodes mylitta).* Widespread; larvae depend on thistles *(Cirsium)* and the invasive knapweeds *(Centaurea).*

Chalcedon Checkerspot *(Euphydryas chalcedona).* North Bend to the Cascade Crest; larvae feed on snowberry *(Symphoricarpos),* mullein, and penstemons.

Edith's Checkerspot *(Euphydryas editha).* Cascades; larvae on paintbrushes *(Castilleja).*

Satyr Anglewing *(Polygonia satyrus).* Widespread; larvae on stinging nettles *(Urtica).*

Faun Anglewing *(Polygonia faunus).* Widespread; larvae feed on willows and relatives (Salicaceae, Ulmaceae).

Hoary Comma *(Polygonia gracilis).* Cascades, usually above 3,000 feet; larvae feed on White Azalea *(Rhododendron albiflorum).*

Oreas Angelwing *(Polygonia oreas).* Widespread; larvae prefer currants (e.g., *Ribes divaricatum).*

California Tortoise-shell *(Nymphalis californica).* Widespread; larvae feed on *Ceanothus.*

Mourning Cloak *(Nymphalis antiopa).* Widespread; many woody hosts for larvae.

Milbert's Tortoise-shell *(Nymphalis milberti).* Widespread; larvae eat only stinging nettles.

American Lady *(Vanessa virginiensis).* Recorded at Seattle but rare with us; larvae favor Pearly Everlasting *(Anaphalis margaritacea)* and various pussytoes *(Antennaria, Gnaphalium).*

West Coast Lady *(Vanessa annabella).* Widespread; larvae favor mallows and relations (Malvaceae).

Painted Lady *(Vanessa cardui).* Widespread; larvae prefer thistles *(Carduus, Cirsium).*

Red Admirable *(Vanessa atalanta).* Widespread; larvae feed mostly on stinging nettles.

Lorquin's Admiral *(Limenitis lorquini).* Widespread; larvae feed mostly on willows.

Satyrs, Browns, Ringlets (Satyridae)

Ochre Ringlet *(Coenonympha tullia).* Occurs on lowlands in western King County; larvae favor various grasses.

Common Wood Nymph *(Cercyonis pegala).* Disjunct populations in the lowlands and the high Cascades;. larvae on grasses.

Dark Wood Nymph *(Cercyonis oetus).* Reported from Snoqualmie Pass and south along the Cascade Crest; larvae on grasses.

Vidler's Alpine *(Erebia vidleri).* Reported from Snoqualmie Pass and north along the Cascade Crest; larvae on pine grass *(Calamagrostis).*

Great Arctic *(Oenis nevadensis).* Reported from Snoqualmie Pass and south along the Cascade Crest; larvae on grasses.

Milkweed Butterflies (Danaidae)

Monarch *(Danaus plexippus).* Reported rarely from the Seattle area; larvae feed on milkweeds *(Asclepias).*

NATIVE TREES

Comprehensive references to the King County flora include Arthur Lee Jacobson's *Trees of Seattle* (1989), *Wild Plants of Greater Seattle* (2001), and the University of Washington's Burke Museum of Natural History and Culture online.

Pacific Yew *(Taxus brevifolia).* Uncommon. Of scattered occurrence in coniferous forests mostly below 1000 feet. One 12 inches in diameter is reported on Squak Mountain (Manning, *The Flowering of the Issaquah Alps,* 1981:14).

Yellow Cedar (also called Alaska Cedar; *Chamaecyparis nootkatensis).* Uncommon, mostly above 5000 feet to timberline.

Western Red Cedar *(Thuja plicata).* Common, mostly below 3000 feet. Often with Sitka spruce in lowland bogs.

Grand Fir *(Abies grandis).* Uncommon. Of scattered occurrence at low elevations, as, for example, near the mouth of Boeing Creek.

Pacific Silver Fir *(Abies amabilis).* Abundant. With Mountain Hemlock, the characteristic tree at 3000-5000 feet. Above, it is gradually replaced by Subalpine Fir. Occurs west to the summit of Tiger Mountain.

Subalpine Fir *(Abies lasiocarpa).* Common above 5000 feet with Pacific Silver Fir, Mountain Hemlock, and scattered Yellow Cedars. Its narrow spires define the timberline profile.

Noble Fir *(Abies procera).* Locally common, particularly on regrown clear-cuts above 4000 feet. A giant, 74 inches in diameter, is marked along the Asahel Curtis Nature Trail. Not known north of Stevens Pass. Note the pineapple-like cones with their exposed bracts.

Western Larch *(Larix occidentalis).* Dave Beaudette reports two wild trees on the south slope of Granite Mountain. They were about 25 feet tall, both producing cones, no seedlings seen. One tree was alive but flat on the ground. The other was alive and upright. This is a snow avalanche area.

Engelmann Spruce *(Picea engelmannii).* Rare. Recorded for the Middle Fork Snoqualmie River. Several were found on the Cascade Crest north of Naches Pass. This area should be checked for Boreal Owls in late September.

Sitka Spruce *(Picea sitchensis).* Uncommon. Typically found in low elevation bogs. Nice examples at the Carnation Marsh Sanctuary. A few individuals in Seattle's parks. Found east at least as far as slightly west of Money Creek on the Skykomish River, along US-2.

Lodgepole Pine *(Pinus contorta var. murrayana).* Rare. Scattered individuals at high elevations such as above Stevens Pass and near Red Mountain Pond. Also a grove—perhaps of the Shore Pine variety *(Pinus contorta var. contorta)* though of questionable origin—at Mukai Pond, Vashon Island.

Western White Pine *(Pinus monticola).* Uncommon to rare. A few scattered individuals at high elevations, a few on Middle and West Tiger Mountains (Manning, *The Flowering of the Issaquah Alps,* 1981:14), plus a substantial stand north of Cottage Lake on the Snohomish County boundary. Those in suburban areas may or may not be native.

Douglas Fir *(Pseudotsuga menziesii).* Abundant. Fast-growing tree of early successional stages on cut-over land, mostly below 3000 feet. A few giants survive, such as the 12-foot-diameter beast on the trail to Trout Lake up the West Fork Foss River.

Western Hemlock *(Tsuga heterophylla).* Abundant. With Western Red Cedar, the climax species of the Puget Sound lowlands. Note how it dominates the understory of our second-growth Douglas Fir forests. It represents the future generation, if given the chance to succeed. Common up to 3000+ feet, as at Snoqualmie Pass, where it occurs with Mountain Hemlock.

Mountain Hemlock *(Tsuga mertensiana).* Abundant. With Pacific Silver Fir, the climax species of the higher mountain forests—those from 3000+ feet. West to the highest elevations of Tiger Mountain (Manning, *The Flowering of the Issaquah Alps,* 1981:13).

Quaking Aspen *(Populus tremuloides).* Uncommon to rare. Scattered clusters mixed with alder, ash, maple, and cottonwood, as for example on the Muckleshoot Prairie at the junction of SE 380th St. and 176th Ave. SE. Also reported near the Bellevue Airfield and on Grand Ridge (Manning, *The Flowering of the Issaquah Alps* 1981:19).

Black Cottonwood *(Populus trichocarpa).* Common, especially along river floodplains. Note impressive gallery forest of this species at Tolt-MacDonald Park near Carnation and along the White River south of Enumclaw. A favorite of Bullock's Orioles and Red-eyed Vireos.

Pacific Willow *(Salix lasiandra var. lasiandra).* Common along streams below 1000 feet. Distinctive long, pointed leaves with warty leaf stalks.

Hooker's Willow *(Salix hookeriana).* Near the beach below the South Bluff at Discovery Park.

Mackenzie Willow *(Salix prolixa).* One of several species of willows along the boardwalk at Marymoor Park.

Piper's Willow *(Salix piperi).* A good-sized individual is labeled as this species on the Marymoor Park nature trail. May be widespread.

Scouler's Willow *(Salix scouleriana).* Common on poorly drained soils, as near the Daybreak Star Center in Discovery Park and on the Foster Island marsh trail. May be a tall and graceful tree. The most abundant "pussy willow" of our area, flowering in February and March. May have reddish hairs on underside of leaves, a unique characteristic.

Sitka Willow *(Salix sitchensis).* Common. Another "pussy willow." Leaves are smaller than Scouler's and silvery on both surfaces. Distinguished by single stamen per male flower. Particularly common on Vashon Island.

Geyer Willow *(Salix geyeriana var. meleina).* One of several species of willows along the boardwalk at Marymoor Park.

Red Alder *(Alnus rubra).* Abundant, mostly below 3000 feet. A fine, tall stand is on marshy terrain behind Tradition Lake above Issaquah.

Sitka Alder *(Alnus viridis var. sinuata).* Common. A shrubby species of avalanche gullies in the mountain zone; extends west to Tiger Mountain (Manning, *The Flowering of the Issaquah Alps,* 1981:7).

Paper Birch *(Betula papyrifera var. commutata).* Rare. Widely naturalized, but a cluster of these birches at Moss Lake southeast of Duvall may well be native. Be careful to distinguish this native from the European White Birch (also called European Weeping Birch, *Betula pendula),* which is well established.

Hall's Swamp Birch *(Betula glandulosa var. hallii).* Rare. Attains the stature of a small tree at Bellefields Nature Park.

Garry Oak *(Quercus garryana).* Rare. An impressive grove in Martha Washington Park south of Seward Park, Seattle, perhaps planted by Indians or by Bandtailed Pigeons centuries ago. Scattered clusters grow on rocky prominences on Tiger Mountain (Manning, *The Flowering of the Issaquah Alps,* 1981:16), and about Muckleshoot Prairie. More than 150 seedlings were hand-planted in Montlake Fill in 1995.

Western Serviceberry *(Amelanchier alnifolia).* Rarely a small tree.

Black Hawthorn *(Crataegus douglasii).* Scarce. Jacobson (1989:125) reports wild individuals at Seward and Martha Washington Parks in southeast Seattle.

Chokecherry *(Prunus virginiana).* Rare. Reported on Rattlesnake Ledge, south of North Bend (Manning, *The Flowering of the Issaquah Alps,* 1981:29).

Bitter Cherry *(Prunus emarginata).* Common at low elevations. Can be a tall and graceful tree, quite unlike the variety east of the Cascades. Numerous in Discovery Park, with Scouler's Willow and Red Alder near the north parking lot.

Oregon Crabapple *(Malus fusca).* Uncommon. Likes low elevation swamps, as at the Carnation Marsh Sanctuary and along Beacon Coal Mine Rd. S in Tukwila.

Bigleaf Maple *(Acer macrophyllum).* Abundant. A characteristic tree of lowland King County. The old, moss-draped specimens along the Railroad Grade Trail in Tolt-MacDonald Park near Carnation are reminiscent of rain forest giants of the Olympic Peninsula.

Vine Maple *(Acer circinatum).* Abundant. An elegant, if shrubby, maple of road edges and forest understory to above 3000 feet.

Rocky Mountain Maple *(Acer glabrum).* Rare. Reported from Rattlesnake Ledge and Tiger and Squak Mountains, on rock outcroppings (Manning, *The Flowering of the Issaquah Alps,* 1981:7). Western varieties, including ours, sometimes also called Douglas Maple.

Cascara *(Frangula [Rhamnus] purshiana).* Common, but scattered throughout the lowlands. Often shrubby. Still supports a minor local industry producing laxative from its bark.

Pacific Dogwood *(Cornus nuttallii).* Common. Flowers twice, in early spring and then again in late summer. At such times it is easy to spot along freeway rights-of-way through our lowland forests.

Pacific Madrone *(Arbutus menziesii).* Common. A tree of sunny aspects. Characteristic of Lincoln and Seward Parks' southwestern exposures. Unmistakable evergreen, magnolia-like leaves and scaly reddish bark.

Oregon Ash *(Fraxinus latifolia).* Common, though less so in the northern half of the county. Near its northern limit here. Particularly conspicuous along the old Black River and about Enumclaw on marshy ground.

Blue Elderberry *(Sambucus cerulea).* Uncommon. A shrub or small tree of sunny aspects. Some tree-sized specimens are north of Enumclaw on the Cumberland-Kanaskat Road and a few more southeast of Redmond. The much commoner Red Elderberry *(Sambucus racemosa var. racemosa)* is but a shrub.

Deerbrush *(Ceanothus velutinus).* Uncommon. A shrub or occasionally borderline tree. Quite unlike its bushy eastern Washington relations. Common on Vashon Island, uncommon elsewhere.

Among the ducks and coots fleeing a Bald Eagle attack at Montlake Fill is one Eurasian Wigeon (the duck with the gold-colored forehead in the center of the photograph). All these birds are seen during Seattle CBCs (© Doug Parrott).

APPENDIX 1. CHRISTMAS BIRD COUNTS

Each Christmas season dedicated birders polish up their binoculars and spotting scopes in preparation for the birding event of the year, the National Audubon Society's Christmas Bird Count, or CBC for short. In the winter of 2010-2011, 62,624 observers manned 2,215 count circles in the United States, Canada, and tropical America, counting 61,359,451 individual birds. The concept was introduced 111 years ago and has been an annual event ever since. Results are carefully tabulated by local compilers, then published in the National Audubon Society's journal, *American Birds.*

The Seattle Christmas Bird Count is a vintage event, first conducted in 1908 by a single observer and run on an annual basis (with the exception of wartime lapses) since 1920. On December 31, 2011, 181observers joined the effort to locate on this single winter day over 50,000 individual birds of 129 species within a 15-mile-diameter circle (the national CBC standard) centered on Pioneer Square.

In 1980-1981, Thais Bock organized the first Kent-Auburn CBC, sponsored by the Rainier Audubon Society. This circle was drawn to include the Green River Valley from Tukwila to Auburn, extending west to Puget Sound at Des Moines and east nearly to Black Diamond. This past winter (January 1, 2012), 64 observers tallied 129 species on this count, equaling the Seattle tally. Eastside Audubon Society initiated a third King County CBC east of Seattle in 1982-1983 to include Lake Sammamish and the Snoqualmie Valley, which had 49 observers in the field on December 17, 2011. They recorded 97 species. Our newest count circle is the Vashon CBC, sponsored by the Vashon-Maury Island Audubon Society, initiated in 1999-2000. Seventy-three observers tallied 117 species in this circle on December 31, 2011. These four count circles are shown on the map on page 208. These counts generate valuable evidence with regard to the long-range impact of our metropolitan expansion. If you would like to participate in a Christmas Bird Count, check the Washington Ornithological Society's website for a list of counts, with dates and contacts.

The Edmonds CBC circle clips the northern edge of King County in Shoreline, Lake Forest Park, and Kenmore, though the majority of that circle is in Snohomish County, and it has not been possible to differentiate birds seen in the King County segment. On the other hand, the Seattle and Vashon circles include bits of Kitsap and/or Pierce Counties, respectively. The occasional Rock Sandpiper on the

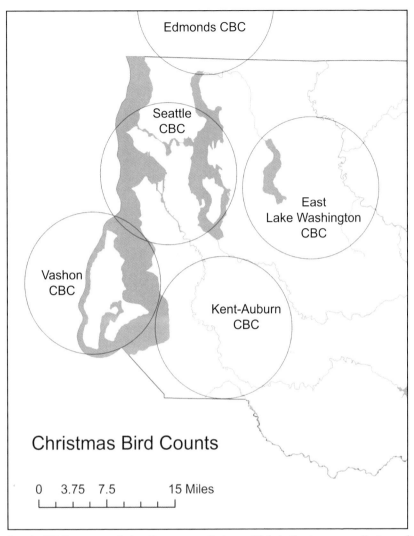

Christmas Bird Counts

0   3.75   7.5   15 Miles

Seattle CBC was recorded at Restoration Point or Blakely Rock, our small piece of Kitsap County.

The tabulated CBC data below (Table 1) reports the average numbers of each species recorded at the four King County CBCs during the past decade (1999-2000 through 2008-2009). Table 2 provides a deeper historical perspective for the Seattle CBC, citing decadal totals since the winter of 1969-1970. (Note that birds seen only during the three days before and after but missed on count day are recorded as "count week" ("cw") birds.

CBCs are a useful barometer of a species' changing fortunes. In Seattle, for example, RUFFED GROUSE were regularly counted until the 1940s, but have not been noted since 1962, as their deep-woods habitat has been progressively eliminated near Seattle. WESTERN BLUEBIRDS were once quite common in Seattle in winter, with up to 100 counted on every CBC between 1924 and 1942. Since 1954, none have been seen on a CBC. By contrast, GADWALL numbers have escalated from less than 10 per count in the mid-1960s to more than 1000 in 1982. ANNA'S HUMMINGBIRDS first appear in the CBC record in 1966 and have been an annual fixture since 1972, with a record 301reported in 2011. EUROPEAN STARLINGS were first counted in 1958, when 75 were seen. This bloomed to 600-plus by 1960 and to more than 7000 by the late 1970s. HOUSE FINCHES appear first in 1953, with five reported, then are seen annually from 1955 to the present. Several hundred are now counted each year. The Christmas Bird Count thus exemplifies the potential scientific contributions of the coordinated efforts of amateur observers.

As noted, Table 2 shows the Seattle Christmas Count circle ten-year averages since 1970 for each species recorded during the past 40 years. I have included columns with the ratios of average numbers in sequential decades, but only for species with a significant count (that is, very small numbers do not provide a solid basis for estimating trends). If the ratio is well below 1.0, the species has apparently declined during the time span indicated. If the ratio is well above 1.0, the species would appear to have increased, at least within the count circle. If the ratio is 2, numbers of that species doubled from one decade to the next; if the ratio is 3, they have tripled, and so forth.

Take the GREATER WHITE-FRONTED GOOSE, for example. During the 1970s and 1980s, it was of less than annual occurrence. During the 1990s, the average quadrupled, though still averaging just 1.2 individuals per year. During the first decade of the 21st century, a continuing increase is noticeable, though not as dramatic as during the 1990s.

BRANTS also exhibit a rising population curve, but one that is more consistent and more substantial, from just 3 birds per year during the 1970s to nearly 100 per year since 2000, with the most dramatic increases noted during the 1990s, when our counts increased 12-fold. CANADA GEESE likewise increased since 1970 through the 1990s but appear to have stabilized during the past decade, perhaps due to control measures.

Our ducks overall show substantial increases, though a careful review of the changes across the past four decades will show a variety of patterns and timing of these increases. Gadwalls, for example, were rare in our area before 1970 but have become locally abundant since 1980 and may have reached a saturation point. It is interesting to note changes in the relative numbers of EURASIAN and AMERICAN WIGEONS, GREATER and LESSER SCAUPS, and COMMON and BARROW'S GOLDENEYES These changes may well reflect real changes or perhaps changes in observers' abilities to differentiate these closely allied species.

Recently, alarms have been sounded with regard to the health of Puget Sound, and there is considerable evidence that several key wintering saltwater species have declined substantially during the past several decades. As noted above, Brants do not seem to have been so affected, nor have the numbers of SURF SCOTERS, BARROW'S GOLDENEYES, RED-BREASTED MERGANSERS, loons, grebes, or cormorants suffered. However, we do note a sharp decline in WHITE-WINGED and BLACK SCOTER numbers during the past decade, and a hint of a drop in WESTERN GREBE numbers, a species flagged as possibly threatened in Puget Sound.

Our two introduced game birds, RING-NECKED PHEASANT and CALIFORNIA QUAIL, have now declined nearly to the vanishing point. This likely reflects the increasing density of our urban environment, though both species have declined throughout King County. Perhaps the Washington Department of Fish & Wildlife has cut back its stocking programs?

By contrast, raptor numbers are generally on the increase, with particularly impressive gains for BALD EAGLES and PEREGRINE FALCONS, both now benefiting from the removal of DDT from our arsenal of insecticides. However, SHARP-SHINNED, COOPER'S and RED-TAILED HAWKS also show strong gains throughout the last 40 years. Curiously, MERLINS seem to have increased as AMERICAN KESTRELS declined.

SURFBIRDS were virtually nonexistent in King County until the late 1980s, with the Seattle CBC birds all from across the Sound at Restoration Point. Since 1990, however, a substantial mixed flock has become regular on the Duwamish and Alki Beach rocks.

Gulls manifest some intriguing shifts. BONAPARTE'S GULLS first increased, then since 2000 have declined precipitously. RING-BILLED GULLS increased through the 1990s but have since tapered off. HERRING and THAYER'S GULL numbers have generally declined, though this may reflect more upon our ability to distinguish them from GLAUCOUS-WINGED x WESTERN GULL hybrids than any real population shift. On the alcid front, PIGEON GUILLEMOTS have done well while MARBLED MURRELETS have dropped off decade by decade, perhaps reflecting the impact of logging of old-growth forests. COMMON MURRES and RHINOCEROS AUKLETS first increased through the 1990s but have declined sharply during the past decade, perhaps reflecting changes in oceanic conditions.

BAND-TAILED PIGEONS, another species of concern due to habitat alteration, appear to have lost ground since the 1980s in our circle. BARN OWLS—never common—are up, while WESTERN SCREECH- and GREAT HORNED OWLS are down, and BARRED OWLS have taken over. Most impressive is the continuing expansion of our ANNA'S HUMMINGBIRD population subsequent to the arrival of these birds from California in the 1960s. Their numbers increased seven-fold since the 1990s.

Our local woodpeckers are increasing across the board. By contrast, HUTTON'S VIREOS are down. The suite of winter forest gleaners, which includes the vireo but is dominated by chickadees, RED-BREASTED NUTHATCHES, BROWN CREEPERS, kinglets, and TOWNSEND'S WARBLERS, show consistent increases, though the magnitude of these changes is not much greater than the overall increase in total individuals of all species counted, thus probably reflecting an increase in the number of observer hours in the field on the Seattle CBC. Similar increases by BEWICK'S and PACIFIC WRENS, SPOTTED TOWHEES, and sparrows in general also likely reflect this increase in coverage rather than actual population shifts.

As you may have noticed, there are lots of crows about, a fact clearly substantiated by the decadel increase in crow numbers, many tallied as they leave their mass colonial winter roosts at daylight. WESTERN SCRUB-JAYS are a recent addition to the Seattle scene and are making themselves at home here, little by little.

EUROPEAN STARLINGS appear to have stabilized since the 1980s. YELLOW-RUMPED WARBLERS continue on a somewhat irregular upward curve. GOLDEN-CROWNED SPARROWS seem to have increased relative to their WHITE-CROWNED cousins, and LINCOLN'S SPARROWS are up rather more than the average of local sparrows, which may reflect some dynamics in these populations.

Undeniable declines are on record for BREWER'S BLACKBIRDS, PURPLE FINCHES, and EVENING GROSBEAKS. The Purple Finch is in retreat to the outer reaches of suburbia, leaving the city to the HOUSE FINCH, while Brewer's Blackbirds seem to have abandoned the inner city for more peripheral mall parking lots. What has transpired with our Evening Grosbeaks remains a puzzle.

In conclusion, a close reading of CBC totals through time offers more questions than answers.

Townsend's Solitaire, North City, January 3, 2010 (© Gregg Thompson).

TABLES

Table 1 at right shows Recent (1999-2008) Totals for Four King County Christmas Bird Counts.

The four counts that are centered in and that include primarily King County territory are: the Seattle CBC (WASE), the East Lake Washington CBC (WAEA), the Kent-Auburn CBC (WAKA), and the Vashon CBC (WAVA). The Edmonds CBC includes just a slice of the northwestern edge of King County and is not included in this tabulation.

Notable differences between our counts are largely explained by the habitats each covers. Obviously, the East Lake Washington count tallies few scoters, since it includes no saltwater shoreline. The East Lake Washington and Kent-Auburn counts include significant open farmland and marsh habitats that attract geese, swans, dabbling ducks, raptors, and sparrows in abundance. Both counts also extend eastward to include foothill woodland, where we might hope to find the occasional Ruffed Grouse, Gray Jay (on the summit of West Tiger Mount in WASE), or American Dipper. Adding all four counts together gives us a fair picture of what birds we might expect to find during a Washington winter, a total of over 123,000 individual birds of 189 species during the past decade.

Northern Pintail drake, Montlake Fill (© Doug Parrott).

Table 1: Recent (1999-2008) Totals for Four King County Christmas Bird Counts

Species	WAEA	WAKA	WASE	WAVA	Totals
circle center latitude N	47.583	47.367	47.600	47.433	
circle center longitude W	122.000	122.200	122.330	122.507	
Greater White-fronted Goose	1.9	2.7	1.7	0.3	7
Snow Goose	1.8	0.6	0.8		3
Brant			94.6	9.9	104
Cackling Goose	71.4	237.9	0.7	1.6	312
Canada Goose	2017.6	988.4	404.6	324.1	3735
Mute Swan			0.1		0
Trumpeter Swan	32.4	3.8			36
Tundra Swan	3.2	0.8			4
Wood Duck	1.9	56.3	23.0	31.4	113
Gadwall	54.6	102.4	827.6	3.4	988
Eurasian Wigeon	0.8	9.4	19.1	7.8	37
American Wigeon	913.2	1908.8	1703.7	2832.6	7358
American Black Duck	0.1				0
Mallard	1333.1	1541.8	1142.6	670.0	4687
Blue-winged Teal		0.2			0
Cinnamon Teal		0.3			0
Northern Shoveler	60.1	224.1	76.8	10.3	371
Northern Pintail	89.6	992.2	216.9	6.8	1305
Green-winged Teal	101.8	661.9	90.4	46.0	900
[Eurasian] Green-winged Teal		*0.3			*0.3
Canvasback	1.1	30.1	440.1	0.4	472
Redhead	0.6	3.7	1.8	0.4	6
Ring-necked Duck	72.4	313.4	424.0	40.2	850
Greater Scaup	5.6	48.2	530.0	163.3	747
Lesser Scaup	15.8	48.0	578.6	9.8	652
Harlequin Duck		20.6	52.0	8.3	81
Surf Scoter		213.0	530.8	851.8	1596
White-winged Scoter		83.2	32.4	551.4	667
Black Scoter		34.1	45.1	14.0	93
Long-tailed Duck			0.3	0.3	1
Bufflehead	234.6	348.1	798.3	461.0	1842
Common Goldeneye	18.2	100.0	287.9	313.2	719
Common x Barrow's Goldeneye			*0.1		*0.1
Barrow's Goldeneye	1.4	79.1	279.7	127.3	488
Hooded Merganser	58.1	109.3	88.9	56.8	313
Common Merganser	50.2	106.1	211.9	178.9	547
Red-breasted Merganser	0.1	14.3	298.8	158.7	472
Ruddy Duck	44.6	201.8	52.7	43.2	342
Ring-necked Pheasant	1.2	1.7	2.4	12.9	18
Ruffed Grouse	0.7			0.1	1
Mountain Quail [Kitsap County]			0.5	1	
California Quail	9.0	17.9	8.6	4.9	40

Species	WAEA	WAKA	WASE	WAVA	Totals
Red-throated Loon		2.2	22.2	37.4	62
Pacific Loon		0.1	19.3	58.1	78
Common Loon	1.0	4.9	13.3	29.1	48
Yellow-billed Loon		0.1			0
Pied-billed Grebe	47.2	60.7	139.3	29.7	277
Horned Grebe	7.9	66.4	276.3	348.9	700
Red-necked Grebe	0.3	18.3	139.0	65.9	224
Eared Grebe	0.2	0.9	7.6	7.0	16
Western Grebe	42.1	9.7	1482.9	1759.6	3294
Clark's Grebe			0.5	0.1	1
Short-tailed Shearwater			0.0		0
Brandt's Cormorant		0.1	209.1	16.6	226
Double-crested Cormorant	92.9	137.2	664.3	466.9	1361
Pelagic Cormorant		2.0	36.6	16.8	55
American Bittern		0.3			0
Great Blue Heron	39.1	38.1	60.9	33.4	172
Great Egret	0.1				0
Green Heron	0.4	1.2	0.6	0.2	3
Osprey	0.1	0.2	0.0		0
Bald Eagle	19.3	26.7	49.6	32.7	128
Northern Harrier	2.1	6.4	0.6	0.2	9
Sharp-shinned Hawk	2.9	9.6	19.6	5.6	38
Cooper's Hawk	5.0	8.1	19.2	4.8	37
Northern Goshawk		0.1		0.1	0
Red-tailed Hawk	42.9	89.3	39.6	17.0	189
[Harlan's] Red-tailed Hawk		*0.2			*0.2
Rough-legged Hawk		0.7			1
American Kestrel	1.3	4.8	0.1	0.9	7
Merlin	0.6	4.3	13.6	1.2	20
Gyrfalcon		0.1			0
Peregrine Falcon	0.7	3.8	5.6	0.8	11
Virginia Rail	2.2	20.2	2.3	2.4	27
American Coot	1158.3	600.2	6393.2	293.6	8445
Sandhill Crane	0.1				0
Black-bellied Plover		3.3	0.0		3
Killdeer	51.0	100.1	81.2	62.9	295
Spotted Sandpiper	0.7	1.0	2.1	3.7	7
Greater Yellowlegs		0.2	0.0	1.8	2
Black Turnstone			124.7	27.4	152
Surfbird			83.4	1.1	85
Sanderling			102.2	59.2	161
Western Sandpiper		1.6		0.7	2
Least Sandpiper		2.2		0.1	2
Rock Sandpiper			0.7		1
Dunlin	22.8	123.7	77.1	34.8	258

Species	WAEA	WAKA	WASE	WAVA	Totals
Long-billed Dowitcher	0.1	4.4			5
Wilson's Snipe	1.8	16.7	4.7	3.1	26
Red Phalarope			0.0	0.2	0
Bonaparte's Gull		0.6	14.4	47.9	63
Heermann's Gull		0.1			0
Mew Gull	1188.7	233.6	939.8	264.3	2626
Ring-billed Gull	150.9	35.4	291.7	2.0	480
Western Gull	2.3	3.1	9.0	2.7	17
Western x Glaucous-winged Gull	*123.1	*394.7	*33.2	*551	
California Gull	8.3	6.7	54.2	7.3	76
Herring Gull	6.3	0.6	9.2	0.6	17
Thayer's Gull		2.3	5.6	3.7	12
Glaucous-winged Gull	239.7	615.9	1714.1	577.3	3147
Glaucous Gull		0.1			0
Common Murre		0.6	42.6	26.7	70
Pigeon Guillemot		2.7	27.2	12.8	43
Marbled Murrelet			1.1	1.4	3
Ancient Murrelet			0.6		1
Cassin's Auklet			0.1		0
Rhinoceros Auklet		0.7	18.3	22.3	41
Rock Pigeon	307.9	845.3	2354.7	237.6	3745
Band-tailed Pigeon	9.3	38.6	87.4	18.3	154
Mourning Dove	7.4	31.8	0.1	25.3	65
parakeet sp.			3.6		4
Barn Owl	1.1	4.7	0.8	0.3	7
Western Screech-Owl		5.2	5.4	0.5	11
Great Horned Owl	0.2	6.2	0.7	3.0	10
Snowy Owl	0.0				0
Northern Pygmy-Owl	0.1				0
Barred Owl	0.1	0.6	2.4	1.6	5
Long-eared Owl			0.1		0
Short-eared Owl	0.1	0.4	0.1		1
Northern Saw-whet Owl		1.8	0.9	1.1	4
Anna's Hummingbird	6.1	14.4	148.2	34.3	203
Rufous Hummingbird			0.1		0
Belted Kingfisher	8.6	17.2	27.6	24.3	78
Yellow-bellied Sapsucker		0.1			0
Red-naped Sapsucker			0.1		0
Red-breasted Sapsucker	3.1	8.2	3.9	6.1	21
Downy Woodpecker	14.4	46.1	68.9	22.1	152
Hairy Woodpecker	6.2	10.0	1.8	4.8	23
American Three-toed Woodpecker	0.2				0
Northern Flicker	54.9	142.1	295.1	82.2	574
Pileated Woodpecker	3.6	10.1	10.4	13.0	37

Species	WAEA	WAKA	WASE	WAVA	Totals
Say's Phoebe		0.1			0
Northern Shrike	0.8	1.8	0.5	0.1	3
Hutton's Vireo	0.6	4.2	6.9	5.4	17
Gray Jay	0.1			0.2	0
Steller's Jay	60.6	132.8	163.1	136.8	493
Western Scrub-Jay		0.6	3.0	0.1	4
American Crow	1109.7	3717.8	12745.0	1040.7	18613
Common Raven	9.6	2.7	0.2	13.7	26
Barn Swallow		0.9	0.4		1
Black-capped Chickadee	225.6	565.3	1480.6	240.4	2512
Mountain Chickadee	0.2	0.2	0.1	0.0	1
Chestnut-backed Chickadee	66.8	152.2	183.2	271.4	674
Bushtit	78.4	439.7	1260.1	74.8	1853
Red-breasted Nuthatch	11.4	26.4	73.9	60.0	172
White-breasted Nuthatch				0.2	0
Brown Creeper	9.8	20.4	60.8	13.1	104
Bewick's Wren	28.9	80.8	243.3	42.6	396
House Wren	0.0				0
Winter Wren	39.4	100.9	191.3	85.7	417
Marsh Wren	5.8	43.7	9.3	2.0	61
American Dipper	1.6	1.4	0.1	0.3	3
Golden-crowned Kinglet	202.9	396.4	1159.7	325.3	2084
Ruby-crowned Kinglet	95.4	183.1	567.8	138.7	985
Townsend's Solitaire			0.7		1
Hermit Thrush	0.1	1.2	6.6	4.2	12
American Robin	585.6	1202.3	3378.4	937.7	6104
Varied Thrush	54.6	42.2	69.6	81.8	248
European Starling	1674.7	4338.8	3998.7	1151.2	11163
American Pipit	0.8	29.7	0.1		31
Bohemian Waxwing			0.4		0
Cedar Waxwing	3.0	10.1	60.0	21.8	95
Orange-crowned Warbler	0.3	1.4	2.3	0.9	5
Yellow-rumped Warbler	7.7	44.2	103.0	1.6	156
Townsend's Warbler	4.6	7.6	21.6	6.6	40
Palm Warbler			0.1	0.0	0
Common Yellowthroat		0.1			0
Wilson's Warbler			0.1		0
Western Tanager			0.2		0
Spotted Towhee	82.0	185.0	248.2	279.3	795
Clay-colored Sparrow		0.1			0
Savannah Sparrow	0.6	6.6	0.5		8
Fox Sparrow	22.8	117.2	182.7	119.6	442
Song Sparrow	159.6	641.2	712.1	385.8	1899
Lincoln's Sparrow	5.6	49.1	18.2	0.8	74
Swamp Sparrow		0.1	0.1		0

Species	WAEA	WAKA	WASE	WAVA	Totals
White-throated Sparrow	0.8	1.3	0.3	2.7	5
Harris's Sparrow			0.2	0.0	0
White-crowned Sparrow	30.8	79.0	48.1	8.9	167
Golden-crowned Sparrow	76.2	205.4	195.4	87.3	564
Dark-eyed Junco	305.7	624.7	803.1	890.2	2624
Red-winged Blackbird	790.4	1083.0	193.1	137.0	2204
Western Meadowlark	18.6	20.6	1.3		40
Yellow-headed Blackbird		0.1			0
Brewer's Blackbird	34.9	423.6	0.3	23.7	482
Brown-headed Cowbird	1.3	92.4	0.2	0.1	94
Pine Grosbeak			0.1		0
Purple Finch	8.7	10.4	8.0	44.4	72
House Finch	220.2	490.1	1125.8	227.4	2064
Red Crossbill	2.1	10.7	3.4	33.7	50
Common Redpoll		0.1	15.2		15
Hoary Redpoll			0.2		0
Pine Siskin	394.4	724.9	1424.4	908.0	3452
American Goldfinch	41.2	137.3	344.7	65.1	588
Evening Grosbeak	6.9	20.8	0.1	0.0	28
House Sparrow	88.2	348.1	992.2	90.7	1519
Number of species	126	156	157	140	189
Number of individuals	**15329**	**28781**	**57607**	**19771**	**121489**

This drake "Common" or "Eurasian Teal," the Eurasian version of our Green-winged Teal, frequented Montlake Fill for several weeks after it appeared on December 5, 2010. While rarities can turn up at any time, this particular rarity is far more likely in winter (© Doug Parrott).

Table 2: King County CBC Decadal Averages and Ratios							
	1970s	1980s	1990s	2000s	80/70	90/80	00/90
Greater White-fronted Goose	0.4	0.3	1.2	1.9	0.8	4.0	1.6
Snow Goose	30.1	0.4	0.1	0.6		0.3	6.3
Brant	3.1	6.3	78.2	98.6	2.0	12.4	1.3
Cackling Goose	0.0	0.0	0.0	1.5			
Canada Goose	201.7	550.5	1184.3	719.8	2.7	2.2	0.6
Mute Swan	0.0	0.0	1.6	0.0			
Trumpeter Swan	0.0	0.0	0.2	0.0			
Tundra Swan	0.2	0.0	0.5	0.0			
Wood Duck	1.9	8.8	23.9	20.8	4.7	2.7	0.9
Gadwall	116.2	995.5	1139.2	871.0	8.6	1.1	0.8
Eurasian Wigeon	3.1	5.4	8.9	20.6	1.7	1.6	2.3
American Wigeon	1529.0	1850.5	2249.7	1609.8	1.2	1.2	0.7
Eurasian x American Wigeon	0.0	0.0	0.3	0.4			
American Black Duck	0.3	0.1	0.0	0.0			
Mallard	1983.0	2631.8	1829.3	1092.4	1.3	0.7	0.6
Blue-winged Teal	0.1	0.0	0.0	0.0			
Cinnamon Teal	0.0	0.1	0.0	0.0			
Blue-winged x Cinnamon Teal	0.1	0.0	0.0	0.0			
Northern Shoveler	105.5	125.3	206.4	80.0	1.2	1.6	0.4
Northern Pintail	819.7	19.6	19.8	237.5	0.0	1.0	12.0
Green-winged Teal	78.8	191.4	52.9	93.4	2.4	0.3	1.8
Canvasback	125.6	106.2	290.6	454.3	0.8	2.7	1.6
Redhead	3.6	1.2	0.9	2.0	0.3	0.7	2.2
Ring-necked Duck	66.5	99.2	201.8	421.3	1.5	2.0	2.1
Tufted Duck	0.3	0.0	0.0	0.0			
Tufted Duck x scaup	0.0	0.0	0.1	0.0			
Greater Scaup	1176.5	401.3	313.9	550.8	0.3	0.8	1.8
Lesser Scaup	231.6	203.8	353.6	562.1	0.9	1.7	1.6
King Eider	0.0	0.1	0.0	0.0			
Harlequin Duck	13.0	27.7	35.1	51.1	2.1	1.3	1.5
Long-tailed Duck	0.7	0.5	0.3	0.3	0.7	0.6	0.8
Surf Scoter	470.5	598.7	574.6	555.5	1.3	1.0	1.0
White-winged Scoter	99.0	72.4	100.3	29.3	0.7	1.4	0.3
Black Scoter	73.7	134.6	164.4	47.3	1.8	1.2	0.3
Bufflehead	288.6	375.5	500.7	827.4	1.3	1.3	1.7
Common Goldeneye	302.3	361.6	294.2	287.0	1.2	0.8	1.0
Common x Barrow's Goldeneye	0.0	0.0	0.0	0.1			
Barrow's Goldeneye	76.2	142.8	198.3	282.3	1.9	1.4	1.4
Hooded Merganser	20.2	57.0	57.9	93.4	2.8	1.0	1.6
Common Merganser	95.4	273.3	231.7	221.6	2.9	0.8	1.0

	1970s	1980s	1990s	2000s	80/70	90/80	00/90
Red-breasted Merganser	136.3	211.6	248.3	295.9	1.6	1.2	1.2
Ruddy Duck	616.2	764.6	317.0	55.8	1.2	0.4	0.2
Ring-necked Pheasant	17.4	39.0	7.5	2.5	2.2	0.2	0.3
California Quail	81.3	46.4	12.5	9.0	0.6	0.3	0.7
Red-throated Loon	6.4	10.4	14.3	20.8	1.6	1.4	1.5
Pacific Loon	3.4	4.3	8.6	13.5	1.2	2.0	1.6
Common Loon	8.5	7.2	11.7	13.3	0.8	1.6	1.1
Yellow-billed Loon	0.1	0.1	0.0	0.0			
Pied-billed Grebe	53.8	113.1	124.4	147.5	2.1	1.1	1.2
Horned Grebe	112.3	168.6	245.4	270.8	1.5	1.5	1.1
Red-necked Grebe	87.0	141.1	144.9	143.3	1.6	1.0	1.0
Eared Grebe	6.2	9.7	5.7	8.1	1.6	0.6	1.4
Western Grebe	880.9	1303.9	1857.2	1447.6	1.5	1.4	0.8
Clark's Grebe	0.0	0.0	0.0	0.4			
Short-tailed Shearwater	0.0	0.1	0.0	0.0			
Brandt's Cormorant	4.2	6.2	5.6	231.5	1.5	0.9	41.3
Double-crested Cormorant	73.2	270.0	509.9	692.3	3.7	1.9	1.4
Pelagic Cormorant	5.7	16.8	42.2	39.1	2.9	2.5	0.9
American Bittern	1.0	0.3	0.1	0.0	0.3	0.3	
Great Blue Heron	26.2	66.2	52.0	63.1	2.5	0.8	1.2
Green Heron	0.6	0.1	0.3	0.7	0.2	3.0	2.4
Black-crowned Night-Heron	0.1	0.0	0.0	0.0			
Bald Eagle	0.5	2.8	19.6	50.4	5.6	7.0	2.6
Northern Harrier	0.0	1.2	0.1	0.3		0.1	3.3
Sharp-shinned Hawk	6.4	8.6	16.6	20.0	1.3	1.9	1.2
Cooper's Hawk	4.5	4.7	9.4	20.5	1.0	2.0	2.2
Northern Goshawk	0.3	0.0	0.1	0.0			
Red-tailed Hawk	5.7	13.8	28.2	39.5	2.4	2.0	1.4
Rough-legged Hawk	0.0	0.1	0.1	0.0			
American Kestrel	1.3	1.3	0.6	0.0	1.1	0.5	
Merlin	2.6	4.4	6.0	13.6	1.7	1.4	2.3
Peregrine Falcon	0.0	0.0	2.9	6.1			2.1
Virginia Rail	3.1	5.5	3.4	2.6	1.8	0.6	0.8
Sora	0.3	0.6	0.2	0.0	2.2	0.3	
American Coot	3238.3	5076.4	7304.3	6647.5	1.6	1.4	0.9
Black-bellied Plover	0.1	0.1	0.0	0.0	0.8		
Semipalmated Plover	0.1	0.1	0.0	0.0	0.7		
Killdeer	67.9	97.0	89.6	77.8	1.4	0.9	0.9
Black Oystercatcher	0.0	0.1	0.0	0.0			
Spotted Sandpiper	5.9	4.1	1.8	2.4	0.7	0.4	1.3
Greater Yellowlegs	0.0	0.2	0.0	0.0			
Ruddy Turnstone	0.3	0.0	0.1	0.0			
Black Turnstone	41.9	34.2	56.8	138.4	0.8	1.7	2.4

	1970s	1980s	1990s	2000s	80/70	90/80	00/90
Surfbird	8.1	24.0	38.0	92.1	2.9	1.6	2.4
Sanderling	60.7	46.1	59.3	90.0	0.8	1.3	1.5
Western Sandpiper	3.7	0.3	0.8	0.0	0.1	2.7	
Least Sandpiper	1.4	3.9	0.0	0.0	2.8		
Rock Sandpiper	0.1	0.6	0.3	0.8	3.9	0.5	2.5
Dunlin	13.0	49.9	135.8	54.6	3.8	2.7	0.4
Long-billed Dowitcher	0.0	0.6	0.0	0.0			
Wilson's Snipe	9.0	18.0	8.8	4.4	2.0	0.5	0.5
Red Phalarope				cw			
Bonaparte's Gull	85.0	366.6	283.6	6.6	4.3	0.8	0.0
Heermann's Gull	0.0	0.0	0.1	0.0			
Mew Gull	1199.0	1187.9	994.3	907.1	1.0	0.8	0.9
Ring-billed Gull	41.1	170.0	437.5	269.3	4.1	2.6	0.6
Western Gull	6.3	4.6	6.2	8.9	0.7	1.3	1.4
Western x Glaucous-winged Gull	2.6	70.2	180.7	350.6	27.3	2.6	1.9
California Gull	21.0	46.4	56.4	51.8	2.2	1.2	0.9
Herring Gull	45.8	19.0	12.1	9.6	0.4	0.6	0.8
Thayer's Gull	28.3	28.0	6.9	5.8	1.0	0.2	0.8
Glaucous-winged Gull	925.1	2482.6	1968.1	1697.9	2.7	0.8	0.9
Glaucous Gull		cw					
Common Murre	28.8	41.1	58.2	37.1	1.4	1.4	0.6
Pigeon Guillemot	8.4	6.0	11.4	28.4	0.7	1.9	2.5
Marbled Murrelet	11.6	2.0	1.9	1.1	0.2	0.9	0.6
Ancient Murrelet	0.0	0.3	2.3	0.6		7.7	0.3
Cassin's Auklet	0.8	0.0	0.0	0.1			
Rhinoceros Auklet	17.1	35.4	76.0	17.5	2.1	2.1	0.2
Rock Pigeon	1109.1	1460.5	1848.7	2466.8	1.3	1.3	1.3
Band-tailed Pigeon	83.6	224.6	133.8	88.6	2.7	0.6	0.7
Mourning Dove	1.1	0.0	0.3	0.1			
Scarlet-fronted Parakeet	0.0	0.0	0.7	3.5			
Barn Owl	0.5	0.2	0.3	0.8	0.4	1.5	2.5
Western Screech-Owl	1.3	4.2	7.6	5.0	3.3	1.8	0.7
Great Horned Owl	1.5	2.3	2.4	0.4	1.5	1.0	0.2
Snowy Owl	1.3	0.0	0.2	0.0			
Barred Owl	0.0	0.1	0.8	2.5		6.4	3.1
Long-eared Owl	0.0	0.2	0.0	0.1			
Short-eared Owl	2.7	1.6	0.8	0.1	0.6	0.5	0.2
Northern Saw-whet Owl	0.3	0.3	0.9	0.9	0.9	3.0	1.0
Anna's Hummingbird	4.5	20.0	23.3	160.0	4.4	1.2	6.9
Rufous Hummingbird	0.1	0.0	0.0	0.1			
Belted Kingfisher	8.7	15.4	16.9	28.0	1.8	1.1	1.7
Red-naped Sapsucker	0.0	0.2	0.0	0.1			
Red-breasted Sapsucker	1.4	4.9	11.3	4.4	3.6	2.3	0.4

	1970s	1980s	1990s	2000s	80/70	90/80	00/90
Downy Woodpecker	16.0	30.2	52.5	71.0	1.9	1.7	1.4
Hairy Woodpecker	1.3	1.0	0.7	1.6	0.8	0.7	2.3
Northern Flicker	80.0	106.6	141.5	308.5	1.3	1.3	2.2
Pileated Woodpecker	2.1	2.9	5.0	10.8	1.4	1.7	2.2
Northern Shrike	1.8	2.2	1.1	0.5	1.3	0.5	0.5
Hutton's Vireo	1.7	4.0	5.7	7.1	2.3	1.4	1.3
Steller's Jay	79.3	42.1	73.6	172.3	0.5	1.7	2.3
Western Scrub-Jay	0.0	0.1	0.7	3.0			4.3
Clark's Nutcracker	0.1	0.0	0.0	0.0			
American Crow	665.6	1379.8	4385.1	12989.4	2.1	3.2	3.0
Common Raven	0.0	0.0	0.2	0.3			1.3
Barn Swallow	0.0	0.0	0.0	0.5			
Black-capped Chickadee	434.4	548.6	866.6	1538.1	1.3	1.6	1.8
Mountain Chickadee	0.9	0.1	0.0	0.1	0.1		
Chestnut-backed Chickadee	63.3	119.2	166.6	194.4	1.9	1.4	1.2
Bushtit	461.7	1003.9	1000.0	1262.0	2.2	1.0	1.3
Red-breasted Nuthatch	15.8	45.2	63.7	75.5	2.9	1.4	1.2
White-breasted Nuthatch	0.3	0.0	0.0	0.0			
Brown Creeper	6.2	14.0	31.0	64.9	2.3	2.2	2.1
Rock Wren	0.0	0.0	0.1	0.0			
Bewick's Wren	46.4	131.0	162.6	243.9	2.8	1.2	1.5
Winter Wren	50.8	137.5	133.7	191.0	2.7	1.0	1.4
Marsh Wren	6.1	15.2	15.7	9.1	2.5	1.0	0.6
American Dipper	0.2	0.6	0.1	0.1	3.8	0.2	1.1
Golden-crowned Kinglet	97.0	640.3	1008.3	1210.9	6.6	1.6	1.2
Ruby-crowned Kinglet	77.0	176.8	277.7	586.0	2.3	1.6	2.1
Blue-gray Gnatcatcher	0.0	0.1	0.0	0.0			
Townsend's Solitaire	0.0	0.0	0.0	0.6			
Swainson's Thrush	0.0	0.0	0.1	0.0			
Hermit Thrush	2.0	2.4	4.6	7.0	1.2	1.9	1.5
American Robin	1304.6	2012.5	2170.7	3488.3	1.5	1.1	1.6
Varied Thrush	79.2	95.9	122.1	69.6	1.2	1.3	0.6
Northern Mockingbird	0.0	0.0	0.1	0.0			
European Starling	2542.4	4141.7	3809.1	3877.9	1.6	0.9	1.0
American Pipit	0.7	6.8	7.6	0.0	10.2	1.1	0.0
Bohemian Waxwing	0.8	1.3	0.0	0.5			
Cedar Waxwing	98.3	39.7	17.2	68.4	0.4	0.4	4.0
Orange-crowned Warbler	0.7	0.3	1.5	2.1	0.4	5.0	1.4
Yellow-rumped Warbler	4.7	17.6	15.1	114.8	3.7	0.9	7.6

	1970s	1980s	1990s	2000s	80/70	90/80	00/90
Black-throated Gray Warbler	0.0	0.1	0.1	0.0			
Townsend's Warbler	2.0	8.0	19.9	21.4	4.0	2.5	1.1
Palm Warbler	0.0	0.0	0.2	0.1			
Common Yellowthroat	0.0	0.1	0.2	0.0			
Wilson's Warbler	0.0	0.0	0.1	0.0			
Western Tanager	0.0	0.0	0.2	0.3			1.3
Spotted Towhee	105.1	128.0	186.0	254.5	1.2	1.5	1.4
American Tree Sparrow	0.6	0.0	0.0	0.0			
Savannah Sparrow	4.0	1.2	1.7	0.6	0.3	1.4	0.3
Fox Sparrow	32.1	73.5	98.5	189.4	2.3	1.3	1.9
Song Sparrow	325.8	429.9	518.3	737.5	1.3	1.2	1.4
Lincoln's Sparrow	1.3	2.2	8.3	18.0	1.7	3.8	2.2
Swamp Sparrow	0.0	0.0	0.1	0.1			
White-throated Sparrow	0.3	0.1	1.0	0.3	0.4	10.0	0.3
Harris' Sparrow	0.1	0.4	0.1	0.1	2.8	0.3	1.3
White-crowned Sparrow	10.8	14.3	21.0	49.9	1.3	1.5	2.4
Golden-crowned Sparrow	15.8	23.9	93.4	205.0	1.5	3.9	2.2
Dark-eyed Junco	508.5	601.3	669.7	787.0	1.2	1.1	1.2
Lapland Longspur	0.9	0.5	0.0	0.0	0.6	0.0	
Red-winged Blackbird	71.4	102.7	143.3	198.4	1.4	1.4	1.4
Western Meadowlark	7.1	7.4	1.5	1.5	1.0	0.2	1.0
Brewer's Blackbird	87.8	40.2	5.8	0.3	0.5	0.1	0.0
Brown-headed Cowbird	0.1	0.0	0.1	0.3	0.0		2.5
Pine Grosbeak	1.7	0.0	0.0	0.1			
Purple Finch	47.6	27.0	10.6	8.6	0.6	0.4	0.8
House Finch	224.7	330.4	821.9	1111.8	1.5	2.5	1.4
Red Crossbill	2.9	20.8	1.6	3.6	7.3	0.1	2.3
Common Redpoll	0.0	0.0	0.4	13.9			34.6
Hoary Redpoll	0.0	0.0	0.0	0.3			
Pine Siskin	1609.4	1108.5	797.7	1541.1	0.7	0.7	1.9
American Goldfinch	72.2	192.2	230.1	372.0	2.7	1.2	1.6
Evening Grosbeak	33.6	26.8	24.5	0.1	0.8	0.9	0.0
House Sparrow	367.1	463.4	758.5	1000.4	1.3	1.6	1.3
Number of Species	110.4	120.7	120.3	121.3	1.1	1.0	1.0
Number of Individuals	26901	39139	47093	59846	1.5	1.2	1.3

APPENDIX 2. KING COUNTY BREEDING BIRD ATLAS

In *Birding in Seattle and King County* (1982), I proposed that birders embark upon "an ambitious new project: compiling an atlas of the breeding birds of King County." The initial plan was for a five-year cooperative state-wide effort to begin in the spring of 1983, to join efforts then underway in New England and California (S. B. Laughlin, D. P. Kibbe, and P. F. J. Eagles, "Atlasing the Distribution of the Breeding Birds of North America," *American Birds* 36:6-19, 1982). The King County Atlas project was to be modeled on the successful British atlas completed in 1976 (J. T. R. Sharrock, ed., *The Atlas of Breeding Birds in Britain and Ireland*, British Trust for Ornithology, Beech Grove, Tring, Herts., England, 1976). The British atlas censused each of 3862 10-kilometer-square quadrangles covering all of Great Britain and Ireland over a five-year period. More than 10,000 observers contributed sightings.

Phil Mattocks took the lead in organizing the Washington State Breeding Bird Atlas project, which began in 1987. We proposed to outdo the Brits, using a survey grid with four times the resolution of the British atlas. We decided to rely on the existing township-range survey lines to define survey quads (see map on page 224). A single township measures approximately six miles square, or 36 one-square-mile sections, which is roughly equivalent to the 10-kilometer-square grid used in Great Britain and Ireland. To refine the scale, we defined our survey quads as a quarter township, dividing each township into four quarters, each three miles on a side, or nine square miles (Mattocks 1988).

The initial five-year timeline was extended through 1993, but the scale of the project—targeting some 7,800 survey quadrangles across the state—proved beyond our capacity. Nevertheless, the results, however incomplete, were published with a "Gap" analysis comparing reported breeding locations with projected breeding ranges based on a sophisticated habitat analysis, as the Washington State Gap Analysis Final Report (Smith et al. 1997). Though township and section boundaries are far from mathematically precise, they have the advantage of being shown on many standard maps.

To conduct a survey, observers might set out early one morning in late spring, targeting one or more quads. Observations from each quad visited on a given day would be entered on a standard field card indicating species and relevant activities

KING COUNTY BREEDING BIRD ATLAS BLOCKS

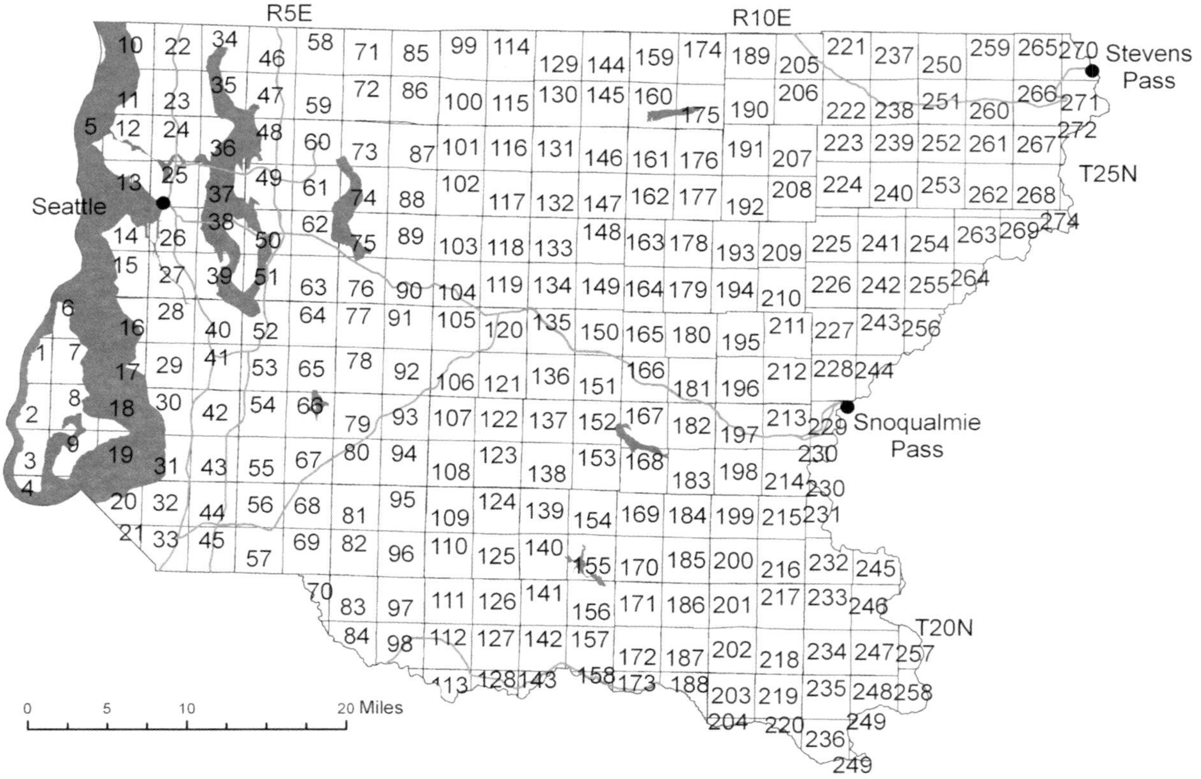

Seattle

Stevens Pass

Snoqualmie Pass

R5E

R10E

T25N

T20N

0   5   10   20 Miles

noted, such as "singing male on territory," "adult carrying food to nest," or "pair copulating." These specific behavioral observations were then translated into three categories: "possible," "probable," and "confirmed" nesting.

Possible if:
√: Species in suitable habitat during nesting season
X: Singing male present in suitable habitat

Probable if:
M: Multiple singing males found during one visit
P: Pair observed in suitable habitat
T: Territory established; also, singing male present at same location on two dates a week or more apart
C: Courtship behavior, copulation, or enlarged cloacal protuberance
V: Visiting probable nest site
A: Agitated behavior from adults
N: Nest-building or excavation of nest cavity

Confirmed if:
PE: Physiological evidence: brood patch or egg in oviduct
DD: Distraction display
UN: Used nest or eggshell (of positive identity)
FL: Recently fledged young incapable of sustained flight
ON: Occupied nest: adults entering, leaving, or incubating, but nest contents unseen
FN: Adult bringing food to nest
FS: Adult removing fecal sac from nest
NE: Nest with eggs
NY: Nest with young seen or heard

Note that we did not record the abundance of breeding birds in each quad, only the presence or absence of nesting evidence for each species.

I was less than satisfied with the results at the conclusion of the state-wide atlas effort and proposed to continue the census with a specific focus on King County's 273 nine-square-mile quads, with the goal of achieving an adequate level of effort in every King County quad. Hal Opperman joined me in recruiting a dedicated cadre of volunteers to this end, beginning in 1994. The key to the effort was rapid feedback of information by continuous updating of a spreadsheet of survey results week-by-week that could be shared with our team of volunteers. We met our goal in 2000. This effort was extended to three adjacent counties: Kittitas, Kitsap, and Island, to produce a comprehensive Breeding Bird Atlas for a transect of the Cascade Range.

The results have been published on Seattle Audubon Society's website as Sound to Sage (http://www.soundtosage.org): "The result of over 10,000 hours of field surveying [3380 in King County] by more than 300 'citizen science' volunteers, Sound to Sage presents maps and accounts of the nesting occurrence of 213 species of birds (86% of those known to nest regularly in the state) in a four-county, 5,000-square-mile swath of Washington extending from the shores of Puget Sound across the Cascade Range to the sagebrush lands adjoining the Columbia River."

The Breeding Bird Atlas did not confirm every species known to breed in the County. The Atlas confirmed just 135 species as nesting, with an additional 16 "probable" and 12 "possible," for a total of 163 species. Table 3 lists Breeding Bird Atlas results, listed in order of the number of census quadrangles for which a species was confirmed or judged probable as a breeding species. Additional species that bred formerly or that have been confirmed as nesting subsequently are appended. The number of species that are positively known to nest (155) or to have nested in the past (5) or that are presumed to nest based on strong if not conclusive evidence (7) totals 167.

Atlas volunteers are currently contemplating a 10-year follow-up survey of a sample of key quads to evaluate changes in breeding bird distributions during the past decade. Stay tuned.

Anytime you're out in the field—whether it's for a citizen-science project or just for fun—you can happen upon a rare visitor to the county. In this case, a Harris's Sparrow was discovered in Bothell in the winter of 2010 and stayed through spring 2011. Birders got to see this male molt from juvenile plumage to the adult splendor shown here (© Gregg Thompson).

Species / # Quads / COnfirmed, PRobable, POssible	CO	PR	CO & PR	PO	CO & PR&PO
American Robin	147	44	191	64	255
Song Sparrow	75	80	155	70	225
Swainson's Thrush	31	118	149	93	242
Dark-eyed Junco	84	61	145	93	238
Chestnut-backed Chickadee	57	74	131	90	221
Pacific Wren	25	106	131	103	234
Pacific-slope Flycatcher	9	118	127	104	231
Cedar Waxwing	31	82	113	82	195
Spotted Towhee	55	58	113	55	168
European Starling	98	10	108	17	125
Barn Swallow	75	28	103	51	154
Wilson's Warbler	18	84	102	113	215
American Crow	60	38	98	72	170
White-crowned Sparrow	42	52	94	77	171
Black-capped Chickadee	54	36	90	54	144
Willow Flycatcher	7	81	88	72	160
Violet-green Swallow	51	33	84	75	159
Common Yellowthroat	33	50	83	38	121
Brown-headed Cowbird	40	43	83	45	128
House Finch	48	35	83	27	110
Common Bushtit	57	25	82	44	126
Mallard	63	18	81	21	102
Steller's Jay	32	49	81	134	215
Varied Thrush	22	59	81	59	140
Rufous Hummingbird	17	59	76	126	202
Red-winged Blackbird	37	37	74	35	109
Golden-crowned Kinglet	22	51	73	142	215
House Sparrow	48	24	72	31	103
American Goldfinch	17	54	71	73	144
Black-throated Gray Warbler	14	56	70	94	164
Bewick's Wren	31	37	68	56	124
Black-headed Grosbeak	14	54	68	88	156
MacGillivray's Warbler	11	53	64	86	150
Red-breasted Nuthatch	21	40	61	121	182
Northern Flicker	31	28	59	140	199
Red-tailed Hawk	23	34	57	83	140
Western Tanager	13	44	57	107	164
Downy Woodpecker	27	29	56	68	124
Warbling Vireo	6	50	56	118	174
Band-tailed Pigeon	6	49	55	85	140
Canada Goose	37	15	52	16	68
Cliff Swallow	39	13	52	40	92
Hairy Woodpecker	21	30	51	74	125

Table 3: BBA Quad Totals

Species / # Quads / COnfirmed, PRobable, POssible	CO	PR	CO& PR	PO	CO& PR&PO
Pine Siskin	11	38	49	99	148
Rock Dove	30	18	48	38	86
Tree Swallow	31	17	48	71	119
Savannah Sparrow	21	27	48	31	79
Orange-crowned Warbler	10	34	44	107	151
Purple Finch	16	28	44	69	113
Townsend's Warbler	4	38	42	76	118
Killdeer	18	23	41	40	81
California Quail	17	22	39	29	68
Hermit Thrush	6	32	38	43	81
Spotted Sandpiper	18	19	37	34	71
Belted Kingfisher	11	24	35	48	83
Western Wood-Pewee	2	32	34	87	121
Brewer's Blackbird	23	10	33	23	56
Olive-sided Flycatcher	2	29	31	98	129
Bald Eagle	25	5	30	15	45
Yellow Warbler	4	26	30	60	90
Marsh Wren	10	18	28	23	51
Gadwall	10	17	27	7	34
Red-breasted Sapsucker	19	7	26	41	67
Common Raven	6	20	26	54	80
Pied-billed Grebe	21	4	25	12	37
Pileated Woodpecker	6	19	25	57	82
Northern Rough-winged Swallow	7	18	25	61	86
Hutton's Vireo	3	22	25	63	88
Gray Jay	16	8	24	25	49
Bullock's Oriole	13	10	23	18	41
Wood Duck	14	7	21	16	37
Brown Creeper	6	15	21	68	89
American Coot	17	3	20	11	31
American Dipper	16	3	19	29	48
Evening Grosbeak	5	14	19	80	99
Common Merganser	14	4	18	30	48
Great Blue Heron	13	4	17	68	85
Green Heron	13	4	17	13	30
Sooty Grouse	12	5	17	28	45
Vaux's Swift	2	15	17	110	127
Red-eyed Vireo	7	10	17	38	55
Yellow-rumped Warbler	3	14	17	44	61
Ruffed Grouse	16	0	16	23	39
Spotted Owl	8	8	16	16	32
Hooded Merganser	9	3	12	12	24
Great Horned Owl	7	5	12	14	26
Lazuli Bunting	3	9	12	4	16

Species / # Quads / COnfirmed, PRobable, POssible	CO	PR	CO& PR	PO	CO& PR&PO
Cinnamon Teal	2	9	11	3	14
Virginia Rail	3	7	10	10	20
Turkey Vulture	0	9	9	30	39
Mourning Dove	5	4	9	22	31
Western Screech-Owl	4	5	9	15	24
Hammond's Flycatcher	2	7	9	60	69
Red Crossbill	0	9	9	73	82
Northern Harrier	4	4	8	8	16
Anna's Hummingbird	2	6	8	10	18
Blue-winged Teal	2	5	7	2	9
Osprey	7	0	7	31	38
Ringed-necked Pheasant	3	4	7	13	20
Fox Sparrow	1	6	7	16	23
Ruddy Duck	4	2	6	3	9
Wilson's Snipe	0	6	6	11	17
Barred Owl	3	3	6	19	25
Lincoln's Sparrow	3	3	6	5	11
Northern Shoveler	3	2	5	2	7
Sharp-shinned Hawk	2	3	5	21	26
Sora	2	3	5	5	10
Glaucous-winged Gull	3	2	5	27	32
Barn Owl	3	2	5	5	10
Common Nighthawk	2	3	5	22	27
Red-naped Sapsucker	4	1	5	6	11
Green-winged Teal	0	4	4	5	9
Pigeon Guillemot	3	1	4	4	8
American Pipit	3	1	4	3	7
Chipping Sparrow	1	3	4	14	18
Common Loon	2	1	3	4	7
American Bittern	1	2	3	7	10
American Wigeon	0	3	3	4	7
Harlequin Duck	3	0	3	6	9
Barrow's Goldeneye	3	0	3	1	4
American Kestrel	2	1	3	20	23
Purple Martin	1	2	3	1	4
Western Bluebird	2	1	3	2	5
Mountain Bluebird	3	0	3	4	7
Solitary Vireo	1	2	3	30	33
Northern Pygmy-Owl	1	1	2	9	11
Northern Saw-whet Owl	0	2	2	5	7
Black-backed Woodpecker	2	0	2	2	4
House Wren	1	1	2	2	4
Pine Grosbeak	0	2	2	3	5
Mute Swan	1	0	1	2	3

Species / # Quads / COnfirmed, PRobable, POssible	CO	PR	CO&PR	PO	CO&PR&PO
Northern Pintail	0	1	1	0	1
Redhead	1	0	1	0	1
Lesser Scaup	1	0	1	0	1
Cooper's Hawk	1	0	1	17	18
Golden Eagle	1	0	1	17	18
Peregrine Falcon	1	0	1	1	2
White-tailed Ptarmigan	1	0	1	2	3
Marbled Murrelet	0	1	1	0	1
American Three-toed Woodpecker	1	0	1	3	4
Dusky Flycatcher	0	1	1	5	6
Scrub Jay	1	0	1	0	1
Ruby-crowned Kinglet	1	0	1	7	8
Townsend's Solitaire	1	0	1	20	21
Hermit Warbler	1	0	1	6	7
Western Meadowlark	0	1	1	3	4
Gray-crowned Rosy-Finch	1	0	1	2	3
Double-crested Cormorant	0	0	0	2	2
Ring-necked Duck	0	0	0	4	4
Bufflehead	0	0	0	3	3
Northern Goshawk	0	0	0	5	5
Merlin	0	0	0	2	2
Northern Bobwhite	0	0	0	1	1
Wilson's Phalarope	0	0	0	2	2
Caspian Tern	0	0	0	1	1
Short-eared Owl	0	0	0	1	1
Black Swift	0	0	0	20	20
Calliope Hummingbird	0	0	0	1	1
Western Kingbird	0	0	0	1	1

Below: Barn Owls nest at Magnuson Park, Seattle (© Gregg Thompson).

GALLERY OF RARE KING COUNTY BIRDS

Clockwise from top left: Brewer's Sparrow, Redmond, April 10, 2007 (© John Tubbs). Yellow-bellied Sapsucker, Shoreline, April 25, 2007 (© Ollie Oliver). Clay-colored Sparrow, Marymoor Park, October 9, 2005 (© Steve Caldwell). Slaty-backed Gull, Renton, January 21, 2007 (© Ollie Oliver). Tundra Swan, Montlake Fill, January 7, 2012 (© Doug Parrott). Tufted Duck, Montlake Fill, February 4, 2012 (© Doug Parrott).

BIBLIOGRAPHY

Aanerud, Kevin. 1989. "Birds Observed at Montlake Fill, University of Washington Campus, Seattle, Washington, from 1972 to 1989." *Washington Birds* 1:6-21.

Aanerud, Kevin R. 2002. "Fifth Report of the Washington Bird Records Committee." *Washington Birds* 8:1-18.

Aanerud, Kevin, and Philip W. Mattocks, Jr. 1997. "Third Report of the Washington Bird Records Committee." *Washington Birds* 6:7-31.

Aanerud, Kevin R., and Philip W. Mattocks, Jr. 2000. "Fourth Report of the Washington Bird Records Committee." *Washington Birds* 7:7-24.

Alcorn, Gordon D. 1962. "Checklist of the Birds of the State of Washington." *Occasional Paper No. 17,* pp. 156-199. Department of Biology, University of Puget Sound, Tacoma. Revised in 1971 as *Occasional Paper No. 43.*

Alcorn, Gordon D. 1972. "Bibliography: Birds of the State of Washington." *Occasional Paper No. 44,* pp. 538-630. Museum of Natural History, University of Puget Sound, Tacoma.

American Birding Association. 1999-2009. "Regional reports." *North American Birds* 53(1)-63(4).

American Ornithologists' Union. 1982. "Thirty-fourth Supplement to the American Ornithologists' Union Check-list of North American Birds." *Supplement to The Auk* 99(3):1cc-16cc.

American Ornithologists' Union. 1998. *The AOU Check-list of North American Birds.* 7th edition. American Ornithologists' Union, Washington, D.C. (with annual supplements published in *The Auk*).

Anonymous. 1921. Untitled note [Snow Bunting sighting]. *The Murrelet* 2(1):5.

Anonymous. 1927. "Osprey near Seattle, Washington." *The Murrelet* 8(2):47.

Balmer, Adam. 1924. "Spotted Owl (Strix occidentalis)." *The Murrelet* 5(1):13.

Balmer, Adam. 1924. "Barn Owl in Washington." *The Murrelet* 5(1):13.

Balmer, Adam. 1924. "Breeding of Pigeon Guillemot near Seattle." *The Murrelet* 5(3):12.

Balmer, Adam. 1925. "Note on the Western Gull (Larus occidentalis)." *The Murrelet* 6(1):13.

Balmer, Adam. 1926. "The Snow Bunting on Puget Sound, Wash." *The Murrelet* 7(1):15.

Balmer, Adam. 1926. "Osprey Nesting at Seattle, Washington." *The Murrelet* 7(3):67.

Beckey, Fred. 1973. *Cascade Alpine Guide: Climbing & High Routes, 1: Columbia River to Stevens Pass.* The Mountaineers, Seattle.

Bell, Brian H. and Gregory Kennedy. 2006. *Birds of Washington State.* Lone Pine Publishing, Edmonton, Alberta.

Bennett, H. Stanley, and Garrett Eddy. 1949. "White-throated Sparrow in King County, Washington, in Winter." *The Murrelet* 30(1):17.

Bennett, H. Stanley, and Garrett Eddy. 1949. "European Starling in King County, Washington." *The Murrelet* 30(1):18.

Binford, Laurence C., and J. V. Remsen, Jr. 1974. "Identification of the Yellow-billed Loon (Gavia adamsii)." *Western Birds* 5(4):111.

Bowles, J. H. 1911. "Notes Extending the Range of Certain Birds on the Pacific Slope." *The Auk* 28(2):169-178.

Brown, D. E. 1921. Untitled note in "General Notes" [sighting of Fox Sparrows and Townsend's Warblers]. *The Murrelet* 2(1):6.

Brown, D. E. 1921. "Nesting of the Green-winged Teal and Ruddy Duck in King County, Washington." *The Murrelet* 2(3):5.

Brown, D. E. 1921. "Late Nesting of the Pied-billed Grebe, King County, Wn." *The Murrelet* 2(3):5.

Brown, D. E. 1922. "Fox Sparrows." *The Murrelet* 3(2):7.

Brown, D. E. 1923. "Notes on the Nesting of the California Cuckoo (Coccyzus americanus occidentalis) in Washington." *The Murrelet* 4(2):17.

Brown, D. E. 1924. "Notes on Fox Sparrows of Western Washington." *The Murrelet* 5(1):11.

Brown, D. E. 1924. "Notes from Western Washington." *The Murrelet* 5(3):11.

Brown, D. E. 1925. "Nesting of Kennicott's Screech Owl (Otus asio kennicotti)." *The Murrelet* 6(2):40.

Brown, D. E. 1930. "Notes from a Country Home." *The Murrelet* 11(l):21-22.

Brown, D. E. 1930. "Additional Notes from a Country Home." *The Murrelet* 11(2):18-19.

Brown, D. E. 1930. "Nesting Habits of the Steller Jay (Cyanocitta stelleri stelleri) in Western Washington." *The Murrelet* 11(3):68-69.

Brown, D. E. 1931. "Notes from a Country Home." *The Murrelet* 12(2):56.

Brown, D. E. 1931. "Additional Notes on the Nesting Habits of the Steller Jay (Cyanocitta stelleri stelleri)." *The Murrelet* 12(2):57.

Brown, D. E. 1935. "Birds Bathing in Icewater." *The Murrelet* 16(1):18.

Brown, D. E. 1935. "Unusual Nest of the Northern Cliff Swallow." *The Murrelet* 16(2):41.

Brown, D. E. 1937. "Some Notes on the Rusty Song Sparrow." *The Murrelet* 18(1/2):29-30.

Brown, D. E., A. M. Winslow, A. D. McGrew, and Thomas D. Burleigh. 1920. "Observation Notes in Vicinity of Seattle." *The Murrelet* 1(1):8.

Burleigh, Thomas D. 1929-1930. "Notes on the Bird Life of Northwestern Washington." *The Auk* 46(4):502-519; 47(1):48-63.

Canning, Douglas J., and Steven G. Herman. 1983. "Gadwall Breeding Range Expansion into Western Washington." *The Murrelet* 64(1):27-31.

Cannon, Violet. 1947 "European Widgeon and European Teal at Seattle, Washington." *The Murrelet* 28(1):13.

Cassidy, Kelly M. 1997. "Snowy Owl Irruption into Washington and Vicinity during the Winter of 1996-1997." *Washington Birds* 6:68-82.

Colby, John F. 1972. "Egg-Tooth Marbled Murrelet in Pierce County, Washington." *The Murrelet* 53(3):49.

Dawson, William Leon, and John Hooper Bowles. 1909. *The Birds of Washington: A Complete Scientific and Popular Account of the 372 Species of Birds Found in the State.* Occidental Publishing Company, Seattle. Two volumes.

Devillers, Pierre. 1970. "Identification and Distribution in California of the Sphyrapicus varius Group of Sapsuckers." *California Birds* 1(2):47-76.

Dunn, Jon L., and Jonathan Alderfer (eds.). 2006. *Field Guide to the Birds of North America.* 5th edition. National Geographic Society, Washington, D.C.

Dvornich, Karen M., Kelly R. McAllister, and Keith B. Aubry. 1997. *Amphibians and*

Reptiles of Washington State: Location Data and Predicted Distributions. Vol. 2 of *Washington State Gap Analysis—Final Report* (K.M. Cassidy, C.E. Grue, M.R. Smith, and K.M. Dvornich, eds.). Washington Cooperative Fish and Wildlife Research Unit, University of Washington, Seattle.

eBird. 2010. [web application] A real-time, online checklist program,...[providing] rich data sources for basic information on bird abundance and distribution. Cornell Lab of Ornithology, Ithaca, New York. Available at: http://ebird.org.

Eddy, Garrett. 1946. "Arctic Tern on Puget Sound, Washington." *The Murrelet* 27(3):53.

Eddy, Garrett. 1951. "Further Notes on the Green Heron Advance in Washington State." *The Murrelet* 32(1):12.

Eddy, Garrett. 1953. "Winter Records of Band-tailed Pigeons (Columba f. fasciata)." *The Murrelet* 34(2):30-31.

Eddy, Garrett. 1956. "Western Willet (Catoptrophorus semipalmatus inornatus Brewster) at Seattle." *The Murrelet* 37(2):25.

Eddy, Mr. and Mrs. Garrett. 1948. "Turkey Vulture Concentration." *The Murrelet* 29(1):11.

Editors. 1951. "Snowy Owls in Western Washington," in "Notes from the Field." *The Murrelet* 32(1):14.

Edson, J. M. 1945. "Wilson Snipe in Winter." *The Murrelet* 26(1):10.

Edwards, R. Y., and D. Stirling. 1961. "Range Expansion of the House Finch into British Columbia." *The Murrelet* 42(3):38-42.

Flahaut, Martha R. 1948. Untitled [note on White-throated Sparrow]. *The Murrelet* 29(3):49.

Goodge, William. 1949. "Glaucous-winged Gull Nesting at Seattle, Washington." *The Murrelet* 30(3):58.

Groth, J. G. 1993. "Evolutionary Differentiation in Morphology, Vocalizations, and Allozymes among Nomadic Sibling Species in the North American Red Crossbill (Loxia curvirostra) Complex" in *University of California Publications in Zoology* 127:1-143, University of California Press, Berkeley.

Grubb, Teryl Gordon. 1976. "A Survey and Analysis of Bald Eagle Nesting in Western Washington." M.S. thesis, University of Washington, Seattle.

Grubb, Teryl G., David A. Manuwal, and Clifford M. Anderson. 1975. "Nest Distribution and Productivity of Bald Eagles in Western Washington." *The Murrelet* 56(3):2-6.

Gunther, Pamela M., Brenda S. Horn, and Geoffrey D. Babb. 1981. "Relative Distribution by Habitat and Brief Literature Reviews of Birds and Mammals in the Skykomish Ranger District, Mt. Baker-Snoqualmie National Forest." U.S. Forest Service, Mt. Baker-Snoqualmie National Forest, Skykomish Ranger District, and Huxley College of Environmental Studies, Western Washington University, Bellingham.

Hagenstein, Walter M. 1936. "Late Nesting of the Band-tailed Pigeon." *The Murrelet* 17(1):21-22.

Hagenstein, Walter M. 1947. "Albinistic Fox Sparrow." *The Murrelet* 28(3):41.

Hagenstein, Walter M. 1948. "Pine Grosbeaks at Sea Level." *The Murrelet* 29(2):27.

Hagenstein, Walter 1950. "European Starling (Sturnus vulgaris) at Medina, King County, Washington." *The Murrelet* 31(1):11.

Hagenstein, Walter M. 1953. "Sight Record of the Tree Sparrow at Seattle." *The Murrelet* 34(1):9.

Hagenstein, Walter M. 1954. "Sight Record of Harris Sparrow at Fall City, Washington." *The Murrelet* 35(3):50.

Haig, Emily Huddart. 1959. "Birds of the Arboretum." *Arboretum Bulletin* 22(4):124, 140.

Hanley, Thomas A., and Richard D. Taber. 1979. *Wildlife Habitat Relationship Guidelines for the Alpine Lakes Wilderness and Management Areas—Mt. Baker-Snoqualmie and Wenatchee National Forests, Final Report.* College of Forest Resources, University of Washington, Seattle.

Hansen, A. J. 1978. "Bald Eagles in the Skykomish Ranger District." U.S. Forest Service, Darrington, Washington.

Hertz, U. L. 1890. "Large Numbers of Sandhill Cranes." *Oologist* 7:51-52.

Higman, H. W. 1944. "Autumn Communal Roosting of Purple Martins within the City Limits of Seattle, Washington." *The Murrelet* 25(3):43-44.

Higman, H. W., and Earl J. Larrison. 1941. "Late Nesting of the Pied-billed Grebe." *The Murrelet* 22(1):19.

Higman, Harry W., and Earl J. Larrison. 1951. *Union Bay: The Life of a City Marsh.* University of Washington Press, Seattle.

Hinchliff, John. 1996. *An Atlas of Washington Butterflies: The Distribution of the Butterflies of Washington.* Corvallis, OR: The Oregon State University Bookstore and the Evergreen Aurelians.

Hunn, Eugene S. 1973. "First Record for the Swamp Sparrow in Washington State." *Western Birds* 4(1):31-32.

Hunn, Eugene S. 1978. "Black-throated Sparrow Vagrants in the Pacific Northwest." *Western Birds* 9(2):85-89.

Hunn, Eugene S. 1979. Untitled [Bird finding insert, Seattle, Washington]. *Birding* 11:288c-288d.

Hunn, Eugene S. 1982. *Birding in Seattle and King County: Site Guide and Annotated List.* Seattle Audubon Society Trailside Series. Seattle Audubon Society, Seattle.

Hunn, Eugene S., and George Gerdts. 1994. "Sighting of a Possible Rufous X Allen's Hummingbird in King County, Washington." *Washington Birds* 3:51-54.

Institute for Environmental Studies, University of Washington. 1974. "Discovery Park Inventory and Natural History Report." Manuscript prepared for Seattle Department of Parks and Recreation.

Jacobson, Arthur Lee. 1989. *Trees of Seattle: The Complete Tree-Finder's Guide to the City's 740 Varieties.* Sasquatch Books, Seattle.

Jacobson, Arthur Lee. 2001. *Wild Plants of Greater Seattle: A Field Guide to Native and Naturalized Plants of the Seattle Area.* Arthur Lee Jacobson, Seattle.

Jewett, Stanley G., Walter P. Taylor, William T. Shaw, and John W. Aldrich. 1953. *Birds of Washington State.* University of Washington Press, Seattle.

Johnson, Linda, and Richard D. Taber. n.d. "Appendix C: Birds and Mammals of the Morse Lake Lowlands." Unpublished manuscript. College of Forest Resources, University of Washington, Seattle.

Johnson, Richard E. 1977. "An Historical Analysis of Wolverine Abundance and Distribution in Washington." *The Murrelet* 58(1):13-16.

Johnson, Richard E. and Kelly M. Cassidy. 1997. *Terrestrial Mammals of Washington*

State: Location Data and Predicted Distributions. Volume 3 in *Washington State Gap Analysis – Final Report* (K. M. Cassidy, C. E. Grue, M. R. Smith, and K. M. Dvornich, eds.). Washington Cooperative Fish and Wildlife Research Unit, University of Washington, Seattle.

Johnston, David W. 1961. *The Biosystematics of American Crows.* University of Washington Press, Seattle.

Jones, Lawrence L. C., William P. Leonard, and Deanna H. Olson (eds.). 2005. *Amphibians of the Pacific Northwest.* Seattle Audubon Society, Seattle.

Kane, Susan M. 1924. "Battle between a Western Robin and Steller's Jay, Witnessed on the Campus at the University of Washington." *The Murrelet* 5(2):9.

Kitchin, E. A. 1925. "Maury Island, Puget Sound, Washington." *The Murrelet* 6(3):64.

Krause, Fayette F. 1974. "A City Marsh Still Lives." *Pacific Search* 8(8):42-43.

Krause, Fayette F. 1975. *Birds of the University of Washington Campus.* Thomas Burke Memorial Washington State Museum, University of Washington, Seattle.

Lambert, Anthony. 1981. "Presence and Food Preferences of the Great Horned Owl in the Urban Parks of Seattle." *The Murrelet* 62(1):2-5.

Larrison, Earl J. 1940. "The Anthony Green Heron in the State of Washington." *The Murrelet* 21(1):1-3.

Larrison, Earl J. 1940. "Water Bird Studies in the University of Washington Swamp." *The Murrelet* 21(2):29-33.

Larrison, Earl J. 1942. "Birds of the Arboretum." *Arboretum Bulletin* 5(9):9-12, 30-31.

Larrison, Earl J. 1942. *A Field Guide to the Birds of the Seattle Area.* Seattle Audubon Society, Seattle.

Larrison, Earl J. 1945. "Blue-footed Booby in the Pacific Northwest." *The Murrelet* 26(3):45.

Larrison, Earl J. 1945. "Albino Purple Martin at Seattle Martin Roost." *The Murrelet* 26(3):45-46.

Larrison, Earl J. 1947. "Miscellaneous Distributional Notes for Washington." *The Murrelet* 28(1):11-13.

Larrison, Earl J. 1947. "Present Status of the Green Heron in Washington." *Condor* 49(2):87.

Larrison, Earl J. 1947. "Sections of the Puget Lowland Belt." *The Murrelet* 28(3):35-36.

Larrison, Earl J. 1947. *Field Guide to the Birds of King County, Washington.* Seattle Audubon Society, Seattle.

Larrison, Earl J. 1952. *Field Guide to Birds of Puget Sound.* Seattle Audubon Society, Seattle.

Larrison, Earl J., and Klaus G. Sonnenberg. 1968. *Washington Birds: Their Location and Identification.* Seattle Audubon Society, Seattle.

Laughlin, S. B., D. P. Kibbe, and P. F. J. Eagles. 1982. "Atlasing the Distribution of the Breeding Birds of North America," *American Birds* 36:6-19.

Laycock, George. 1994. *The Bird Watcher's Bible.* Doubleday and Company, Garden City, New York.

Lewis, Mark G., and Fred A. Sharpe. 1987. *Birding in the San Juan Islands.* The Mountaineers, Seattle.

Longwell, William K., Jr. 1981. *Guide to Trails of Tiger Mountain.* Issaquah Alps Trails Club, Issaquah.

Maddock, H. J. 1925. "Nesting of the Western Belted Kingfisher *(Ceryle alcyon caurina)* on Puget Sound, Washington." *The Murrelet* 6(3):59-60.

Manning, Harvey. 1982, 1986, 1987, 1990. *Footsore: Walks and Hikes around Puget Sound.* Vols. 1, 2, 3, and 4. Mountaineers Books, Seattle.

Manning, Harvey. 1981. *Guide to Trails of Cougar Mountain and Squak Mountain: Including prospectus for a Cougar Mountain Regional Park.* Issaquah Alps Trails Club, Issaquah.

Manning, Harvey. 1981. *The Flowering of the Issaquah Alps.* Issaquah Alps Trails Club, Issaquah.

Manuwal, David A., Philip W. Mattocks, Jr., and Klaus O. Richter. 1979. "First Arctic Tern Colony in the Contiguous Western United States." *American Birds* 33(1):144-145.

Marzluff, John M., and Tony Angell. 2005. *In the Company of Crows and Ravens.* Yale University Press, New Haven.

Masta, Susan E. 1992. "The Winter European Starling Population in Seattle, Washington, in Relation to the Populations of Three Species of Woodpeckers." *Washington Birds* 2:36-41.

Mattocks, Philip W., Jr. 1988. "The October Frigatebird and Other Sightings." *Washington Ornithological Society Newsletter* 1:1-2.

Mattocks, Philip W., Jr., Eugene S. Hunn, and Terence R. Wahl. 1976. "A Checklist of the Birds of Washington State, with Recent Changes Annotated." *Western Birds* 7:1-24.

McCaskie, Guy. 1970. "Blue Jay in California." *California Birds* 1(2):81-83.

McCaskie, Guy, and Paul DeBenedictis. 1966. *Annotated Field List, Birds of Northern California.* Golden Gate Audubon Society, San Francisco.

McInerny, Christopher J. 2002. "Shorebird Passage at the Montlake Fill, University of Washington, Seattle, 1996-1997." *Washington Birds* 8:19-28.

McKnight, Donald E. 1960. "Cinnamon Teal near Kent, Washington." *The Murrelet* 41(2):27.

McMannama, Zella. 1948. "King Eider Taken at Seattle, Washington." *The Murrelet* 29(3):48.

Michael, John H., Jr. 1992. "Intertidal Nest of Northern Rough-winged Swallow." *Washington Birds* 2:23-24.

Miller, Robert C., and Elizabeth L. Curtis. 1940. "Birds of the University of Washington Campus." *The Murrelet* 21(2):35-46.

Mlodinow, Steven G., and Kevin R. Aanerud. 2006. "Sixth Report of the Washington Bird Records Committee." *Washington Birds* 9:39-54.

Mlodinow, S. G., P. F. Springer, B. Deuel, L. S. Semo, T. Leukering, T. Doug Schonewald, W. Tweit, and J. H. Barry. 2008. "Distribution and identification of Cackling Goose *(Branta hutchinsii)* subspecies. *North American Birds* 62:344-360.

Morgan, Brandt. 1981 "Pilling's Pond." *Audubon Magazine* 83(4):102-105.

Morse, Robert, Tom Aversa, and Hal Opperman. 2003. *Birds of the Puget Sound Region.* R.W. Morse Company, Olympia, Washington.

Muller, Martin J. 1995. "Pied-billed Grebes Nesting on Green Lake, Seattle, Washington." *Washington Birds* 4:35-59.

Muller, Martin J. 2000. "Pied-billed Grebe Scavenging a Dead Bird." *Washington Birds* 7:44-45.

National Audubon Society. 1949-1970. "Regional reports." *Audubon Field Notes.* Vols. 1-24.

National Audubon Society. 1971-1994. "Regional reports." *American Birds.* Vols. 25(1)-48(1).

National Audubon Society. 1994-1998. "Regional reports." *Field Notes.* Vols. 48(2)-52(4).

Nellis, Carl H. 1973 "Staggered Hatching of Robins." *The Murrelet* 54(3):38.

Nichols, H. Kenneth, Jr. 1947. "White Pelicans Seen at Redondo, Washington." *The Murrelet* 28(1):6.

Nysewander, David R., Joseph R. Evenson, Bryan L. Murphie, and Thomas A. Cyra. 2005. Report of Marine Bird and Mammal Component, Puget Sound Ambient Monitoring Program, for July 1992 to December 1999 Period, final revision of 2001 manuscript. Prepared for Washington State Department of Fish & Wildlife and Puget Sound Action Team. WDFW Wildlife Management Program, Olympia.

Nystrom, Gunnar. 1969. "Sight Record of Common Teal at Seattle, Washington." *The Murrelet* 50(3):36.

Opperman, Hal, et al. 2003. *A Birder's Guide to Washington.* American Birding Association, Inc., Colorado Springs.

Palmer, R. H. 1928. "Relative Abundance of Bird Species in Southeastern Idaho; Fresno County, California; Santa Clara County, California; and King County, Washington." *The Murrelet* 9(2):28-38.

Paulson, Dennis R. 1992. "Interior Song Sparrow in Western Washington." *Washington Birds* 2:42-43.

Paulson, Dennis R. 1995. "Sharp-shinned Hawk Hunts from Thermal." *Washington Birds* 4:60-61.

Paulson, Dennis. 1999. *Dragonflies of Washington.* Seattle Audubon Society, Seattle.

Paulson, Dennis. 2009. *Dragonflies and Damselflies of the West.* Princeton University Press, Princeton.

Peterson, Roger Tory. 1961. *A Field Guide to Western Birds.* Houghton Mifflin Company, Boston.

Pistrang, Marvin A. 1981. *Bedrock and Bootsoles: An Introduction to the Geology of the Issaquah Alps.* Issaquah Alps Trails Club, Issaquah.

Puget Sound Action Team. 2007. *State of the Sound 2007.* Publication No. PSAT 07-01. Office of the Governor, State of Washington, Olympia.

Pyle, Robert Michael. 2002. *The Butterflies of Cascadia: A Field Guide to All the Species of Washington, Oregon, and Surrounding Territories.* Seattle Audubon Society.

Ransom, Webster H. 1950. "Some Observations of Winter Waterfowl at Green Lake Refuge, Seattle, Washington." *The Murrelet* 31(2):35.

Ransom, Webster H. 1954. "English Sparrows and Other Birds Eating Tent Caterpillars." *The Murrelet* 35(1):14.

Ransom, Webster H. 1950. "Memorial Day, 1950, Inventory of Wild Ducks, Geese, and Coots at Green Lake, Seattle, Washington." *The Murrelet* 31(3):48.

Ransom, Webster H. 1955. "Another White-Throated Sparrow Recorded for State of Washington." *The Murrelet* 36(1):11.

Rathbun, Samuel F. 1902. "A List of the Land Birds of Seattle, Washington, and Vicinity." *The Auk* 19(2):131-141.

Rathbun, S. F. 1911. "Notes on Birds of Seattle, Washington." *The Auk* 28(4):492-494.

Rathbun, Samuel F. 1915. "List of Water and Shore Birds of the Puget Sound Region in the Vicinity of Seattle." *The Auk* 32(4):459-465.

Rathbun, S. F. 1921. "A Day's Trip to Mount Si, Cascade Mountains." *The Murrelet* 2(3):9-10.

Rathbun, Samuel F. 1922. Untitled [note on duck abundance in King County]. *The Murrelet* 3(2):7.

Rathbun, S. F. 1922. "Some Notes on the Vaux Swift *(Chaetura vauxi)* at Seattle, Wn." *The Murrelet* 3(2):11-14.

Rathbun, S. F. 1927. "Casual and Accidental Occurrences of Certain Species of Land Birds in the Northwestern Portion of the State of Washington." *The Murrelet* 8(2):29-34.

Rathbun, S. F. 1935. "Unusual Places Chosen by Birds for Nesting Purposes." *The Murrelet* 16(2):38-39.

Ratoosh, Ellen S. 1995. "Birds of the Montlake Fill, Seattle, Washington (1979-1983). *Washington Birds* 4:1-34.

Ratti, John T. 1981. "Identification and Distribution of Clark's Grebe." *Western Birds* 12(1):40-46.

Reichard, Timothy A. 1974. "Barred Owl Sightings in Washington." *Western Birds* 5:138-140.

Richardson, Frank. 1957. "Cooper's Hawk Knocked down by Crows." *The Murrelet* 38(3):37.

Richardson, Frank. 1959. "Winter Roost of Starlings at Union Bay, Seattle." *The Murrelet* 40(1):8-9.

Rieck, Carroll A. 1962. "A Common Egret in Western Washington." *The Murrelet* 43(3):52.

Rieck, Carroll A., Eugene S. Dziedzic, and Robert G. Jeffrey. 1971. "A High Density of Pheasants at Seattle, Washington." *The Murrelet* 52(1):7-9.

Robbins, Chandler S., Bertel Bruun, and Herbert S. Zim. 1966. *A Guide to Field Identification: Birds of North America.* Golden Press, New York.

Scattergood, Leslie W. 1948. "Autumn Census of Lake Washington Waterfowl in 1937." *The Murrelet* 29(1):5-8.

Scattergood, Leslie W. 1949. "Notes on the Little Piked Whale." *The Murrelet* 30(1):3-16.

Scheffer, Victor B. and John W. Slipp. 1948. "The Whales and Dolphins of Washington State with a Key to the Cetaceans of the West Coast of North America." *American Midland Naturalist* 39(2):257-337.

Scheffer, Victor B. and Karl W. Kenyon. 1963. "Elephant Seal in Puget Sound, Washington." *The Murrelet* 44(2):23-24.

Schultz, Zella M. 1955. "Odd Fatalities in Ruddy Ducks." *The Murrelet* 36(3):41.

Schultz, Zella M. 1958. "Sight Record of a Hybrid Male Goldeneye." *The Murrelet* 39(1):11.

Schultz, Zella M. 1966. "Sight Record of a Common Grackle *(Quiscalus quiscula)* in Seattle, Wash." *The Murrelet* 47(1):19-20.

Schultz, Zella M. 1967. "Sight Records of Franklin's and Sabine's Gulls in Seattle, Washington." *The Murrelet* 48(1):19.

Schultz, Zella M. 1970. "The Occurrence of the Yellow-billed Loon in Washington." *The Murrelet* 51(2):23.

Schultz, Zella M. 1970. "Sight Records of the Tufted Duck *(Aythya fuligula)* at Seattle, Washington." *The Murrelet* 51(2):25.

Schwartze, C. D., and Gordon D. Alcorn. 1960. "House Finches' Feeding Menaces Cultivated Blueberries." *The Murrelet* 41(1):8-9.

Servheen, Christopher. 1978. "Mountain Beaver as a Prey Species of the Golden Eagle." *The Murrelet* 59(2):77.

Sharrock, J. T. R. 1976. *The Atlas of Breeding Birds in Britain and Ireland.* T. & A. D. Poyser Ltd., Berkhamsted, England.

Shipe, Stephen J., and William W. Scott. 1981. "The Great Blue Heron in King County, Washington." Washington Game Department Urban Nongame Program. Seattle.

Sibley, David Allen. 2007. *The Sibley Guide to Birds.* Alfred A. Knopf, New York.

Sidles, Constance. 2009. *In My Nature: A Birder's Year at the Montlake Fill.* Constancy Press, LLC, Seattle.

Sidles, Constance. 2011. *Second Nature: Tales from the Montlake Fill.* Constancy Press, LLC, Seattle.

Slipp, John W. 1941. "Breeding of the Shoveller in Western Washington." *The Murrelet* 22(2):32-35.

Slipp, John W. 1941. "Notes on the Mourning Dove in the Northwest." *The Murrelet* 22(3):59-60.

Slipp, J. W. 1942. "California Brown Pelican on Southern Puget Sound." *The Murrelet* 23(1):20.

Slipp, John W. 1942. "The Tube-Nosed Swimmers of Puget Sound." *The Murrelet* 23(2):54-59.

Slipp, J. W. 1947. "Notes on Finches of the Genus Carpodacus in Western Washington." *The Condor* 49(2):86-87.

Smith, Kurt. 1981. "Swan Lake *au Naturel.*" *Seattle Post-Intelligencer,* Section E, pg. 1. June 12, 1981.

Smith, M.R., P.W. Mattocks, Jr., and K.M. Cassidy. 1997. Breeding Birds of Washington State. Vol. 4 in *Washington State Gap Analysis–Final Report* (K.M. Cassidy, C.E. Grue, M.R. Smith, and K.M. Dvornich, eds.). Seattle Audubon Society, Seattle.

Spring, Vicky, Ira Spring, and Harvey Manning. 1993. *100 Hikes in Washington's Alpine Lakes.* The Mountaineers, Seattle.

Stepniewski, Andrew. 1999. *The Birds of Yakima County, Washington.* Yakima Valley Audubon Society, Yakima.

Stiles, F. Gary. 1972. "Age and Sex Determination in Rufous and Allen Hummingbirds." *The Condor* 74(1):25-32.

Stinson, Derek W., James W. Watson, and Kelly R. McAllister. 2007. *Washington State Status Report for the Bald Eagle.* Washington Department of Fish and Wildlife, Wildlife Program, Olympia.

Storer, Tracy I., Robert L. Usinger, and David Lukas. 2004. *Sierra Nevada Natural History.* University of California Press, Berkeley.

Suckley, Geo. and J. G. Cooper. 1860. "No. 3: Report upon the birds collected on the survey" in Part III.—Zoological Report, in *The Natural History of Washington Territory and Oregon, with much related to Minnesota, Nebraska, Kansas, Utah, and California, between the thirty-sixth and forty-ninth parallels of latitude, being those parts of the final reports on the survey of the Northern Pacific Railroad route, relating to the natural history of the regions explored, with full catalogues and descriptions of the plants and animals collected from 1853 to 1860.* Bailliere Brothers, New York.

Swan, Ed. 2005. *The Birds of Vashon Island: A Natural History of Habitat and Population Transformation 1850-2005.* The Swan Company, Vashon Island, Washington.

Taber, Richard D. n.d. (study was active from July 1, 1973-June 30, 1974). "Current Status of Ten Uncommon Birds and Mammals in Snoqualmie National Forest and Vicinity." Manuscript. School of Forestry, University of Washington, Seattle.

Taylor, Walter P. 1923. "Upland Game Birds in the State of Washington, with a Discussion of Some General Principles of Game Importation." *The Murrelet* 4(3):3-15.

Taylor, Walter P. and William T. Shaw. 1929. "Provisional List of Land Mammals of the State of Washington," *Occasional Papers of the Charles R. Conner Museum,* No. 2. State College of Washington, Pullman.

Thorson, Thomas. 1941. "The Occurrence of Escaped Parrots in and Around Seattle." *The Murrelet* 22(3):64.

Thrush, Coll. 2007. *Native Seattle: Histories from the Crossing-Over Place.* University of Washington Press, Seattle.

Tirre, William J. 1947. "The Emperor Goose at Seattle, Washington." *The Murrelet* 28(3):41.

Tweit, Bill, and Dennis R. Paulson. 1994. "First Report of the Washington Bird Records Committee." *Washington Birds* 3:11-41.

Tweit, Bill, and Jeff Skriletz. 1996. "Second Report of the Washington Bird Records Committee." *Washington Birds* 5:7-28.

Udvardy, Miklos D. F. 1977. *The Audubon Society Field Guide to North American Birds: Western Region.* Alfred A. Knopf, New York.

Van Velzen, Aldeen C. 1969. "Status of Yellow-headed Blackbird in Western Washington." *The Murrelet* 50(2):21.

Wahl, Terence R. 1995. *Birds of Whatcom County: Status and Distribution.* T. R. Wahl, Bellingham.

Wahl, T. R., and D. R. Paulson. 1981. *Guide to Bird Finding in Washington.* Terry Wahl, Bellingham, Washington. Previous editions (some published by Whatcom Museum Press) 1971, 1972, 1973, 1974, 1977. Subsequent editions through 1994.

Wahl, Terence R., Bill Tweit, and Steven G. Mlodinow (eds.). 2005. *Birds of Washington: Status and Distribution.* Oregon State University Press, Corvallis.

Weber, John W. 1977. "Blue Jay Influx into Washington during the 1976-1977 Winter." *The Murrelet* 58(3):84-86.

Wheeler, Richard J. 1965. "Pioneering of Blue-winged Teal in California, Oregon, Washington and British Columbia." *The Murrelet* 46(3):40-42.

Zimmerman, Dale A. 1973. "Range Expansion of Anna's Hummingbird." *American Birds* 27(5):827-835.

INDEX

This index includes citations only to birds and places. To locate a given map, check the List of Maps on page viii. For a list of individual photographs and/or photographers, check the Photography Credits on pages vi-viii. Birds are listed by their common name, not by their latin name. Italicized page numbers indicate where a given bird can be found in the frequency charts. Boldface page numbers indicate where a photograph of the bird appears. Indices to place names cover only those pages where the author discusses a given place in detail. Most places are indexed by the first word in their names. Individual parks, lakes, and wildlife areas are also grouped generically by type of site.